MW00682425

Property Management Reinvented

How to Convert Maintenance and Energy Expenses to Profits

Nov. 21/88

MEL A. SHEAR

To Lois with my sincerest best wishes

M Shear

PRENTICE HALL, Englewood Cliffs, New Jersey 07632

Library of Congress Cataloging-in-Publication Data

Shear, Mel A.
    Property management reinvented.

    Includes index.
    1. Real estate management   I. Title.
HD1394.S52   1988   333.3′068   87–18852
ISBN 0–13–731191–5

Editorial/production supervision and
    interior design: Madelaine Cooke
Cover design: Diane Saxe
Manufacturing buyer: Peter Havens

© 1988 by Prentice Hall
A Division of Simon & Schuster
Englewood Cliffs, New Jersey 07632

Printed in the United States of America

10 9 8 7 6 5 4 3 2 1

ISBN   0-13-731191-5   025

Prentice-Hall International (UK) Limited, *London*
Prentice-Hall of Australia Pty. Limited, *Sydney*
Prentice-Hall Canada Inc., *Toronto*
Prentice-Hall Hispanoamericana, S.A., *Mexico*
Prentice-Hall of India Private Limited, *New Delhi*
Prentice-Hall of Japan, Inc., *Tokyo*
Simon & Schuster Asia Pte. Ltd., *Singapore*
Editora Prentice-Hall do Brasil, Ltda., *Rio de Janeiro*

This book is dedicated to my family, the people who were associated with me at 55 St. Regis Crescent North, Downsview, Ontario, Canada, and the people now involved with me in the EBM Group (Effective Building Management Group), a company dedicated to providing information, professional consulting services, support services, and contemporary educational programs for the construction and building management industry.

All have contributed and are still contributing to the process of reinventing property management.

A special thanks to my production editor, Madelaine Cooke, for the professional way in which she helped me complete the project, and to the Apple Corporation for their Macintosh computer, without which this book would never have been completed.

Contents

Preface

While writing the *Handbook of Building Maintenance Management,** it occurred to me that the maintenance and energy management programs developed during my tenure at Cadillac Development and Cadillac Fairview were so valuable that they should be made available to the design, construction, and building management industry. I decided that because my experiences in the industry for more than 20 years were so unusual—and not likely to be repeated by anyone else—they should be documented in a special book. *Property Management Reinvented* is the result of that decision.

The system explained in this book establishes a framework that unites all the people and disciplines involved in the industry. At the same time, it allows each person to achieve his or her goals. The system identifies problems, collects pertinent information about them, and then assigns the responsibility to the right people to solve them without creating new ones. The coordination of all these activities is not possible unless we use the new strategies suggested in this book as the basis for a new approach to managing property.

To reinvent property management, I am suggesting that the construction and building management industry agree on a commonly recognized on-site and supportive management team operating under the umbrella of a common purpose, using a common chart of expense accounts, and supported by a com-

---

*Mel A. Shear, *Handbook of Building Maintenance Management* (Englewood Cliffs, N.J.: Prentice-Hall, 1983).

mon recordkeeping and information system. One benefit of a system such as this is that it allows the industry to be linked by computer networks that enables it to use common data bases for decision making.

It has been predicted that, in the future, information, people, and profits will be inexorably linked. Human capital will replace dollar capital, and information will surpass material goods as a basic resource.* This means that when we identify the management team, business unit, or profit center, we are also identifying the people who are needed on that team. Once we identify their functional responsibilities, we can identify what they need to know to be successful. To reinvent property management and to make it work, management needs the right information in the hands of the right people. Skills development, then, becomes a priority in our industry. *Property Management Reinvented* was written to explain a management system that will help you do the right things right—through other people.

It is not easy to communicate the technical information that people need to make a maintenance and energy management program successful. I have found that if explanations are too wordy, people don't read them, or they find them hard to understand.

When I needed to use a typewriter to convey a message, it was difficult to edit and rewrite things so that I was actually saying what I meant to say. Illustrations were another problem that plagued me during my career in property management. Not only was it difficult to create the forms we used, it was costly and time-consuming to edit and change them, especially if we had printed a supply and were forced to wait until they were used up before we reprinted.

All this changed when I purchased a computer. You will find that in this book most of the information is contained in charts and forms I was able to create with the computer. I believe that it is much easier for readers to comprehend what I mean when I am able to explain it with a chart, a form, an example, or a picture. In effect, this book could be considered a verbal-visual communication tool.

This book may not provide all the answers to the problems you are facing. If it helps you understand, helps you organize your thinking, and helps you save maintenance and energy dollars, then it will have served its purpose. The maintenance and operations of buildings are so complex that it is impossible to create the perfect book on the subject. It is for this reason that I encourage feedback from readers that would help improve this book's contents in future editions.

---

*John Naisbitt and Patricia Aburdene, *Re-inventing the Corporation* (New York: Warner Books, 1985), p. 4.

ACKNOWLEDGMENTS

During my career I saw many innovations initiated, tried, improved, and often discarded. The contents of this book are the end result of those experiences. Many unique and talented people were involved in our maintenance management process; I was merely the medium through which these ideas were channeled and the central human data base around which they were refined, organized, directed, and controlled.

Some of the special information and support resources available to me were Joseph Berman, executive vice-president of the residential division, who supported the program; Earl Lyons, manager of housekeeping services; Jack McConnell, manager of electrical-mechanical services; Don Clark, manager of structural services; John Sutherland, manager of groundskeeping services; Andy Zuliani, manager of maintenance services; John Norris, recruiter and trainer of building operators; my secretaries, Judy Stevens and Fran London; and Paul McNab, manager of mechanical vending. Although many other people, too numerous to mention, made significant contributions to our multi-faceted maintenance program, and although everyone on our maintenance and operations team contributed to our success, it was these people who made their specialized functions something unique. It was my pleasure to have worked with them all.

Introduction

The construction and building management industry must learn how to manage the future rather than the past. To "manage tomorrow" requires an agreed-upon system of management that links under a single workable system all the disciplines involved in design, construction, management, operations, and support services. A system such as this was developed by Cadillac Development Corporation and Fairview Corporation, two major Canadian real estate developers that, in 1974, merged to form the Cadillac Fairview Corporation.

During a 20-year period, a system evolved in which the creation of an effective information system and the use of functional specialists to support on-site staff allowed management to organize and harness talent and information so that maintenance and energy expenses could be realistically and efficiently managed.

I.1 BREAKING WITH TRADITION

At Cadillac Development and, later, at Cadillac Fairview, the residential maintenance and operations department dared to break with the traditional approach to property management; in fact, we reinvented it.

Cadillac Development took the bold step of separating management into three distinct key functions: marketing and leasing, administration, and maintenance and operations. When Cadillac created this separation, most people thought property management was only marketing, leasing, rent collections, and administration. This idea is still common today.

Design, construction, and renovation management should also be part of the management team's responsibility, headed by someone who can manage all the functions. Management of a building begins when it is conceptualized and ends only when the building is destroyed, and it is for this reason that a management team must include the developer, the designer, the builder, the manager, the operator, and the people who provide consulting and support services, not just the people who lease space and collect rents.

Traditionally, the people who plan, design, and construct a building project are called the *project management team;* the people who manage it after it is built are called the *property management team*. This distinction is unfortunate. If we expect to overcome industry problems, everyone must be part of the same team and have the same long-term goals and objectives.

I.2 A NEW CONCEPT

During my management career, it was always my tendency to concentrate on my weaknesses, rather than on the things I liked or my strengths. In 1964, when I first became involved in property management, my biggest concern was the myriad maintenance problems existing in our buildings. As I searched for answers to them, I became very much involved with construction, operations, and service specialists. It seemed only natural that the company assign the responsibility for maintenance and operation to me. In any case, no one else was eager to take it on.

Initially I found problem diagnosis difficult because of my lack of knowledge about structure and electrical-mechanical equipment. I found it difficult to obtain all the relevant information about a problem. There were several reasons for this, but it was mostly because the symptoms were not fully investigated or because the available information was incorrect. It was practically impossible to investigate structural or electrical-mechanical problems properly without having access to specialists with the know-how to investigate and assess problems, recommend solutions, and supervise the work needed to correct them.

In many cases, the effect of the remedial work was opposite to what was, in fact, required. I found that errors of this kind were not only ineffective and expensive but on occasion actually made a condition worse, making more extensive work necessary. There is a great need for the right kind of consulting and support services to help management diagnose problems and overcome them. Many people in these kinds of services complain that management does not understand the value of their services and would rather call on them only when there is a crisis. They claim that building owners are not receptive to those who want to sell them the programs and systems they need.

I found that once I gathered around me specialists in housekeeping, groundskeeping, structural, and electrical-mechanical services, the pieces of the puzzle started to fit into place; that emergency calls were reduced to a minimum; and that the results began to show on the bottom line of each building's financial statement. It is time for the design, construction, and building management industry to realize the importance of these specialists and do something about developing them. At the same time, it is as important for the consulting and support-service industry to develop the right programs and to have professionals available to carry them out as it is for the design, construction, and management people to be receptive to them.

1.3 A SYSTEMS APPROACH TO PROPERTY MANAGEMENT

People are important, but so is information. The planning, budgeting, and accounting systems that were developed by Cadillac's residential maintenance and operations department are another essential part of this reinvented building management process. Without these systems, it would be difficult to plan, organize, staff, direct, control, monitor, and improve a management program. It is from these records that I am able to discuss the results of our maintenance and energy management program.

1.4 OUR OBJECTIVE

Our goal was to maximize income while reducing the cost of maintenance and energy to their lowest possible levels without downgrading the structure, the electrical-mechanical systems, or the comfort and sense of well-being of the residential buildings' occupants.

We achieved this goal during a period of extreme inflation and during a time when we were forced to spend money overcoming horrendous problems that were built into our buildings. In spite of this, and with little support from the company, we were able to reduce the operations and maintenance costs and still maintain a reputation as the best landlords in Toronto.

1.5 THE INFAMOUS TORONTO APARTMENT FLIP

The saving of approximately $5 million through our maintenance and operations program was significant for several reasons. In 1981 and 1982, the profit generated by Cadillac Fairview's residential apartment portfolio was about $16 or $17 million. Our maintenance and operations program contributed one-third of that profit. Without the program it would have been necessary to raise the rents by that amount to achieve the same results. The development arm of the residential division made many poor decisions; they not only used up the profits generated by the buildings but actually showed a substantial loss.

In 1981, the company showed a net loss of $4.9 million on an income of $784.3 million. Without our contribution, the company would have shown a loss of $9.9 million. During that year, the company wrote down the value of its investments in lands for residential buildings by $43 million.

In 1982 Cadillac Fairview decided to sell off its entire residential division and in doing so shocked the real estate industry. This led to the infamous flipping of these apartment buildings that increased the price of the buildings from $270 million to $500 million in one day. The flak from this activity has still not been resolved, and the two people involved have left the country. There have been many theories about why the buildings were sold. Certainly the location of the buildings and the reputation of the company as being good managers were big factors in the inflation of the mortgages to accommodate the $500 million price tag. No one has been able to identify the owners of the ten numbered companies that supposedly purchased the buildings. Two of the people involved owned the trust companies that held the new mortgages on the properties. The two companies were put into receivership, and the three key participants are facing fraud charges.

Many believed that they were sold because of rent control. The truth was that the company needed the cash to overcome some of the bad development decisions made by the residential and other divisions. Since that time the main role of the company has been that of money manager rather than entrepreneur developer. At the time of the sale, when the mortgage interest rate was 18 percent, the company not only realized a substantial amount of cash from the sale but was potentially able to earn more money from second mortgages than from owning and managing the buildings.

When Cadillac Fairview sold the buildings, it received a $40 million down payment and now earns the second-mortgage interest without having to manage the buildings. In the process it sold off some irreplaceable prime locations in Toronto. These locations may have been more important than the short-term gains of the moment. It is my opinion that some of the best locations should not have been included in the sale, especially one mixed-use project that was extremely successful. This decision also negated the problem of rent control that kept the rental income below market levels. Owning shopping centers and office buildings seemed to be a much better financial investment than one in apartments that were controlled by rent control legislation.

When we review the generally understood criteria for a successful real estate venture, however, we find that investments in real estate must be cognizant of location, quality of design and construction, properly financed, and professionally managed. Once the buildings were flipped a couple of times, they certainly weren't properly financed; saddling the buildings with second and third mortgages would now have a great effect on the way they are being managed.

Today in Toronto, apartment buildings are still full, and office buildings are having a vacancy problem. The construction and building management industry has always tended to overbuild. This is the reason why it is not necessary to impose rent control: The industry traditionally regulates itself.

The buildings that meet the success criteria mentioned previously will always be successful; any that have not met even one of the criteria will be much less successful. One of the factors that make real estate developers believe that they can be successful is the use of a net lease, commonly used in commercial buildings, that allows them to charge back to the tenant all increases in operating expenses over a base year. This is not one of the criteria for a successful real estate venture. Being able to charge back all inefficiencies to the tenants cannot substitute for professional management.

In Toronto, in 1985, the office building market was greatly overbuilt, and many buildings that were full a few years before were having problems attracting tenants. Buildings that met the success criteria did not have those problems, but those that would be considered second class or lower found it difficult to keep their buildings full or their rents at the proper level.

All buildings, whether commercial, residential, industrial, or institutional, need to be designed, built, and managed properly if their owners expect them to be successful. I believe that professional management is the key to success, and effectively managing the maintenance and operations functions can contribute significantly to that success. This book explains how to do just that.

Issues and Answers
for Building Managers

1.1 HOW IT ALL STARTED

Before 1968 most people in the construction and building management business looked upon property management as an occupation that quite simply leased apartments, collected rents, and dealt with tenant complaints; however, building management may have all begun in rural schoolhouses and early offices, where it was considered part of the duties of the teacher or junior clerk to "sweep out and fire up." As buildings became larger and central heating was developed, teachers began to hire older boys to stoke the furnace. When school boards and office managers realized that these duties were interfering with schoolwork or office routines, it seemed logical to hire someone specifically to deal with building maintenance.

In the twentieth century, buildings of all types—schools, offices, hospitals, factories, shopping centers, and apartments—have become more and more sophisticated, and more skill and expertise is needed to keep them operating smoothly. The modern building, in spite of automation, requires managers, operators, consultants, and support-service specialists with qualifications that are far removed from the school janitor who shuffled around the building kicking up dust with the broom and a feather duster.

Even in the early 1960s, the roles that people were expected to play on the management team were still quite vague. One job description explained that the property manager's role was to allow "the owner-entrepreneur to develop new projects without being bothered by the tenants." The development of new projects appeared to take priority over managing them after they were built.

Entrepreneurial Philosophies

In the past, most buildings being built were either very heavily mortgaged or "mortgaged out." In many cases the developer actually put no money into a new building and even made a profit. It was because of this that most people in the construction and building management business believed that they were only in the development business. Overmortgaging (by inflating the pro forma cost projections) and building as cheaply as possible was the objective, not the construction of decent manageable buildings. (It should be understood that 100 percent mortgages are not necessarily objectionable, provided that the buildings are properly built, maintained, and operated.)

Buildings with 125 percent mortgages or those that are saddled with two or three mortgages, especially when mortgage rates are very high, burden a building with a debt load that can be overcome only by raising the rents. If high rents force vacancies and the rental income is too low, it is impossible to pay the debt load and operational expenses.

In the early 1960s, some developers faced very serious problems because, in Toronto, entrepreneurs quickly saturated the market, and many apartment units were vacant. With huge mortgages to pay, developers panicked, and many offered months of free rent and other incentives to fill the buildings. Eventually, the buildings did fill and have stayed full since.

Rent controls helped to keep them that way, as many tenants who could afford more expensive accommodations stayed in the buildings protected by rent control legislation, and people in the lower income bracket live in subsidized housing that is paid for by the taxpayers. Today, there is such a demand for apartments in Toronto that tenants are subletting their apartments and receiving as much as $3,000 "key money" for their lease. Rent controls have kept their rents much below market while they are gouging other tenants.

It is not that all developers, landlords, and tenants are greedy. Many landlords who own buildings with good tenants never kept their rents at market levels for fear of losing their tenants. When rent controls were imposed, these owners' rents were too low. Many tenants have been enjoying these below-market rents, yet they are unashamedly asking for key money.

Strange as it may seem, even after these same landlords found their overmortgaged and poorly built buildings difficult to manage, there were always buyers. Even the Ontario Housing Corporation bought many of these buildings for subsidized housing. The taxpayers have been paying ever since. Many people believe that the best hedge against inflation is to own real estate, so they keep buying buildings that are overmortgaged and poorly built. These conditions could not have existed only in Toronto, Ontario, Canada; other areas must surely have had similar situations. Many of these buildings were bought by foreign money and are now owned by absentee landlords who do not seem to worry about making a profit. Their objective was to get their money into Canada, and buying buildings seemed to be the best way of doing this.

In Toronto, the problem of a building's initial heavy debt load was overcome in two ways. First, the population increase in Toronto since the 1960s has been phenomenal; second, inflation seems to have swept the inflated prices of the buildings under the rug.

These second- and third-time owners, however, with even heavier debt loads of second and third mortgages, found that they needed substantial increases in rents to keep from losing their investments. At the same time, many of them believed that the only way to save money was to ignore maintenance until it was absolutely necessary. This philosophy created a situation where landlords raised rents and at the same time ignored the upkeep of their buildings, creating an image problem with the tenants. The resultant publicity, when the media exploited and publicized extreme cases, panicked the Ontario government into imposing rent controls. Overmortgaging, poor initial design and construction, misapplication of equipment, poor management, inadequate or nonexistent training programs, poor or nonexistent recordkeeping systems, low productivity, fragmented communications, high costs, government interference, and poor decision-making processes are all problems facing the construction and building management industry, and rent control is not the answer for solving them.

It is a matter of utmost urgency that an industry responsible for shelter, a basic necessity of life, develop some initiatives to overcome all of these problems as soon as possible.

What Business Are We Really In?

There was a general misconception at that time that is still prevalent today: Companies in the construction and building management industry believe they are in the development business and not in the business of protecting their assets by efficient and effective management, even though they own buildings that have an expected life span of 50 years.

In 1968 a management consulting company was hired by Cadillac Development to study its property management group. It was during this consulting exercise that we were first introduced to management theory; the planning and decision-making process; objectives; goals; budgets; and other management strategies. Although many on our management team had been working in the industry and managing various enterprises for many years, we had never heard of a job description. One of the most significant recommendations made by the consultants was that Cadillac add a house-and-grounds specialist to its maintenance and operations department.

The Basic Problems

Because many people in the design, construction, and building management industry do not have sufficient knowledge about structure or electrical-mechanical systems, they are forced to make decisions about maintenance and operations activities by gut feel and ignorance, often providing stopgap treatment that eventually necessitates complete removal and replacement of major structural or electrical-mechanical components when they fail completely.

You will find that because of the short-term objectives of real estate development entrepreneurs, poor design and construction, and misapplication of equipment are prevalent. A good example of this is the energy-savings retrofit explained in Chapter 12. Equipment that had to be replaced was installed originally to save $20,000. By the time the retrofit was completed, the extra cost of the fuel and the retrofit was 25 times the original savings.

The Importance of the Design, Construction, and Building Management Industry

Many billions of dollars are spent on construction in the United States and Canada. The annual expenditure of more than $30 billion on building construction in Canada alone is responsible for more than 18 percent of the country's gross national product (GNP).* If the services used by property management are added to these statistics, the entire design, construction, and building management industry could possibly account for as much as 30 percent of the GNP.

The Institute of Real Estate Management has existed for more than 50 years, and its certified property manager's (CPM) program is recognized among the best in the world. In 1987, 7,890 CPMs managed more than $872.5 billion in public and private real estate assets and supervised more than 8.05 billion square feet of commercial space in office buildings, shopping malls, retail strip centers, and industrial properties, along with 11.2 million residential units, encompassing apartments, condominiums, cooperatives, and federally assisted housing in the United States. Any study related to the trends and problems of the construction industry would not be complete without input from property management and support-service industries. It is estimated that there are 2 million people employed managing and providing support services to buildings in Canada and the United States.†

In the greater metropolitan Toronto area alone, it is estimated that there are 3,000 building owners and property managers, 20,000 building operators,

---

*Statistics provided by the Ontario Ministry of Housing in its brochure for Building Tomorrow, an international forum on the business of building held in Toronto, November 2–6, 1986.

†IREM Fact Sheet, July 1987.

and 20,000 support-service technicians. More than 60,000 people are employed
in residential, commercial, industrial, and institutional buildings in over 800
schools, 50 hospitals, 6,000 apartment buildings, 640 office buildings, and
many industrial facilities in that area.*

1.2 DESIGN, CONSTRUCTION, AND BUILDING
MANAGEMENT PROBLEMS

The Construction Sciences Research Foundation Study

In 1978 the Construction Sciences Research Foundation, an independent research affiliate of the Construction Specifications Institute,† commissioned the
Kellogg Corporation‡ to study construction problems and trends that would
be of concern to the construction industry during the 1980s. Because of certain
beliefs within the industry, this study did not include any research into the
problems already built into buildings.

    Traditionally, the design, construction, and building management indus-
try has been split into two groups. The first is the design and construction
group; the second is the property management group that takes over buildings
after they are built. Because the construction industry believes that a project
ends when the building is built, the study does not include input from property
managers. As a result, the study, which made some amazingly accurate observations and recommendations, is much less meaningful.

Issue Categories Identified by the Kellogg Study

In spite of the fact that management, consulting, and support services were
not included in the study, the Kellogg Corporation's findings are important.§
The issues documented must be addressed if we are to overcome the problems
plaguing our industry.

    A review of the methodology used in the study should help support the
validity of its findings. It consisted of personal interviews, two mail surveys,
and a February 1979 workshop in Denver at which two rounds of discussion

*In 1982 and 1983 my colleagues at the EBM Group and I conducted several studies of our
industry. Unless otherwise attributed, the industry statistics provided in this book are conservative extrapolations from the results of that research. I have assumed that the United States
market is ten times that of Canada, the Canadian market, ten times that of Ontario, and the
Ontario market, twice that of Toronto.

†Construction Specifications Institute, Inc., 1150 17th St., NW, Suite 300, Washington,
DC 20036.

‡Kellogg Corporation, 5601 South Broadway, Suite 400, Littleton, CO 80121.

§*Construction Trends and Problems Through 1990* (Washington, D.C.: Construction
Sciences Foundation Inc.). Copyright 1981.

took place. Eighty-one leaders from throughout the construction industry participated and were asked their opinions in questionnaires. Each successive questionnaire focused more narrowly on specific recommendations for coping with key issues identified in earlier questionnaires.

The Key Issues

The fifty-five problems identified by the experts were fitted under seven major categories:*

1. The cost of regulation
2. Improving management and supervision
3. The effective utilization of physical and technical resources
4. The effective utilization of labor resources
5. Improving risk management
6. Control of costs
7. Improving industry organization

If management were included in the study the following problems would have been added to the list:

1. Overmortgaging
2. Rent controls or other unnecessary government regulations
3. Poor and fragmented communication between the developer, designer, builder, manager, consultant, operator, and the people who service a building
4. An inadequate decision-making process that has been traditionally based on hunch, rule of thumb, conventional wisdom, or ignorance
5. Recordkeeping and information systems that are poor or nonexistent about the past history of existing buildings, their structural and electrical-mechanical components, and previous, present, or future costs
6. A lack of suitable training programs for the people on design, construction, and building management teams, especially related to maintenance services and especially in management skills

Many of the problems identified by both construction and building management have a common thread, mainly because both are involved in buildings, and every effort should be made to deal with them. The cost of regulation is identified as one such problem, and this includes the issue of rent controls

*Construction Trends and Problems Through 1990, pp. 12 and 13.

and other regulations imposed federally, at the state or provincial levels, and at local levels.

Improving Management and Supervision Is Practically Impossible

Improving management and supervision was identified as one of the most significant and costly problems facing the industry. Correcting this problem is extremely difficult, and perhaps even impossible, unless there is a concentrated effort to improve the industry organization. There are several reasons why this industry lacks cohesive direction and the united front that are so necessary if these issues are ever expected to be resolved:

1. The widely dispersed market in the United States and Canada prevents the concentration of the industry in any one locale. The traditional concept of buildings being different also tends to fragment the industry into commercial, residential, industrial, and institutional groupings—all trying to achieve the same goals but without strength in numbers and without actually properly identifying their goals.
2. The labor-intensive nature of the construction, management, operation, and servicing of buildings has made it relatively easy for anyone to enter the business without necessarily assuring that the people involved are suitably qualified for the jobs that they do.
3. High-risk entrepreneurs tend to be attracted to the potential of making a lot of money in the construction and building management business. They tend to inflate cost projections and build cheaply so that they can "mortgage out" a new project, keep and milk the property for a few years after it is built, fill it with less-than-desirable tenants, and then dump it when the cost of maintenance or all of their tax shelter benefits have been exploited. Amazingly enough, they generally find a buyer, but there are many extreme examples of these buildings just being abandoned.
4. The industry cannot take a strong leadership position in these matters because it is so fragmented. There are several reasons for this fragmentation; they should be identified and steps taken to overcome them: (a) The design, construction, and building management industry considers the design and building stages as project management's responsibility, the "after-it's-built stage" as property management's responsibility. (b) The industry believes that residential, commercial, industrial, and institutional buildings are different and as such that each product line must have its own management team. Many companies, because of this misconception, organize their management teams by these product lines and in doing so duplicate their development, design, building, management, operation, and service groups in each division.

The Problem of Fragmentation

Fragmentation of the design, building, and management teams, as well as fragmentation by product line, makes improvement in productivity, efficiency, and effectiveness practically impossible. It also prevents the industry from making its voice heard in legislative and public forums. The voices that are heard lack the in-depth understanding of many of the key issues as they have been identified here and thus tend to beat to death gut issues that are quite obvious. They are constantly fighting a rearguard action as they react to government-legislated roadblocks. Many of the real issues are not being identified because they are not understood. The obvious pet issues are constantly being presented, but nothing is really done about them. Fragmentation makes it difficult to respond to issues that affect the industry and more or less removes the possibility of dealing with them in a less formal and flexible manner. It eliminates the possibility of identifying problems before they become serious and dealing with them at that time, rather than after the government has already acted.

Fragmentation reduces the opportunity for defining a common purpose, for developing suitable specifications, for using a common planning procedure, for using a common chart of expense accounts, for establishing common data bases that can be accessed by the industry through computer networks, for the possibility of getting feedback from everyone on management teams, and for the possibility of attacking all the problems that were identified and eliminating them.

If the design, construction, and building management industry accepted the fact that buildings are buildings—that each building is its own profit center or business unit; that they all have structural and electrical-mechanical equipment of varying degrees of sophistication; and that they all need housekeeping and groundskeeping; that it does not matter whether they are used for commercial, residential, industrial, or institutional purposes—the industry would be more accepting of constructive recommendations.

A Building's Life Cycle

A building goes through four stages in the course of its generally accepted life cycle of 50 years (Figure 1.1).

1. The conception stage includes the purchase of land, financial arrangements, gaining approval for the project, and could take a minimum of three years.
2. The design stage may consume one or two years. This stage includes preliminary design and working drawings, estimates, specifications, and contract documents.

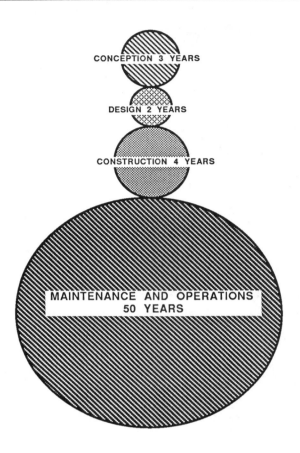

CONCEPTION 3 YEARS

DESIGN 2 YEARS

CONSTRUCTION 4 YEARS

MAINTENANCE AND OPERATIONS
50 YEARS

Because a building has a generally accepted life span of 50 years, the people who make value analysis decisions about a building's location, the way it is designed, the quality of construction, the way it is managed, operated, and serviced, its debt load, and its purpose must make them on the basis of long- rather than short-term benefits.

For any existing building that is plagued with poor location, design, and construction and generally mismanaged, it is necessary that the owner and/or manager have the right information and be qualified to make decisions that will assure the best return on the dollars being spent to operate it.

Figure 1.1 The various stages of a building's life span (From Mel A. Shear, *Handbook of Building Maintenance Management,* © 1983, p. 4 [A Reston Publication]. Adapted by permission of Prentice-Hall, Inc., Englewood Cliffs, New Jersey).

3. The construction time depends entirely upon the size and scale of the project; however, it may take up to four years to complete.

4. Leasing the building or selling the units, if it is a condominium, should be considered part of the ongoing life of the building. Accountants usually consider 50 years as the average life of a building; however, the Wrigley Building, in Chicago, is more than 60 years old and is still beautiful and functional. Thus, the maintenance and operational services required by a building span a much longer period than the initial development, design, and construction stages and deserve more serious consideration than they receive at present.

Life-Cycle Costs

Traditionally, designers and builders use initial cost as their main criterion when designing and building, but this should not be the case. When decisions are made by design, construction, management, consultants, or support-service specialists about the purchase of structural or electrical-mechanical equipment, consideration must be given not only to the initial cost but to the expected life span and the cost of operating the equipment over that life span (see Figures 1.2 and 1.3).

Many problems and unnecessary expenses are incurred by buildings when things are purchased that are not suited to their intended application. If mistakes are made while a building is under construction, the cost to remove and replace a component could be as much as three to ten times the initial cost. Poor materials and workmanship and cheap equipment always eat into a building's profits (see Figure 1.4 for another comment on this subject).

The *life-cycle cost* of a piece of equipment is the amount of money needed to buy it, to have it installed, and to provide an annuity that will cover the cost of its operation for a specified lifetime. When a building is completed, management should be provided with a *building profile* that identifies the components that will wear out and need replacement (see Figure 1.5). Each piece of this equipment should be tagged and color coded for easy identification. Maintenance programs should be recommended and included in the turnover documents.

Management should plan to provide funds to replace components before they fail. A properly planned maintenance program can double the life of a component; however, when the time for replacement comes, immediate action should be taken. Nothing is worse for a building's image than worn carpets, chipped, unsightly paint, or other signs of neglect.

Never defer maintenance as a means of improving cash flow. The problems will not go away; in fact, they will only get worse, and as they back up, you will be forced to resolve them as the components fail completely. You may pay now or pay later, but you must pay—there is no escape.

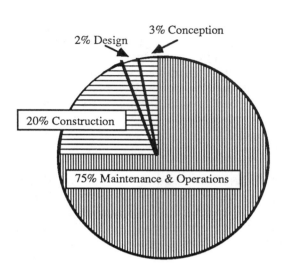

2% Design   3% Conception

20% Construction

75% Maintenance & Operations

Decisions about a building's structure and electrical-mechanical equipment during the development, design, and construction stages are critical and must be made by considering not only the initial cost but also the cost to maintain and operate over the building's life cycle. See Figure 1.4 for anticipated life spans of major components.

Figure 1.2 A building's life-cycle costs. (From Mel A. Shear, *Handbook of Building Maintenance Management*, © 1983, p. 5 [A Reston Publication]. Adapted by permission of Prentice-Hall, Inc., Englewood Cliffs, New Jersey).

1.3 IMPROVING INDUSTRY ORGANIZATION AND MANAGEMENT

Match the Management Team to the Needs

The Kellogg report cites improving industry organization and improving management skills as being two key issues.* The people involved in design, construction, and building management should all be considered as being on one

*Construction Specifications Institute, *Construction Trends*, pp. 5–7, 9–10.

If management expects to maximize income and reduce the cost of management services to its lowest possible level without downgrading the structure and the electrical-mechanical equipment, it cannot be saddled with inferior workmanship, the wrong structural components, or misapplication of the electrical-mechanical equipment.

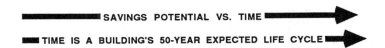

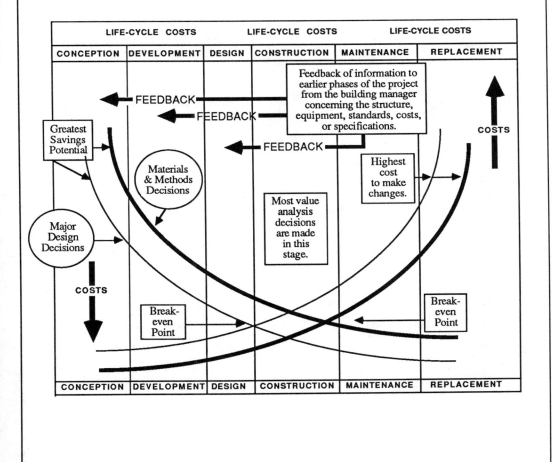

Figure 1.3 The importance of making the right design, materials, and methods decisions before beginning construction.

RECREATIONAL FACILITIES	Years	INTERIOR FINISHES	Years
Swimming Pool	20 - 25	Carpets	10 - 20
Pool Fence	10 - 20	Terrazzo	50
Pool Deck	15 - 25	Painted Plaster	10
Equipment & Change Rooms	15	Wallpaper	10 - 15
MECHANICAL EQUIPMENT		Ceramic Tile	30
Fans	25	Vinyl Tile	20 - 25
Chillers	20	Suite Entrance Doors	35
Fan Coil Units	20	**HARD LANDSCAPE**	
Fire Hoses	30	* Asphalt Roads & Parking Lots	50
Sprinkler Heads	50	* Concrete Sidewalks & Curbs	50
Stand & Distribution Piping	50	Ramps To Underground	15
Alarm System	25	Lamp Standards	30
Compactor	20	Signage	30
Refuse Chutes	35	Fountains	20 - 25
Elevator Equipment	50	**BUILDING ENVELOPE**	
Elevator Cab	25	* Masonry	50
Pumps	20 - 25	Exterior Painting	5
Snow Melting Equipment	15	Painted Flashing	5
Unitary Air Conditioners	20	Balcony Slabs	50
Heating Boilers	25	Balcony Railings	15 - 20
Boiler Breeching	20	Built-Up Roofing	20
Domestic Hot Water Storage Tank	20	Inverted Roofing	50
Domestic Water Heater	15 - 20	Entrance Doors	20
Valves	20 - 30	Sliding Patio Doors	25
Pressure Reducing Valves	15	Parking Garage Doors	25 - 30
Cushion Tanks	35	* Windows	25 - 30
Compressors	20	Roof Flashings	20
Domestic Hot Water Piping		Metal Siding	25
Cast Iron	15 - 20	Metal Gratings	30
Copper	50	* Front Canopies	30 - 40

There are several reasons why information about the anticipated life span of major components found in buildings is useful. Building owners, especially condominium owners, may want to set up a reserve fund so that the funds for retrofitting and replacement will be available when needed. It could also be useful when designers are making decisions about components when a building is being built or when retrofitting or replacing them. It is recommended that management have available to them the as-installed prices for all major components. Building owners and/or managers would then have the opportunity to keep records of the initial cost, as well as of the cost to maintain and operate. The accounting system recommended in this book will allow management to monitor the cost to operate, maintain, and replace. Experience has shown that regular inspections and preventive maintenance will double the life of a component.

Those components marked with an asterisk show a life span on this chart; however they should be regularly inspected and repaired on a recurring basis. With this kind of maintenance it should not ever be necessary to remove and replace them unless the building owner wants to change the designs.

Figure 1.4 The anticipated life spans of major components.

IT'S UNWISE to pay too much,
but it is unwise to pay too little.
When you pay too much, you
lose a little money; that is all.
When you pay too little, you
sometimes lose everything,
because the thing you bought
was incapable of doing the thing
you bought it to do.

The common law of business
balance prohibits paying a little
and getting a lot - it can't be
done. If you deal with the
lowest bidder, it's well to add
something for the risk you run.
And if you do that, you will
have enough to pay for
something better.

-- JOHN RUSKIN

People who develop, design, build, and manage buildings
should use a system of value analysis that involves a method
of critical reasoning about the specifications and the cost for the
products, equipment, materials,chemicals, tools, parts, supplies,
and services that are used in buildings when they are built and
when they are renovated or retrofitted during their life span.

Figure 1.5 Something to
remember when making development, design, construction, or
operations decisions.

team and should jointly develop a suitable organizational hierarchy for that
team (see Figures 1.6 and 1.7).* Not only should there be agreement about the

*Because each building is a separate business unit, or profit center, each building must have
its own management team. Although I sometimes use the term *property manager* to describe the
person who heads that team and has total responsibility for the management of a building through
all its stages, this person should be thought of as *the head of a building business unit* to avoid
thinking of him or her as merely an office administrator who leases space and collects rents.
Throughout the book, when discussing reinvented property management, I use these terms inter-
changeably.

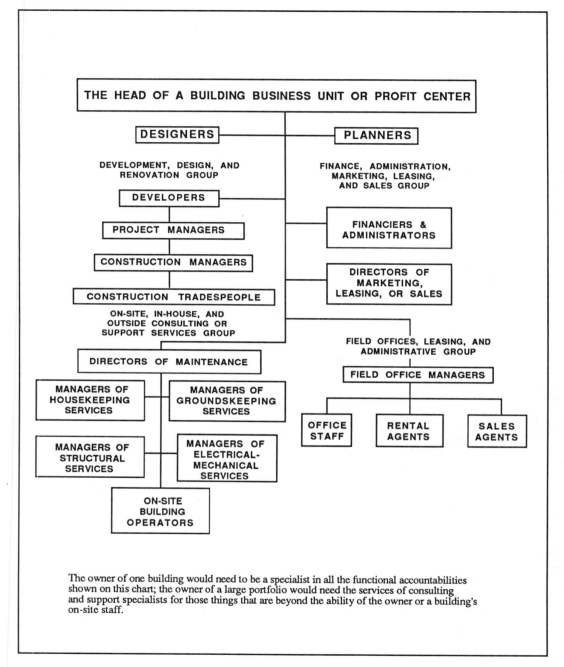

The owner of one building would need to be a specialist in all the functional accountabilities shown on this chart; the owner of a large portfolio would need the services of consulting and support specialists for those things that are beyond the ability of the owner or a building's on-site staff.

Figure 1.6 An organizational hierarchy for a building business unit or profit center.

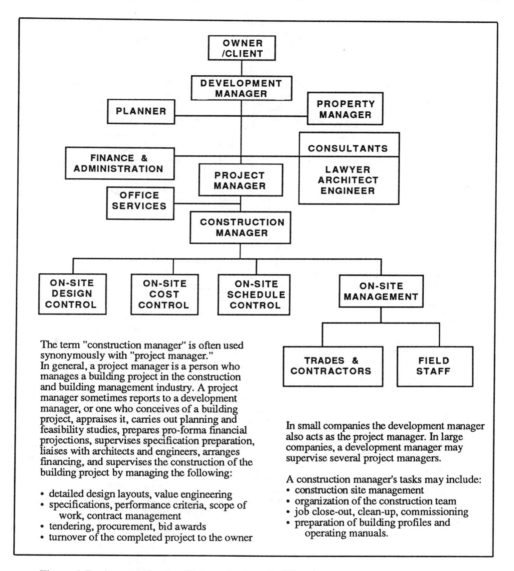

The term "construction manager" is often used synonymously with "project manager." In general, a project manager is a person who manages a building project in the construction and building management industry. A project manager sometimes reports to a development manager, or one who conceives of a building project, appraises it, carries out planning and feasibility studies, prepares pro-forma financial projections, supervises specification preparation, liaises with architects and engineers, arranges financing, and supervises the construction of the building project by managing the following:

- detailed design layouts, value engineering
- specifications, performance criteria, scope of work, contract management
- tendering, procurement, bid awards
- turnover of the completed project to the owner

In small companies the development manager also acts as the project manager. In large companies, a development manager may supervise several project managers.

A construction manager's tasks may include:
- construction site management
- organization of the construction team
- job close-out, clean-up, commissioning
- preparation of building profiles and operating manuals.

Figure 1.7   An organizational hierarchy for a building construction team. The building owner or a representative of the owner is the head of this group.

team and titles that are given to the players, but there should also be agreement about the purpose of the team and also about its responsibilities (see Figures 1.8 and 1.9). Without this agreement it is practically impossible to improve the industry organization or to improve the effectiveness of management. How can the industry decide about training programs without agreement about the people on the team or what they need to know to be successful?

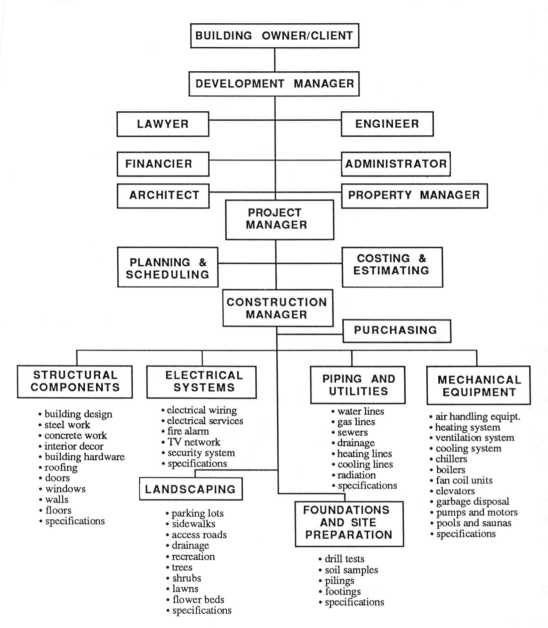

Figure 1.8 Functional activities of the people on a design, construction, and building management team.

The objective of all construction and building management companies is to maximize income for building owners, while reducing the cost of management services to its lowest possible level without downgrading the structure, the electrical-mechanical equipment, the ambience, or the comfort and sense of well-being of the building's occupants.

This objective applies to all buildings, whether they are used for commercial, residential, industrial, or institutional purposes, or whether for the owner of one building or for owners of many buildings. The objective of managers of publicly owned buildings is to maximize income and reduce subsidies to their lowest possible levels.

It is with this objective in mind that this organization of the specialists and their functional responsibilities was developed.

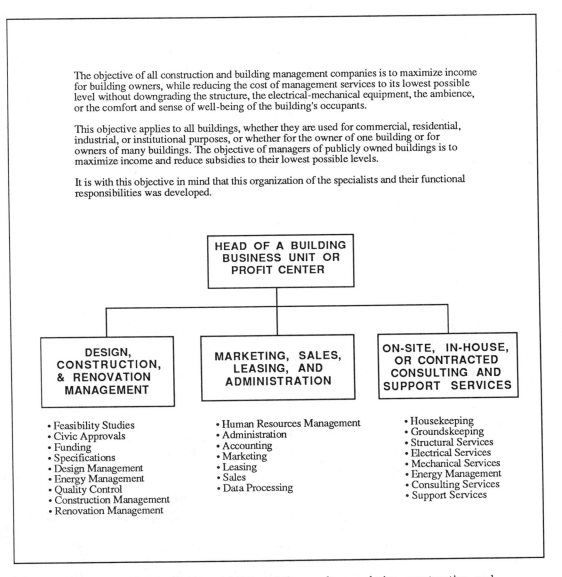

Figure 1.9 Functional accountabilities of the people on a design, construction, and building management team.

Most of the people needed on the team are often not included in the Canadian government's directory of occupations; if they are mentioned, the descriptions of their responsibilities are vague or completely incorrect. This may be the situation in the United States and, perhaps, in many countries.

The industry will get support from the government only when industry problems are clearly defined. One of these problems is to identify the people involved in the industry and what they do. The construction and building management industry must consider this a most urgent matter and take steps to correct any misconceptions about the people, their titles, and what is expected of them as a condition of employment.

In the book *Re-inventing the Corporation*, John Naisbitt and Patricia Aburdene explain the importance of people by stating that "in the new information society, human capital has replaced dollar capital as the strategic resource. People and profits are inexorably linked."* They claim that successful companies, especially successful construction and building management companies, must build a reputation for respecting people and offering them a chance to grow personally. Once we identify the management team and the roles that people play on that team, it will be easier for people to identify their career paths. By having the right information and the right training programs, the industry can help people develop and reach realistic goals for the industry and themselves.

Roadblocks to Improving Management

In Ontario, the Ministry of Government Services owns and manages 9,000 buildings, employs 80,000 people, and owns $5 billion worth of land, buildings, and equipment. They spend $320 million annually on major expenses and renovations and $130 million on operations and maintenance. The Ontario Ministry of Municipal Affairs and Housing owns and manages 85,000 apartment units. Canada Mortgage and Housing, in 1982, held mortgages on 200,000 subsidized units in Canada. The Department of Public Works owns and manages thousands of buildings in Canada, including all the airports. These buildings are worth $60 billion and cost $6 billion annually to operate. The Canadian government employs 35,000 people in these buildings.† To approximate the U.S. government's real estate investment, multiply these figures by 10.

In view of all this, it seems strange yet understandable that because of fragmentation the design, construction, and building management industry has not been able to decide on the organization of its management team or the roles that people must play on them.

The Kellogg report found that "industry fragmentation" was one of the key issues. This is the reason why the industry has not been able to come to grips with the basic and fundamental need to identify and organize its manage-

---

*John Naisbitt and Patricia Aburdene, *Re-inventing the Corporation* (New York: Warner Books, 1985), p. 4.

†These statistics have been compiled from the Ontario Ministry of Government Services 1984–85 annual report; from "Management of Government (Real Property)," a task force report published in 1986 by the Minister of Supply and Services Canada, p. 13; and from my own consulting reports.

ment team. Until this shortcoming is resolved nothing else will fall into place. This situation is strange, given the fact that most governments in the world are the biggest developers, designers, builders, managers, and operators of buildings and that the industry is responsible for 30 percent of the gross national product and provides shelter, a basic necessity of life.

The cost of regulation was identified as another of the key issues faced by the design and construction industry. It was found by the study that the cost of compliance was far more costly than the regulations indicate. It concluded that the problems of regulation must be examined on a twofold basis: the necessity of the regulation in the first place and, second, its clear, consistent, and rational implementation.

It seems that if the industry would overcome the problem of fragmentation many problems with regulation would be overcome, as a unified design, construction, and building management industry dealt with the problems from a position of strength.

Management Theory

Management is management. Management has been defined as the management of "agreed upon goals" using a minimum of resources. Resources are defined as "time, dollars, tools, equipment, ideas, people and space." Management is also considered "getting the right things done right through other people."* To be successful, managers must know how to delegate, motivate, communicate, and evaluate, and how to improve themselves and others. The interesting thing to remember is that once you know how to manage, you can manage any enterprise, whether it is a hot-dog stand or a multimillion-dollar real estate development. Management is management. The principles of management are the same, the differences are the products, the goals, and the people.

The construction and building management industry, to manage the future, must agree on a system of management that will link all the disciplines involved in design, construction, management, operations, and the servicing of buildings under a single workable system. The system must establish a meaningful framework that unites all the disciplines and, at the same time, allows each of them to achieve the goals of their enterprises and themselves.

The management system used by most corporations does not do this. The system used in the Cadillac Fairview's residential maintenance and operations department did provide a framework that united all the specialists.

The first thing that their system did was to identify problems, collect pertinent data to help solve them, and follow up to assure that the problems were indeed solved, without creating new ones. Too many managers, especially

---

*These terms were defined by Dr. Harvey A. Silver at a Cadillac Fairview in-house management seminar, April 20–30, 1977.

in the construction and building management industry, tend to manage "yesterday rather than tomorrow." Success hinges on five basic management activities. A brief outline of these activities will help you understand them and encourage you to develop a management plan that includes them all.

Planning building maintenance needs.   Planning must include the establishment of clear-cut, well-defined organizational goals and strategic plans that provide the basis for systematic planning at the lowest level of the company. To do this Cadillac decided that a building would be a business unit and provide the basis for all of planning, organizing, staffing, directing, and control. Once the organization was separated and structured on the basis of work specialization and task identification that matched the needs of a building, the company needed a way to communicate the specialists' intentions, the costs for their recommendations, and the results expected. After each support-service consulting specialist was allotted an appropriate role on an organizational chart, job descriptions and more formal charters of accountability detailing all the functional accountabilities, specifications, patterns of authority, work flow, and a system of assuring feedback was developed.

All of this was part of the overall planning process for managing maintenance and operations expenses in which Cadillac clearly defined the objectives of the program and set out a means of attaining these goals. It was a way of deciding in advance what needed to be done in every building and then deciding who was to do it and when. The basis for this planning process revolved around specialized building inspections—the information gathered about each building and included in a building profile and any other records about maintenance requests, work and purchase orders, renovation, and retrofit proposals—and the costs to correct problems.

One of the major challenges facing people who own and manage buildings is to find an effective way of planning the myriad tasks that need to be done, getting them done, and then measuring the results of the program, a means of identifying problems and means of directing activities if they do not conform to the company's purpose. The forms created and successfully used for this purpose are illustrated in Chapter 5.

Organizing.   Every design, construction, and building management company should develop a management organizational hierarchy similar to ones used by baseball or hockey teams or any other sports organization. In Cadillac Fairview's residential maintenance, consulting, and support-service division these responsibilities were organized into housekeeping, groundskeeping, structural, and electrical-mechanical services. All management teams should be organized on the basis of task identification and work specialization. As in any sport, the first thing you must do is identify the game you are playing so that you can staff your team with the right kind of people. The second step is to staff the team with people skilled to handle the various specializations that were identified.

Job specifications and channels of communication should be identified by vertical lines in a tiered structure and should be defined by an organizational chart backed up by the assignment of functional accountabilities, procedures, and regulations. The organizational chart should show patterns of authority, work flow, and feedback.

Staffing.   Staffing is the recruiting, interviewing, hiring, position assignment, performance assessment, training, upgrading, and, when necessary, firing of the people filling the positions identified on the organizational hierarchy. To succeed, you need people, and those people must be trained to handle the responsibilities assigned to them. Once the organization of the team has been agreed upon by the design, construction, and building management industry, a whole new field of opportunities will open for architects, engineers, project managers, property managers, building operators, and the people who will provide consulting, support services, supplies, materials, parts, equipment, and chemicals for them.

Directing.   The success of the directing function depends on the style, nature, and skill of the top, middle, and first-line managers. All must be endowed with the right portions of human, conceptual, and technical skills if they expect to lead, motivate, and give direction to their staffs.

Controlling.   Controlling is having a system of management that provides a means of measuring inputs of information, energy, and materials against the output from the efforts of the management team. Controls are a means of measuring performance, identifying problem areas, and redirecting them to conform with corporate purpose. The management information system that is used by management to achieve the required controls should inform, appraise, and support the managers who should be qualified to intelligently react and correct or redirect problem situations. To be successful, managers must have a system that measures progress toward clearly defined objectives and measurable results.

Traditionally people in senior property-management positions handle paper and people functions. It is for this reason that we think only of leasing, rent collections, purchasing, and accounts payable activities when we think of management data bases. The truth is that most of the money invested in buildings is for the structure and the electrical-mechanical equipment, and the industry will have to become more expert in dealing with the decision-making process when designing, building, managing, and operating buildings. To control the money invested in buildings, decision makers need the right information.

Management's Seven Strategic Areas of Activity.   In property management there are seven strategic areas of activity that repeat themselves each month and require controlling:

1. Leasing
2. Occupant turnover (move-ins and move-outs)
3. Rent collection and bad-debt recovery
4. Inspections (housekeeping, groundskeeping, structure, electrical-mechanical, and in-suite)
5. Purchasing (supplies, services, materials, chemicals, parts, equipment, and tools)
6. Accounting (receivables, payables, payroll, repair and maintenance expenses, the cost of on-site staff salaries, fuel, electricity, water, renovations, retrofits, mortgages, taxes, legal insurance, taxes, etc.)
7. Maintenance tasks (daily, weekly, monthly, semiannual, and annual recurring and nonrecurring maintenance services tasks), carried out by the on-site and support-services people

Feedback.   Feedback is the only way to test whether the assumptions on which decisions have been made are valid, or whether they have become obsolete. Organized information is needed for feedback, and it must be accurate if effective results are to be achieved. There are several needs that require satisfying by building owners if they expect to be successful: the need for the right information, the right consulting and support services, the right people, both in-house and on-site, and the availability of consulting and support information and services that are beyond the ability of the owners and their staff.

The criteria for a successful real estate venture.   Cadillac Development brought with it when it merged with Fairview two key management policies. First, it always set its rent levels by market demand. This was achieved by raising the rents until it forced a vacancy. The second policy was guided by generally acknowledged criteria for a successful real estate venture. These criteria state that a building must be properly located, properly designed, properly built, properly financed, and effectively and efficiently managed. This policy certainly paid off because the buildings were always full of good tenants and were always kept at a high level of maintenance. Both policies were important, but the policy related to the location, the quality of product, and the maintenance and operation of the buildings was the main reason for attracting and keeping good tenants. It earned the company the reputation of being the best residential landlord in Toronto. These were the conditions that existed in 1973, when rent controls were imposed in Ontario.

Landlords who did not get market rents or who did not keep their buildings at a high level of maintenance were caught with their rents down and a backlog of deferred maintenance that ate away at their profits as they were forced to correct maintenance problems on a crisis basis. Buildings with these conditions always attracted less-than-desirable tenants who usually paid rents that were much below the market.

Keeping a record of problems and improving knowledge.   It was important to have a system of managing maintenance that would assure that all of the recurring and nonrecurring maintenance was properly planned, organized, directed, and controlled. The on-site staff and the support-service people, whether in-house or provided by an outside contractor, knew exactly what they were supposed to do on a daily, weekly, monthly, semi-annual, and annual basis to keep the buildings in top shape. At the same time, they all strived to keep the costs at their lowest possible level and the occupants of the buildings comfortable. This is not easy, and that is why the industry has problems making it work.

It is important for a property manager to know exactly what is being done, by whom, and at what cost. To do this Cadillac developed and used a system of recordkeeping that began with a maintenance request, which kept records of problems handled by the on-site staff, a work order for keeping records of work done by the in-house support-service technician, and a purchase order for keeping records of work done by the contractor. A renovation proposal form was used to document renovations and retrofits. All these forms are illustrated and explained in Chapter 4. Saving the forms for one year and analyzing them provided some very valuable information:

- It helped identify all the maintenance problems.
- It helped organize them into specific services and electrical-mechanical systems.
- It highlighted the need for more input into the planning process for new buildings and prompted the creation of a technical committee that studied the problems and recommended solutions for them.
- It identified the need for developing specialists in marketing, leasing, administration, housekeeping, groundskeeping, and structural and electrical-mechanical services. As these in-house consulting specialists researched problems and recommended solutions, they became better and better. Initially they were not actually trained to manage their specialty, because people with the management skills needed were just not available. By allowing them to concentrate on their specialty, and because they worked within our management system, they became very professional in the way they handled their jobs.

A Common Budgeting and Recordkeeping System

Once Cadillac discovered the wisdom of organizing its maintenance management team by the specialized functional accountabilities of housekeeping, groundskeeping, and structural and electrical-mechanical services, it seemed logical to also organize its repair and maintenance expense accounts in the same manner. These account classifications are all illustrated and explained in Chapter 5.

Because all buildings require the control of these same expense classifications, it seems logical that the construction and building management industry use a common chart of maintenance and operations expense classifications. The answers to the following questions can help clarify and value analyze this recommendation:

How should the information be organized?

What does management need to know about the income and expenses for a building?

How can the information be used to help manage maintenance and energy expenses?

What kind of information do we need to manage recurring maintenance tasks?

How often are the recurring tasks carried out?

What kind of information do we need to help us manage the myriad recurring and nonrecurring maintenance, renovations, and retrofits; the on-site staff; the in-house support services; or work carried out by an outside contractor?

How can we control the nonrecurring, or capitalized, expenses?

How much will it all cost?

What kind of results or benefits do we expect?

What kind of information do we need to keep in data bases?

What is the best way to use this information to help management develop, design, build, manage, and operate a building?

What is the best way to use this information to help management plan, organize, staff, direct, and control all the activities required to maximize income and reduce the cost of management services to its lowest level without downgrading the structure, the electrical-mechanical equipment, the ambience, or the comfort of a building's occupants?

The organization of information related to the maintenance and operations of buildings is usually included as a total expense in the repair and maintenance account. It is difficult, and practically impossible, for management to properly plan, organize, staff, direct or control renovations and retrofits, the repair and maintenance expenses, the cost of on-site staff salaries, and the cost of fuel, electricity, and water without having an account classification to match each activity and then knowing how best to use the information.

**Match the Building Components
to the Expense Classifications**

After much study, Cadillac decided to match up the expense account classifications with the services and electrical-mechanical systems found in all buildings. Records were kept of all components that required maintenance or that would wear out and need replacement. The activities needed to maintain a continuity of care program for these components were then built into the budgets by using the budget-builder working papers that are illustrated in Chapter 5. In this way a building became the system.

Once the information was organized, it seemed quite logical that people who specialized in those functions would be called upon to help decide about the tools, equipment, supplies, materials, parts, and services that were needed by each building. Everyone involved in specific functions participated in the preparation of specifications for them. The account classifications were organized to match the building components and were further broken down to assure that there was a classification for everything that needed to be done. This ensured that all the information that managers needed was in a logical place.

As the budgets were prepared for each building, the budget-builder planning process assured that everyone on the management team participated. It was especially important that people who specialized in one of the functions, or who headed up each business unit, inspect all the components or the equipment in each building to assure that they were being maintained to expectations and to determine the need for component or equipment replacement or upgrading.

There are several things about inspections that warrant mentioning:

- Not everyone can do maintenance-services inspections—people need to be trained to properly carry them out and to report their findings.
- Managers should take their on-site staffs with them when they inspect. It provides an excellent opportunity for communication.
- Inspections should be carried out daily by the on-site building operator, quarterly by the manager, and annually by the building owner.
- Problems uncovered during the inspection should be identified and corrected as soon as possible. Problems that will need to be corrected in the future should be included in the budget-builder working papers and added to the next budget. Problems indicating the need for training and upgrad-

ing the on-site staff should be handled by setting up special one-on-one clinics to help them overcome a specific problem.

A Study of Management

Management is often perceived as a problem for most development companies for several reasons. Development and construction people seem to be immune to the problems that construction builds into buildings; the heavy mortgage debt load; the many structural and electrical-mechanical problems; the fact that, in residential buildings, less desirable engineers and tradespeople are sometimes used; and they are not held accountable for the financial, structural, and electrical-mechanical problems passed on to management. In 1968, because Cadillac was planning for a 20,000-apartment rental portfolio, a consultant was asked to study the property management group.

Why Just the Management Group

At that time, the company had built only apartment buildings, and this had the advantage of allowing the development, design, construction, and management teams to work together on this one product line. When we started to build shopping centers and office buildings, the company decided to set up separate product-line divisions for each type of project. Both of these new divisions completely ignored the management systems that were already in effect (based on the recommendations of a consulting firm). These systems had been used, studied, and refined to a point where the company was considered one of the best management groups in Toronto.

In each of the product-line divisions, authority and responsibility misconceptions arose because it seemed to senior management that the management of the buildings started after the buildings were completed and not when they were first conceived. The development, design, and construction team could do virtually as it pleased without being held accountable for the problems it created. That is why the person at the head of the management team must be qualified to handle the entire development, design, construction, management, and operations of each building or all the buildings in a company's portfolio.

That the 1968 management study included only the people who managed after the building was built, and not the entire company, was a big mistake and had a great bearing on the future of Cadillac's residential group. Then the company was called Cadillac Development, but this decision not to include the developer, designer, and builder in the management study also spilled over into the management decisions made by the Cadillac Fairview residential division after Cadillac and Fairview merged. Both Cadillac and Fairview paid dearly for misconceptions relative to the nature of the business that they were in and the fact that the developer, designer, and builder were not considered part of, or contributors to, the success of each building project. Further problems resulted because they considered commercial, residential, and industrial buildings; homes; new communities; and condominiums as different from one another, and each of them had duplicated management hierarchies.

This is mentioned here not to point a finger at Cadillac Fairview but rather to suggest that the construction and building management industry take a close look at the way it has traditionally perceived its business and take steps now to change any misconceptions.

Action Recommendations

"Construction Trends and Problems Through 1990" made several recommendations to the design and construction industry. The recommendations are excellent, and we could use most of them to help improve the management of buildings, perhaps adding a few recommendations of our own:

- Education and training are needed on many levels to handle the different facets of the problems.
- Train users in employment of a management systems approach.
- Train system designers in the needs and problems of the users, so the system supports the user and not vice versa.
- The owners of design, construction, and building management companies must understand and support the need for the use of the best management systems available to help improve the present situation.
- Funding must be made available immediately to develop these systems and to provide education for all those presently employed in developing, designing, building, or managing buildings to help improve their weaknesses in either their human, conceptual, or technical skills. These programs should also be made available to those wishing to seek careers in this industry.
- Most recommendations made by the study pointed to improvement in the educational and communications process. Guidelines were prepared involving such matters as organization; risk determination and allocation; designer and contractor selection; useful management systems; the use of computers, whose data bases and software systems would be helpful to small and medium-sized companies and the development of suitable information systems that would be made easily available to small companies.

A Joint Effort Is Essential to Success

In the study, the Construction Sciences Research Foundation recommends a joint effort of technical and professional organizations and lists the Construction Specifications Institute, the American Society of Civil Engineers, American Institute of Architects, American Association of Cost Engineers, and the Project Management Institute. The American Society of Heating, Refrigeration and Air Conditioning Engineers; Refrigeration Service Engineers Society; Plant Engineers Society; the Hotel-Motel Association; the Institute of Real Estate Management; the International Council of Shopping Centers; Building Owners and Managers Association; and any other organizations developing, designing, building, managing, or providing support services to commercial, residential, industrial, or institutional buildings should also be included.

Not only is there a need to develop the right information and management system, but it is essential to get the information about what is available and effective to those who actually would use it. It was with this in mind that the foundation also suggested the following:

- Study the management process from a more scientific point of view and develop better performance-measurement techniques of managers and management tools.
- Develop an efficient time-share management information service to allow small firms to use sophisticated systems properly.
- Support an appropriate study into the ways and means of introducing new management techniques into the construction and building management industry.
- Develop more seminars, workshops, and continuing education to get the word out to those who use it.

The study emphasized that it was important to develop measurement techniques so that designers, builders, managers, operators and the support service industry can measure the benefits in terms of time and costs from the adoption of improved management techniques. The systems that were developed and explained in this book do just that.

1.4 A SYSTEMS APPROACH TO PROPERTY MANAGEMENT

The Decision-Making Process

The management of buildings is one continual decision-making process; because of this, the decision-making function deserves special attention. The decision-making process actually begins when someone conceptualizes a new building project, and it continues through the design, building, management, and operations stages for the rest of the project's life. Decisions made by people in each of the design, construction, management, operation, and service groups have varying degrees of effect on the rest of the groups involved with the building, depending on their responsibilities. For example, decisions made by senior executives have a significant impact on their entire organization, its performance, and its results. Everyone on the management team makes decisions every day that have varying degrees of influence on the rest of the organization and also on the tenants or occupants of the buildings he or she manages. Decisions about location, financing, the quality of the structure and the electrical-mechanical equipment, as well as the daily operational decisions all have an impact on the viability and financial success of the project.

There are several elements related to each decision-making process that should be kept in mind and understood. The person responsible for making a decision must:

1. Have a clear understanding of the problem being resolved.
2. Know the specifications required to correct the problem.
3. Be qualified to think through what is "right" for a solution to satisfy the specifications.
4. Be able to build in, initiate, and monitor the action required to correct the problem.
5. Be receptive to feedback about the decision and whether it did correct the problem without creating new ones.

The Need for New Strategies

Since the end of World War II the construction and building management industry has exploded throughout the world. Buildings are bigger and more sophisticated, and the people in the industry are called upon to make more and more multidisciplined decisions about the way we develop, design, build, manage, operate, and provide support services for buildings. Within each of these specialized fields are subgroups and people who manage these functions for commercial, residential, industrial, and institutional buildings. All these specialists are making decisions about buildings and about people.

Coordination of the activities of the people involved in managing, operating, and providing support services for all buildings will never become a reality unless we develop new management strategies that will allow the industry to organize, embrace, and harness all these talents into a property management team under the umbrella of a common purpose.

The General Systems Approach

The *general systems approach* to property management must be such that it links all the disciplines involved in buildings under a single workable system. The system must establish a meaningful framework that unites the disciplines and, at the same time, allows them to achieve the goals of the entire organization and themselves.*

Whether to solve a single problem or to devise a means of systematically solving a common recurring problem, a systems approach can be used. It applies the concept of identifying problems, collecting pertinent data to help solve them, and following up to assure that the problems have indeed been solved without creating new ones. It involves identifying the various specialists who command special techniques, possess knowledge, and have acquired the right kind of experiences for solving the problems that are identified.

The systems theory of management. In the construction and building management industry we find that we have systems within systems, each one contributing to the success or failure of the other. This systems theory of management is primarily *an attitude* of looking at the organization as a whole structure, taking into account its interrelated and dependent parts or subsystems. It recognizes that no one part can perform effectively without the others and that any action of one will affect the balance of the organization or even of the entire industry.

A construction and building management organization, rather than being a closed entity, is itself a subsystem of the social, political, and economic community involved in the development, design, construction, management, operations, and service cycles of all types of buildings.

The system of property management recommended here is *pragmatic*, because its actions are directed to respond to real world needs. It is *organized*, because it assembles information from a vast number of resources, including multidisciplined specialists, generalists, and experience, and places it into organized packages that can be used by everyone involved in the process. It is empirical and *theoretical*, because it quantifies this tremendous input of data and, employing theoretical models, generates several solutions. Once you have people with the right specialized skills available as a support for building owners and they have access to the right information, they will be able to continually isolate problems, attack them, and eliminate them. It is worth repeating that while these specialists are involved in this process they get better and better at their specialty. *This system of management grows and improves as it is being developed and used.*

---

*The systems developed and used successfully by Cadillac Development and then by Cadillac Fairview residential divisions' maintenance and operations department over a 17-year period were generally based on the general systems theory explained herein; however, those of us in the department were unaware of the theory at the time.

Although I knew that the system that we used produced some fantastic results, it was difficult to explain how or why it did work. Professor Ken R. Blowatt gave me a copy of his book *Project Management Theory* (Brock University, 1976), and it was from information that I read in his book that I was able to explain our systems approach to property management developed and used from 1964 to 1981.

A way of thinking—a method of analysis.   The general systems approach is based on a philosophy that permits the head of each building unit, or profit center, to view problems and interrelationships with a "whole" view. It includes the ability to solve problems, to analyze systems in which all variables are considered, weighed, and computed to an optimal program of action. Finally, these solutions are applied to the system, recognizing all the subsystem relationships. Thus the systems approach is a way of thinking, a method of analysis, and, finally, a managerial style.

The objectives.   The systems approach has six objectives in support of the managerial process:

1. To provide management with as much information as possible for guiding and controlling the enterprise.
2. To foster the formulation of long-range plans and objectives, thus establishing a framework for subsystem cohesion.
3. To balance future developments with current problems.
4. To develop discrete plans and objectives for individual programs.
5. To keep abreast of new ideas and technology that may affect the organization.
6. To discharge these objectives efficiently and effectively.

A Matter of Utmost Urgency

The objective of the design, construction, and building management industry should be to develop a common management system that would encompass all the various areas of specialization and organize them under a common organizational management hierarchy; to agree about job titles for members of the management team; to agree on a common chart of expense accounts; to use a common planning and budgeting process; and to use common recordkeeping and accounting systems. In this way each specialist not only will be able to contribute to improving the system but will have available relevant information from all the other participants.

In an industry where there is such a multitude of theories and such diversification of specialized activities that could be made manageable and workable by making available the right information, the right consulting and support services, and the right training programs, the need for this common concept of property management becomes a matter of utmost urgency.

To assure success, support is required from the disciplines associated with the design, construction, and building management industry; professionals involved in building sciences, energy, computer technology, residential, commercial, industrial, and institutional building management; financial management, architecture, and engineering; and those entities that provide materials, parts, supplies, tools, equipment, chemicals, labor, and vehicles.

The challenge is to control the renovations and retrofits, the repair and maintenance expenses, the on-site staff salaries, and the cost and consumption of fuel, electricity, and water by the right system of management. The decisions about location, quality of construction, proper financing, and professional management begin with the developer and do not end after the building is built, but continue for the life of the property.

If any of the criteria for success is missing, then the building will not be successful. Once this is understood, the organization of the team, its goals, objectives, and career paths; the information and support that they need; and their training become relatively easy.

1.5 A CHARTER FOR THE INDUSTRY

The use of a charter of accountability provides a means of analyzing industry purposes and objectives and helps define industry responsibilities. The charter is the foundation for structuring the business unit or profit-center team, a means of providing a yardstick against which management's performance can be measured. If this charter has validity, then the industry can use it as a basis for developing or expanding charters for others on the team. The charter provides a means of organizing responsibilities and information about our industry or the people involved that is logical and easy to understand.

It is essential that people on management teams have a clear understanding of their responsibilities or there will be conflict. When we analyze the construction and building management industry, we will find that people are responsible for everything from a single building to companies with several different kinds of buildings valued at billions of dollars.

The heads of small companies may be responsible for the development, design, building, management, and operation aspect of a building's life. Some companies may not develop, design, or build buildings; they may just buy existing buildings. In these cases, the development functions would not be included in their functional accountabilities, but some of the decision-making about a building's viability and about renovations or retrofits would still be functional responsibilities of management. All the other functions in the charter apply to all building owners or managers, whether they own residential, commercial, industrial, or institutional buildings. Only the relationship with the occupants would vary among different types of buildings. (Charters of accountability are further discussed in Chapter 6.)

Purpose of the Charter

1. To define the development, marketing, leasing, administrative, and maintenance services accountabilities for a construction and building management company.

2. To set objectives and standards against which the company's performance can be measured.

Purpose of a Construction and Building Management Company

1. To successfully develop, design, build or buy, and manage or operate a building or buildings by maximizing profits for a privately owned building and reducing subsidies for buildings that are owned publicly.
2. To assure that the building's ambience and the comfort and safety of the occupants are better than can be obtained elsewhere.
3. To protect a company's reputation for quality and integrity and the investment in the property.
4. To achieve company goals using a minimum of time, dollars, tools, equipment, ideas, people, and space.
5. To achieve predetermined objectives through other people by coordinating labor, machinery, time, and materials. Getting the right things done by delegating, motivating, communicating, evaluating, and improving the skills of the company leaders and the other people on their management team.

Objectives of a Construction and Building Management Company

1. To identify the people needed on its management team, their goals and objectives and functional accountabilities.
2. To satisfy the emotional needs of the people on its team and the occupants of the buildings being managed.
3. To provide, today and tomorrow, all the qualified people needed to develop, design, build, manage, operate, and provide support services for the buildings it builds or retains in a management portfolio.
4. To assure the safety, security, and comfort of the occupants of the buildings being managed and the members of the management team.
5. To maximize profits for the buildings it builds and sells or keeps and manages.

Corporate Intent

Building owners should delegate to their management team a large measure of initiative and self-direction. The people on their development, design, building, management, operations, or support-services teams are expected to manage as carefully as they would if they were taking care of their own businesses. They should expect them to control expenditures as if the money were coming from their own pockets. Everyone on the management team should be as critical of any flaw in courtesy, friendliness, and service in a building as the tenant paying the highest rent.

To accomplish this, construction and building management companies must assure that they have qualified people on their management team. Everyone on that team from the chief executive officer down to the person providing on-site service to the tenants must be qualified to carefully apportion time among improving tenant relations; overseeing all the development and construction, renovation, or retrofit services; and the marketing, sales, leasing, administrative, technical, and maintenance services illustrated on the management chart attached to the charter, and by assuring that someone qualified is inspecting the building's housekeeping, groundskeeping, structure, and electrical-mechanical equipment on a regular basis.

The owners of construction and building management companies should assure that the people on their management teams resist giving too much time to the functions in which they might be most experienced and interested. People on their management teams should be taught to place the greatest emphasis on those functions in which they are least experienced. Construction and building management companies should, using the assistance of people with the specialized skills shown on the support-services chart and through other industry-recognized educational institutions, be continually encouraging their management staff to expand the skills—human, conceptual, and technical—they will need to become most competent to handle the responsibilities assigned to each member of the management team.

Accountability

To adequately manage the services needed to develop, design, build or buy, and manage or operate a building, the chief executive officer of a large construction and building management company or the owner of one building would need to be knowledgeable about all the services detailed as functional accountabilities in the charter and illustrated on the function accountability chart attached to and forming a part of the charter (see Figures 1.6 to 1.9).

BUSINESS MANAGEMENT

1. Develop a management organizational team that suits the business of the company.
2. Define the functional accountabilities for the middle- and first-line managers identified by that organizational hierarchy.
3. Assure that management recruits, hires, motivates, trains, develops, assesses performance, and upgrades people to professionally and adequately fill the roles identified by that organizational hierarchy.

4. Assure that management develops and achieves adequate policies, specifications, and standards.
5. Assure that when required management sets up suitable management or field offices.
6. Establish short- and long-term planning goals.
7. Assure that management develops a system of preparing realistic income and expense budgets for each building in the management portfolio.
8. Analyze the results of the management program and take the appropriate steps to overcome any problems identified by those results.

FINANCE AND ADMINISTRATIVE

1. Assure that there is a finance and administrative system that adequately supports and value analyzes the feasibility of new ventures, acquisitions, renovations, or retrofits.
2. Assure that there is an administrative system that controls revenue received from leasing and other sources, as well as the expenditures for new buildings or acquisitions, renovations, retrofits, staff salaries, repair and maintenance, fuel, water, electricity, taxes, insurance, legal fees, and other management expenses.
3. Assure that there is adequate legal, tax, insurance, personnel, marketing, sales, leasing, and other operational services for the portfolio being managed.
4. Assure that management provides adequate bridge, mortgage, and other financing when required.
5. Assure that there are proper financial audits and other management controls and an adequate information system.

DEVELOPMENT

1. Assure that there is adequate concept, design, specifications, project management, construction management, and maintenance support services to value analyze the acquisition of an existing property, to complete a renovation or retrofit, or to build a new building.
2. Assure that management identifies the major components of a building and establishes and maintains a current cost for them so as to monitor the initial and ongoing cost for these components over their life span.
3. Assure the acquisition of land or new properties to satisfy the future needs and goals of the enterprise.
4. Liaise with the people responsible for maintenance support services about built-in problems and be aware of the costs to correct them.
5. Assure that management develops realistic pro forma financial projec-

tions for each department, each building in its management portfolio, and for any new projects.

6. Assure that, when required, someone is qualified to seek municipal approvals for projects.

7. Assume responsibility for buildings being built and those included in the management portfolio.

8. Assure that the project management team participates with the on-site staff and those who will be providing maintenance, consulting, and support services during formal turnover of a new property and that everyone participates in the preparation of a building profile.

9. Assure that, wherever possible, management is provided with as-built drawings and microfilm of the structure, landscaping, and electrical-mechanical systems for all properties being managed or being added to the portfolio.

10. Keep everyone on the management team informed about plans for developments, acquisitions, renovations or retrofits, either at management meetings or by written reports.

MAINTENANCE SERVICES

1. Assure that management develops maintenance services standards and specifications for the buildings being managed and assure that they are being maintained.

2. Assure that management defines the on-site, in-house, and outside maintenance, consulting, and support services required to manage each building in the portfolio. Arrange to publish and keep up-to-date a suppliers and services guide showing the specifications, the services, and the people recommended, what they do and how much they charge.

3. Assure that management develops operations budget projections for each building in the management portfolio that include a planned maintenance and energy management program; costs for custodial care, recurring and nonrecurring repairs, on-site staff costs, consulting and support services, capitalized expenditures for renovations and retrofits; and the consumption goals and projected costs for fuel, water, and electricity.

4. Assure that the company has the statistical data required for short- and long-term acquisition, construction, or building management planning.

5. Assure that management develops, implements, and monitors a planned maintenance and energy management program.

6. Assure that management properly defines, specifies, documents, obtains quotations for, and completes all major renovations or retrofits that have been approved in each budget year.

7. Liaise with proper consulting and support-service specialists when considering the purchase or development of a new project.

8. Assure that management formally takes over all new buildings that are added to the management portfolio.

9. Assure that management develops a building profile, energy audit, and master action plan for all buildings being managed (see Chapter 4).

10. Assure that management keeps up-to-date all as-built plans and microfilm files for them.

11. Assure that management prepares at least one annual written report for each building being managed that would include an inspection of the structure, the housekeeping and groundskeeping conditions, as well as an inspection of the electrical-mechanical systems.

12. Assure that management defines the on-site and maintenance support services for each building being managed; sets job specifications for in-house and on-site staff; recruits, hires, trains, motivates, assesses performance, and upgrades the support staff; and develops specifications for all recurring and nonrecurring maintenance functions, renovations or retrofits, tools, equipment, supplies, parts, and materials required for each building in the portfolio.

13. Assure that senior management keeps the company and the members of the management team informed about maintenance and operations activities, either at management meetings or by regularly submitting written reports.

LEASING, SALES, AND ADMINISTRATIVE

1. Define and provide leasing, sales, and administrative services that help ensure safety, comfort, and ambience for the people living or working in the buildings being managed and that satisfy the needs of the building owner.

2. Arrange for adequate management of all leasing or sales functions if the building is a condominium. Set rent rolls, assure that management documents all move-ins and move-outs, and manage any rent subsidies or other special programs relative to the occupants' needs and services.

3. Formulate policies in relation to occupant eligibility criteria.

4. Liaise orally and in writing with administration, development, and maintenance support services concerning plans for all new projects. Assure that there is adequate feedback about any problems along with recommendations for correcting them for all existing and new buildings.

5. Assure that management recruits, hires, trains, motivates, assesses performance and upgrades people who provide leasing, sales, and other on-site office or head-office management services for the tenants.

6. Assure that management develops office and administrative budgets for each building in the portfolio.

7. Assure that management develops and maintains the necessary administrative recordkeeping control.

8. Assure that management develops and maintains an up-to-date client profile of all applicants on a waiting list, a directory of all the present tenants, and vacancy and availability records.

9. Assure that management prepares revenue budgets for each building being managed and maintains adequate statistical data for long- and short-term planning.

10. Assure that everyone on the management team maintains a high level of public relations and that people are taught to never argue with a tenant.

11. Cooperate and participate with any government ministry or other institution or agency that is involved with developing, designing, building, managing, operating, or servicing the construction and building management industry.

Maintenance Management

2.1 HOW THE PROGRAM STARTED*

In 1970 Cadillac Development experienced a problem that alerted it to the need for a more effective maintenance and energy management program. The company's electrical-mechanical specialist discovered an unbelievable problem with in-suite heating convector valves that had seized in either the open or shut position. By inserting a magnet-tipped probe into the body of the valve, he discovered that the heating water contained a black magnetic substance that was analyzed as iron oxide. These metal filings were the reason the valves were seizing, and the test provided the evidence of corrosion in the heating systems (Figure 2.1).

To overcome this problem the specialist found a chemical called Nutek,† which, when introduced into the heating water, neutralized the electrolysis and put the ferrous oxide back into solution. The only problem was that Nutek cost $50 per gallon, and the company was reluctant to allow the staff to arbi-

---

*Sections 2.1 and 2.2 are adapted from Mel Shear, *Handbook of Building Maintenance Management*, © 1983, p. 563 (A Reston Publication), by permission of Prentice-Hall, Inc., Englewood Cliffs, New Jersey.

†Nutek is manufactured by Nuclear Technology Corporation, P.O. Box 1, Amston, CT 06231.

The components of a Flair electric radiator valve illustrated make up an electric zone valve used in apartments to regulate the flow of the heating system water. It opens when the thermostat calls for heat and closes when the desired temperature has been reached. The chrome-plated stem, because it is machined to fit precisely, was quickly seized up when the oxidized iron fouled it up. It is possible that even with proper water treatment, valves will still require periodic maintenance.

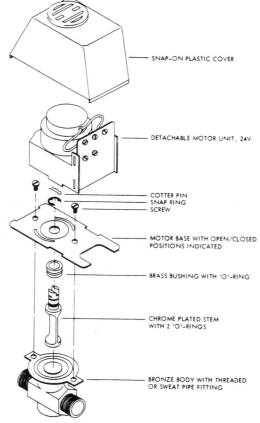

SNAP-ON PLASTIC COVER

DETACHABLE MOTOR UNIT, 24V.

COTTER PIN
SNAP RING
SCREW

MOTOR BASE WITH OPEN/CLOSED POSITIONS INDICATED

BRASS BUSHING WITH 'O'-RING

CHROME PLATED STEM WITH 2 'O'-RINGS

BRONZE BODY WITH THREADED OR SWEAT PIPE FITTING

A magnetic probe was inserted into the body of an in-suite heating convector zone valve and picked up a black substance from the heating system water. An analysis of this substance revealed that it contained oxidized iron. It was this fact that provided evidence that the heating systems in Cadillac's buildings were corroding.

After much research a water treatment chemical was introduced into the heating systems. The unusual thing about this chemical was that it put the oxidized iron back into solution and at the same time pacified the electrolysis condition between the copper convectors and the iron piping.

The high cost of the chemical forced Cadillac to explore and initiate a comprehensive maintenance and energy management program to help offset the expense and justify the program. It was at this point that Cadillac actually began reinventing property management.

Figure 2.1 Cadillac used a magnetic probe to remove a black substance from a valve body. The blow-up of the parts illustrates why the finely machined valve seized up.

trarily add this expensive chemical to the heating systems of a 10,000-suite portfolio.

To find a way to offset the high cost of the chemical, the maintenance and operations department of Cadillac Development's residential division studied ways of improving the productivity of the department and of making the maintenance programs more effective and efficient.

It was necessary to upgrade the knowledge of senior management, all the in-house support-service consultants, the building operators, the property managers, and the people who provided outside consulting and support services. In many cases the company was able to guide the outside contractors who provided supplies, services, and products so that they were able to do things that were identified in its master action plan but that the in-house staff was unable to do.

2.2 THE CHALLENGE

In effect, it meant identifying all the problems with the structure and the electrical-mechanical equipment and initiating a program for overcoming them and of keeping records of the results. Fortunately, previous records of utility consumption and repair and maintenance expenditures were available to help set a yardstick for the program. It took some time to develop the program, introduce water treatment, correct leaks, set up a system of testing the water, overcome resistance to change and obtain support for the program.

It was felt that because people were now very conscious about problems the benefits of this type of program would show up in the bottom line of each building's profit as the cost of maintenance and the cost of energy used in the buildings were reduced. The department pledged that it would save much more than the cost of the chemical or the cost of any additional staff that was needed to carry out the program.

2.3 A PRESCRIPTION FOR SUCCESS

In 1970, to convince the company to allow them to introduce the $50-per-gallon chemical into the heating systems, and after much research and study, the maintenance and operations department of Cadillac Development's residential division made several recommendations. They offered to develop a maintenance and energy management program that would save the company at least 10 percent of its maintenance expenses and 20 percent of its energy expenses. They planned, organized, staffed, directed, and controlled the program so as to:

- Systematically test the water in the heating systems to assure that the correct amount of chemical was being introduced initially to stabilize the corrosion problem.

- Train the electrical-mechanical consulting specialists to sample, test, add chemicals, monitor the results, and assure that the correct amount of chemicals was introduced into the heating systems initially and when required after that.

- Double the life of components that wear out and need replacement by initiating a "continuity of care" recurring and nonrecurring maintenance program for the structure and the electrical-mechanical equipment installed in the buildings.

- Develop_ and initiate a zero-base planning and budget-building procedure that would allow management to build into each building's budgets funds for the recurring and nonrecurring expenses associated with the proposed maintenance and energy management program.

- Organize the repair and maintenance expense account classifications used in the budget-builder working papers so that they matched the functional services of a building; for example, housekeeping, groundskeeping, structural services, and electrical-mechanical systems. In this way, the consulting and support-service specialists responsible for each of these functions could help the property manager build in the funds for all the recurring and nonrecurring maintenance and operations expenses associated with his or her specialty using a logical, easy-to-understand format.

- Organize the accounting records for repair and maintenance expenses; on-site staff salaries; fuel, water, and electricity expenses; the cost of building additions, replacements, and equipment additions and replacements; and any construction deficiencies in the first five years of a building's life to match the budget-builder working paper classifications to provide management with a means of comparing the results of the program with the budgeted plan.

- Reduce the need for corrective maintenance.

- Identify the in-house, consulting, and outside support-service specialists needed for this program. These specialty functions were classified as housekeeping, groundskeeping, and structural and electrical-mechanical services.

- Seek outside support-service specialists who would be qualified to carry out the program as outlined in the support-service charter of accountability developed along with the specifications for each function.

- Recruit, hire, train, assess, and upgrade, where necessary, the on-site staff, consultants, and in-house support specialists and assign to them the responsibility for those functions that could not be purchased from outside the company.

- Initiate regular "look, listen, and touch" inspections by the on-site staff and regular hands-on building inspections by the in-house consultant specialists in housekeeping, groundskeeping, structural services, and the electrical-mechanical systems.
- Immediately correct any problems uncovered by these inspections—unless the cost to correct them was under an amount specified by the owner—after seeking approval for the expense from the building owner.
- Report, in writing, about what the inspections uncovered, both favorable and unfavorable, and seek approval to correct any problem that would cost more than an amount predetermined by the owner unless the expense was part of an approved recurring maintenance activity.
- Develop a renovation proposal procedure so that all recurring expenditures of less than an amount predetermined by the owner and not budgeted or all nonrecurring expenses over that amount were properly researched, approved, and documented before the money was spent.
- Reduce maintenance and operations expenses to their lowest possible levels without downgrading the structure, the electrical-mechanical equipment, the building's ambience, or the comfort of the tenants.
- Efficiently operate the electrical-mechanical equipment already installed in a building before spending any money on nonrecurring retrofits or energy-saving measures.
- Assess all potential energy-saving measures to assure that the ones providing the greatest return on investment would be commenced first.
- Develop historical records of each building's structure and electrical-mechanical equipment to document everything that would require maintenance or wear out.
- Develop work loads and schedules of duties for the on-site staff and for any support-service people who would be carrying out maintenance functions in each building.
- Develop a method of providing maintenance and energy goals for each building in the management portfolio and measuring the success of the program.
- Continue the program until there were no further opportunities to reduce maintenance and energy expenses.

These recommendations led to a successful maintenance and energy management program. Some of the savings achieved are discussed in Chapter 12. Two entries are worthy of special mention.

The first is the $1 million per year in laundry machine profit. The machines were first installed in our buildings by a contractor who was in the business of supplying this service. For providing the laundry room, the hot water, and the electricity, we received a percentage of the income. During the time this arrangement was in effect, the tenants complained bitterly because the machines were constantly breaking down, so we decided to take over this service ourselves. Once we had control, the income was kept at market level, and our maintenance program doubled the life of the machines to ten years.

The second entry of note is the savings earned from a long-term elevator-service contract. After the problems with the laundry machines, the next biggest headache was with elevators. We were able to convince Cadillac to purchase one of the better elevators, and it became the company's policy to use them in all its buildings.

Fairview also made it a policy to use the same elevator equipment in their office buildings and shopping centers. When Cadillac Development merged with Fairview, we met with the people in the office building group and suggested that we combine our buying power to negotiate a long-term deal for elevator service. At that time, we had 450 of the top-quality elevators in our buildings and signed a 20-year full-maintenance contract for service. In 1982 this contract saved Cadillac Fairview $400,000. Of equal importance was the fact that the elevators were always in top shape. This is a good example of how expenses can be reduced to their lowest possible level without downgrading the equipment.

This was the only time we were able to take advantage of an opportunity to combine our buying power. Although this kind of unity of action could have been a very big source of revenue for the company, the division of the company by product line would not allow such things to happen. It is for this reason that construction and building management companies should be organized by function and not by product line.

2.4 FROM SAVINGS TO PROFITS

In 1970 Cadillac Development's maintenance and operations department also pledged to save 20 percent of the energy costs. The results of that program are further discussed in Chapter 12. These results do not include the saving of 30,000 MCF of natural gas in the three buildings in which we replaced the heating plants. At the rate of $4.50 per MCF of natural gas, this translates into a further saving of $135,000 per year.

2.5 THE PLAN OF ACTION

Because buildings come in such a variety of designs and because they are used for so many different purposes, it was necessary to reduce the portfolio to individual buildings. Each building would have its own budget-builder working papers and its own chart of income and expense accounts. It is not uncommon for accountants to use common mortgages or common heating and cooling plants to determine how the financial statements for a building should be structured.

Each Building As Its Own Profit Center

Buildings, although they are used for apartments, offices, industry, or as institutions, all have walls, roofs, windows, doors, floors, and various levels of sophisticated electrical-mechanical systems. Each building should be considered as its own profit center or business unit and should compete only against itself. It is recommended that building management portfolios be broken down into individual building units for planning, budgeting, and accounting purposes.

This was the way Cadillac planned, organized, staffed, directed, and controlled the maintenance management of its portfolio. On a building-by-building basis the company identified every component that required maintenance and included the information in individual building profiles. From this information daily, weekly, monthly, semiannual, and annual maintenance activities to maintain the structure, the grounds, and the electrical-mechanical systems were decided. It was determined whether the work would be done by the on-site staff, the in-house support services, or by an outside support contractor. Cadillac analyzed how long a task would take, when it would be done, why it was being done, and what the end results and cost would be.

Once the opportunities were identified and priorities established, action plans were developed that attacked each area in a logical, systematic fashion. It was then relatively easy to plan and schedule day-to-day maintenance and operations activities.

A System of Value Analysis

Cadillac developed a system of value analysis that involved a critical-reasoning exercise by the in-house consultants about the products, equipment, materials, chemicals, supplies, parts, and services that were used by the residential construction and building management staffs. In concert with the development and construction team specifications were developed that were used by the residential division. It is strange that all of this knowledge and information was not shared by the shopping center, office building, or industrial divisions of the company who were also building and managing buildings. It seemed logical that the company would want to control this planning exercise from a corporate level. Even if everyone on the management teams knew exactly what to do, the corporate organization, and the lack of the right organizational climate, would not allow the right things to happen.

Some important value analysis questions that we asked were:

- What is it?
- What is its purpose?

- What other products, equipment, materials, services, parts, chemicals, or supplies will achieve the same or better results?
- What does it cost?
- What products, equipment, materials, services, parts, chemicals, or supplies will satisfy the needs of the building?
- When will the company be satisfied with the performance of the equipment, products, materials, services, parts, chemicals, or supplies?

Strategic Planning Is Important

Strategic planning allows management to skillfully select from many possible opportunities. The concept is to apply zero-base budget planning techniques to each identified opportunity to drive up the *achieved performance* to its highest level and the remaining *savings potential* to its lowest level. Once the opportunities were identified and priorities established, action plans were developed that attacked each area in a logical, systematic fashion.

2.6 CHARTERS OF ACCOUNTABILITY FOR A BUILDING BUSINESS UNIT

Cadillac developed charters of accountability for the property managers, the on-site staff, the consultants, and the support-service specialists on the management team. Charters rather than job descriptions were used because the company felt that it was important for people to know exactly what their purpose was, their objectives, and the details of their functional accountabilities. Although an attempt was made to avoid overlapping of responsibilities, the organizational hierarchy would not allow this to happen, and many problems were created as people banged heads with those having overlapping responsibilities.

From these charters training programs and functional performance tasks were developed for the people in the residential maintenance and operations department. On an annual basis supervisors met with their staffs to review their functional performance tasks, the goals that they set for themselves, and the status of each task. This exercise was actually a form of performance evaluation. During the meeting a very valuable dialogue took place between supervisor and staff.

2.7 THE ADVANTAGES OF ORGANIZING BY FUNCTION

Cadillac Fairview's residential maintenance and operations department was organized by specialized functions, and there are many advantages to this approach:

- Everyone is linked by a common purpose.
- Specialized roles that people play on construction and building management teams can be standardized, accredited, and recognized.
- People become more knowledgeable when they concentrate on a specialty. The construction and building management industry should make a concentrated effort to agree on the structure of management teams involved in the industry, what they want to call those people, how they are organized, and, most of all, agree about what they are expected to do and know as a condition of employment.
- The industry should use a common chart of income and expense accounts and common forms and systems. This makes more sense if the management teams are organized by function. All the planning, organizing, staffing, directing, control, and monitoring seems more logical when things are thought of in this way.
- Many large construction and management companies waste a lot of money and talent when they organize by product line, because there is much overlapping and duplication of development, design, construction, management, on-site operations, consulting, and support services in each division.
- Many companies also spend a lot of time on problems that are common to buildings in a division even though another division has already researched and put into practice the solution. There have been cases when two development officers in the same company were anonymously bidding up the price of the same piece of land.
- There is great potential for savings when value analysis, specifications, and buying power are assigned to someone who is qualified to be responsible for a specialized function and that person negotiates the best prices for the whole company and monitors the results of his or her decisions.
- There are also many benefits available to companies and individual building owners when everyone uses the same budget-builder working papers and the same income and expense account classifications. Data bases can be developed, quantities can be computerized, and such things as tools, parts, chemicals, supplies, equipment, and services can be organized, standardized, and bulk purchased by management.
- Recurring purchases of supplies and services can be contracted for and scheduled with one purchase order detailing the needs for all the buildings. It would be necessary for owners of only one building to avail themselves of these benefits in association with others with similar needs. The Construction Science Research Foundation aptly recommends that the construction and building management industry develop an efficient time-share information system that would be made available to small companies.

2.8 MAINTENANCE MANAGEMENT AND RENT CONTROLS

Cadillac operated on the premise that the construction and building management business was a long-term one and that the company's existing buildings and any new developments must be properly located, suitably financed, well built, and professionally managed.

Any construction and building management company that does not have a similar policy could be caught with its rents low and its buildings at a low level of maintenance when rent controls are imposed, as many were in Ontario in the mid-1970s. Before that most tenants were on two-year leases, and landlords hesitated to raise the rents for fear of losing good tenants. Many landlords were happy if their buildings were full of people who didn't cause too much trouble. They offset the lower rent levels by deferring maintenance or by responding to problems only as they arose.

In Toronto, in the 1960s, landlords even gave free rent and paid their building operators for signing up new tenants or for renewing an existing tenant. Many landlords painted each apartment every two years whether the unit needed painting or not. Since the imposition of rent controls in Ontario, many tenants are painting their own apartments, and their landlords are saving this expense.

Before rent controls, because many buildings were "mortgaged out" or heavily leveraged, the debt load for a building with a vacancy rate of more than 5 percent was too much to absorb, landlords were forced to take drastic action to fill their buildings. In Toronto, inflation and the dramatic growth of the city quickly overcame this problem for building owners.

In the 1980s there is such a shortage of rental units in Toronto that many tenants are now asking for key money by selling to the incoming tenants their worn carpets or old draperies. There are very few lease renewals because few stay for the full term of their leases. They sublet before the renewal date and get the key money from the new lessee so that they will have it to pay for another apartment.

After rent controls were imposed, most tenants had yearly leases, and rents were automatically raised by 6 percent each year. In 1986 the Ontario government developed a new formula for calculating the percentage of increase. Although this system may not keep rents as high as they would be without rent controls, it is a better way for landlords to maintain their income levels than the way in which most of them operated before rent controls. Any building owners who kept their buildings well maintained and their rents at market level found rent controls less of a problem than they were for those who let their buildings run down. Well-maintained buildings not only demand higher rents but attract and keep much better tenants. This fact alone should be the main incentive for landlords to get better control of their maintenance and operations expenses.

Many believe that rent controls encourage landlords to neglect their buildings; however, landlords who neglect their buildings do so because of the wrong attitude vis-à-vis maintenance, and that attitude was there even before rent controls. Some do not support rent controls because they believe that they create more problems than they solve and that they interfere with the free marketplace that usually finds its own level of value and is so important to the free enterprise system.

Rent controls and their effect on the thinking of people who build and manage buildings are not mentioned here to offer any miracle answers to the problems that their imposition creates—books and debates have covered the causes and effects of this negative approach to problem solving; what is being emphasized is the importance of knowing what business you are in, the purpose and objectives of the industry, and the importance of knowing how to do the right things.

It is important to assure that you receive the highest possible price for your product and at the same time to know how to reduce the cost of management services to its lowest possible level. When management overcomes the lost opportunity to save what existed previously and at the same time adds the savings to its profit, it doubles the savings. Conversely, if management does not initiate a program, every opportunity to save what is missed becomes a loss and reduces the profit available for a building. The other thing to remember is that contrary to common belief, rental income is not the only source of revenue available to building owners. Why not increase your return on investment from both the income and expense sources?

3

Specifications, Standards and Contract Management

3.1 CONTRACTS

The Contract Documents

Whether it is called an *offer, tender, quote, bid, estimate,* or *contract*, a piece of paper that describes certain work to be done and gives a price for doing it becomes a legal document that is binding on both parties once they have signed it.

Before we can discuss the different types of contracts under which renovations, retrofits, and maintenance contracts are negotiated, we must have a basic knowledge of what are termed *contract documents*. Obviously, the formal contract between the manager, building owner, or someone designated by the owner to negotiate these contracts, forms part of these contract documents. It is generally understood that these documents include the terms and money, but they also should include design drawings, specifications, and standards when they involve new constructions, renovations, and retrofits. Addenda that revise the original plan are also considered part of the contract documents.

After considering the contract documents, one must consider how these documents will be negotiated with the people who will be doing the job. Contracting systems generally fall into several types.

Lump-sum contracts.   Under this system the contractor, after making careful estimates of the amounts and unit costs of work or material shown on the contract documents, proposes to complete the project for a certain amount of money. This amount of money will not change regardless of future additional costs due to miscalculation, price rises in materials or wages during the term of the contract, or other items such as cost increases for subcontracts. However, in lump-sum contracts and with other types of contracts, the contractor is protected from responsibility of what is termed *acts of God*. That is, the contractor will not be held accountable for circumstances or conditions that could not be anticipated when estimates were made and the bid submitted. Such things as unseasonal rains, hurricanes, tornadoes, and community-wide strikes are considered as acts of God.

Cost-plus-fixed-fee contracts.   There are often reasons a contractor cannot, or will not, risk a lump-sum contract. In this situation, the contractor agrees to keep precise records of all money spent for labor and material and the cost of subcontracts, bills the customer for these costs, and adds on an agreed upon fixed fee for the entire project.

In some cases, this type of contract includes an *upset-sum clause*. This clause stipulates that the contractor will guarantee that the costs plus the fee will at no time ever exceed a contract-stipulated top sum. In this type of contract the contractors' only incentive is to protect their own interests; they may not be trying to keep the costs reasonable.

An Additional Clause for Profit Incentive.   The problem with a cost-plus contract is that the contractor may not make sufficient efforts to ensure that the project is built as efficiently as possible. Costs are allowed to build up until they endanger the contractor's profit margin.

To overcome this problem, a contract is used that gives the contractor a share of the cost and the upset sum set forth in the original estimate. In this type of contract the contractor estimates that the total cost of the project will not exceed a certain sum and that the fee for this work will be X dollars. In addition, the contractor guarantees that the cost of the contract, plus the fee, will not exceed a certain amount.

In addition to the guaranteed cost plus fixed fee, the contract stipulates that the contractor will receive a share (quite often 25 percent) of the difference between the original cost estimate and the actual cost. If the cost goes above the original estimate, the contractor bears this cost.

Additions to Contracts

The building owner–customer may have additional needs, the designer may have omitted a requirement, or conditions may entitle the contractor to additional funds. In these circumstances, the contractor will list the items involved and will price each item. As with most management activities, communication among the people involved will keep everyone informed about the situation, and when the time comes to settle these extras, they will be negotiated without too many problems.

Term of Service Contracts

The initial term of service contracts should be one year. Once management is satisfied with the workmanship and cost of the service, it is wise to negotiate for longer periods. In some cases, long-term contracts can be negotiated at a discount. A popular form is an initial contract with several one-year renewals at the building manager's option. All contracts should be subject to thirty days' notice of termination without cause by either party. During the initial term of the contract, the contractor cannot cancel the contract (except in the case of nonpayment), and the building manager may, after written warnings, cancel only for cause such as nonperformance or poor performance of the specification.

Many building managers feel that they can put greater pressure on contractors and give themselves maximum flexibility by not specifying a contract term at all or, if they do, by giving themselves the option of canceling the contract at any time without cause. There are several reasons for not adopting this policy.

- A constant change of on-site staff or contractors disrupts the maintenance program in a building and upsets the occupants.
- A reputable contractor will spend a lot of time, effort, and expense setting things up in a building, hiring and training staff to assure that they will do a good job. If they sense that management may, perhaps, unreasonably throw them out, the initial effort by the contractor to do a good job will be lessened.
- A continuity of care develops when managers, contractors and their staffs, and the building on-site staff develop a relationship that provides for the smooth handling of preventive and responsive maintenance. The people involved become very familiar with the building, its needs, and the needs of the tenants. It takes time for each new contractor to get to know the people, the building, and the electrical-mechanical systems. Thus, continuity of the people involved and the services are very important, and carefully choosing the right people initially will be a big contributing factor to making a building successful.

Periodic Payment Less a Percentage

Most contracts stipulate that the purchaser will pay the contractor periodically, especially for big contracts, to the extent of the contractor's costs less 10 or 20 percent. This percentage reduction in payment is called a *hold-back* or *retainage* and applies particularly to new construction, renovation, and retrofit contracts.

Escalation Clause

It is unreasonable to expect a contractor to continue providing service with no price increases, especially if labor costs increase for reasons beyond the contractor's control, such as:

- An increase in the minimum wage.
- An increase in wage costs because of a new union contract or the unionization of the contractor's company.
- An increase in tax contributions or insurance.

Costs to Be Included

The contract should define in detail the cost included in the price and the costs that are excluded. Management should seek more than just a single quoted price; rather, it should require that each bidder supply additional information such as payroll,* total payroll cost, equipment and supplies cost, and subcontracting cost.

The bidder should also provide a list of all equipment that the contractor will place in the building to use in carrying out the contract. This information is important for it enables the manager to evaluate the quality of the bid. Clearly a bid with only a small percentage of the price spent on payroll, equipment, supplies, and subcontracting costs is less attractive than a bid in which a larger percentage of the price is allocated to these items. Comparison of such data may reveal inconsistencies to be probed before making a decision.

These data should be kept on file (in the building profile manual) to enable the person responsible for the service to check in event of poor service or a request by the contractor for a price increase based on an increase in labor and supervision costs.

Define Insurance Requirements

The amount of insurance coverage required by the contractor should be specified in the instructions to the bidders. Contractors should supply management with certificates that show that they have the following bodily injury and property damage liability coverage:

---

*Productive man-wages × wage rate = productive wages; lead-man man-hours × wage rate = lead-man wages; supervisor man-hours × supervisor wage rate = supervisor wages; and man-hours for relief for paid leave × wage rate = paid-leave wages.

1. Comprehensive automobile liability
     Basic automobile liability
     Uninsured motorists
2. Comprehensive general liability
     Owner's, landlord's, and tenant's liability
     Care, custody, and control liability
     Contractual liability
     Manufacturer's liability
     Owner's and contractor's protective liability
     Personal injury liability
     Extended property damage liability
3. Employee fidelity bond, including third party legal liability
4. Workmen's compensation employees' liability
5. Umbrella excess third party liability

Care, custody, and control. Standard comprehensive general liability policies exclude coverage for property directly in the care, custody, or control of contractors' employees. This exclusion should be included in the contractor's insurance coverage.

Extended property damage. Including this clause in the contractor's insurance broadens the definition of property damage to include theft and mysterious disappearances of property for which the contractor is legally liable. This clause is very important for building owners and their managers, as most insurance carriers will respond only to losses involving damaged property.

Third-party legal liability. This clause covers contractors' legal responsibility for the dishonest acts of their employees against their customers. Inclusion of this coverage should be a major consideration of building owners and their managers when selecting a service contractor.

The amount of coverage for the different types of insurance might be set forth and legislated by local governments; however, the limits should be checked out by your own insurance company to assure that they are satisfied that the contractor is sufficiently covered.

Property managers must also make every effort to protect the building and to assure that, aside from normal safety practices, the people who carry out contract work in their buildings do so in as safe a manner as possible.

3.2 CONTRACT CONSIDERATIONS FOR RENOVATIONS AND RETROFITS

Several things must be included when negotiating a contract for special jobs such as renovations and retrofits:

- A detailed description, with drawings, of exactly what is being contracted and subcontracted for and with whom.
- Assurance that all necessary permits will be obtained by the contractor and that all work will be done according to local building codes.
- A statement of all warranties, explaining exactly what is covered and for how long.
- Certificates of insurance.
- Firm starting and completion dates.
- Price and terms of payment.

Holdbacks

For large jobs, it is common practice to make interim payments: such things as a deposit (10 percent of the contract price) or as payment for the work that has been done. Avoid *progression clauses* that require payments at specific times, regardless of the amount of work that has been done. Some money should always be held in reserve to ensure satisfactory completion of the work.

Another reason for withholding some of the money on all payments, including the last one, is to protect yourself against liens that can be placed on your building by suppliers or workers who were not paid by the contractor. In effect, a lien holds your property as security for the contractor's debts, even if you paid in full.

The proper procedure is to hold back from all payments the amount of your liability that is stipulated in the local lien laws, and for the time stipulated for creditors to register a lien on your property. This amount could be anywhere from 10 to 20 percent, and the period varies from 30 to 60 days after the contracted work is completed.

Making Final Payment

In some areas you will be notified by the courthouse, land registry, or land titles office if a lien has been placed against your property, but it is much safer for you or your lawyer to check with them directly before paying the holdback to the contractor at the end of the stipulated time period. If there is a lien, make no more payments until you receive notice that it has been discharged.

Do not make the final payment or sign a completion certificate, or any other document that releases the contractor from further responsibility, until everything you were promised has been done. If the contractor assures you that he or she will be back in a few days to finish everything off, tell the contractor that you will make the final payment then.

3.3 BASES FOR AWARDING CONTRACTS

Lowest Bidder

Most government contracts are awarded to the lowest bidder. Because of this, many reputable service companies do not even bid for government contracts. To assure that the public is getting the best value for the dollars spent on contracts, it is absolutely essential that the people preparing specifications and design and working drawings are highly qualified and experienced. Supervision of the work being done by contractors is also very critical when one value analyzes the workmanship for these projects.

Highest Bidder

The following are a few of the reasons for awarding a contract to someone other than the lowest bidder.

1. The chosen bidder has the ability to complete the project in a shorter time, thus bringing the new facility into use sooner and offsetting the extra cost.
2. One of the bidders has more experience and has a proven track record for giving value for the money charged.
3. Past experience with the bidder has shown that the people making the decision about the contract have confidence in the workmanship and dependability of the contractor.

Selective Bidding

The principle of selective bidding is to thoroughly screen potential bidders before bidding and to restrict the number of bidders; three is recommended. The basic assumption is that any one of the bidders is qualified to do the job and that price will be a major factor in the final decision.

The reason for screening beforehand is that the small number of bidders enables you to spend adequate time with each one. The purpose of this action is to thoroughly explain the specifications, carefully showing the building, introducing key tenants or occupants, and providing a "feel" for the standards that are expected. If there are too many bidders, there is not enough time for detailed meetings and communication of the building's needs to each bidder. Consequently, contractors could underbid or overbid the job.

3.4 CRITERIA FOR SELECTION OF BIDDERS

When you restrict your bidders, it makes the choice of those who bid an important one. Contractors are as professional as accountants, lawyers, or doctors, and similar criteria are useful when picking any one of them, especially their reputation in the industry. Other checks can be performed as well, and the following are a few of them.

- *Reputation:* Ask for a list of the contractor's local contracts similar in size and scope to your buildings. Ask for the name and phone number of all references. Another way is to ask various contractors you are considering to list the three best contractors (besides themselves) in your area. Chances are that the same two or three names will keep cropping up.
- *Financial and General Stability:* Appraise the contractor's financial stability to determine whether he or she is able to handle your contract. This information can be verified by asking for bank and other credit references. How long has the contractor been in business in your area? How many years has the local manager or owner been in his or her current position?
- *The Contractor's Office and Shop:* Make it a point to visit the office and shop of the potential contractor to get a feel for the way that the business is managed; make a general assessment of the mood and order within the office. Particularly observe the following:

    The caliber of management and support staff

    Personnel practices and records

    The relationship the contractor has with the union

    The technical backup and resources

    Staff training and motivation program
- *Management Efficiency:* Meet and assess the people who own and manage the company you might be doing business with. Get a feel for their philosophy of management and the integrity of the people who work for them. Would you feel comfortable negotiating and working with them? Would they treat the buildings you are managing as if they were the owners paying the bills? Do they have management depth, or is the organization dependent on one person?

    If it is a large organization, how many people would be reporting to one supervisor? Try to assess the caliber of the supervisors. Does it have a training program? Does it use the latest equipment and methods?

    Inspect the company's work. Pick out at random a couple of the buildings it is currently servicing, and inspect them without advance warning.

3.5 CHOOSING A CONTRACTOR

One of the more important decisions that managers make is the *make-or-buy decision*, whether to use in-house or on-site staff, or an outside service contractor for handling the maintenance services required by a building. The right service contractor, working closely with the on-site operating staff and the manager, actually becomes part of the management team. The contractor's prime objective should be the same as the manager's: to help management make each building a successful business unit. Just as it would be if the manager were hiring on-site or in-house services; communication between the manager and whoever is doing the maintenance has to be such that they know exactly what is expected of them as a condition of employment or of the contract.

Having selected three bidders, any one of whom you would be happy to have service your buildings, the next step is to thoroughly acquaint them with your specifications, standards, and expectations. It is advisable to set a day and time by which the three bids will be given to you. It is not advisable to discuss the proposals with them when the bids are submitted. Once all the prices are in, you can meet with each contractor and have each proposal explained in detail. Because the initial screening should ensure that the three bidders are competent and responsible businesses, price will be a major factor in your selection. In most cases, differences will be related to the cost of labor and supervision if the bidder has complied with all the conditions of the bid request. If all three bids are very close, then nonmonetary factors—perhaps revealed through the screening checks—could influence your selection of a contractor other than the low bidder.

Agreement on Specifications and Standards

Specifications are a detailed, precise presentation of something or of a plan or proposal for something, a statement of particulars, as of dimensions or materials. *Standards* are conditions that are substantially uniform, well established, and acceptable. Specifications are necessary for any major new construction, renovation, or retrofit project; standards are particularly appropriate for housekeeping or groundskeeping conditions. As an example, hospitals require definitions of cleanliness different from those required by an apartment building. A good way to define the level of cleanliness in a building is from the reaction of its occupants.

Levels of cleanliness could be defined as follows:

Prestige Cleaning or Groundskeeping: A standard that will provide unsolicited compliments from building occupants or visitors, one that would make a cleaning complaint a rarity.

Adequate Cleaning or Groundskeeping: A standard that would provide neither compliments nor serious criticism.

Minimal Cleaning or Groundskeeping: A standard that results in criticism by building occupants or visitors. In this system, complaints usually trigger periodic *special cleanups* to avoid losing the contract or the tenants.

Experience has shown that when the people doing the housekeeping or groundskeeping are professionally trained to carry out the tasks assigned to them, the result is a prestige job at minimal cost. It is like getting two dollars' worth of value for one dollar. Unprofessional people waste time, materials, and supplies; cause equipment breakdowns; and keep management busy fighting conditions that are not acceptable. In summary, the first step in selecting a housekeeping or groundskeeping contractor is to define the standards.

Define the Contract That Meets the Building's Needs

Detailed specifications are needed to describe a list of tasks to be performed, the frequency with which each task is to be performed, and some indication of the thoroughness with which each housekeeping and groundskeeping task is to be performed. Managers should document the tasks that would apply to any in-house staff carrying out the various daily functions in a building. Both on-site and in-house staff should be treated as you would an outside contractor.

The make-or-buy decision-making process. Management should be constantly weighing the advantages and disadvantages of buying services against doing the work themselves. In fact, to make the right decisions about what is best for a building, management must compare the costs against clearly defined specifications and standards for everyone bidding for a contract. That decision-making process would also apply when considering using on-site and in-house staff. The same process of elimination would apply to the people you hire, as would the specifications and standards that you follow.

Make the specifications and standards realistic. Unless the specifications are realistic, bidding contractors are faced with the dilemma of either bidding to the specs literally, thus pricing themselves out of contention or bidding to the specs while costing to carry out a job to a much lower standard because that is what they sense that the customer really wants. This situation is bad for everyone because it encourages a lack of integrity and professionalism, and it makes it difficult for management to receive truly comparable bids, because each bidder is only guessing at the standards that the customer really wants.

To help develop a suitable specification and standard, management should develop checklists and learn from the bids made by reputable contractors. Specifications can be broken down into four steps:

1. Analyze the standards required in each specialized maintenance function.
2. Determine the frequency of the tasks that are necessary to meet the standards that are established.
3. Express these frequencies and tasks in a detailed written format.
4. Define what is meant by each task.

3.6 MONITORING THE CONTRACTOR'S PERFORMANCE

Once you have chosen a contractor, it is in your interest that the contractor succeed. Regard him or her as a partner, not as an adversary. The contractor's staff become a part of your management team. The following are some practical ways in which you can help them:

- Once you have decided, sign a contract as soon as possible.
- Provide adequate lead time to start the contract. Ask how long the contractor needs; encourage him or her not to state a very short time span just to impress you. The contractor needs to take the time to properly plan, organize, and staff the project.
- Suggest that you use this lead time to help the contractor set the stage:
    Arrange for adequate storage space for equipment, supplies, tools, chemicals, and spare parts that the contractor needs to do the job properly.

    Make sure that all the tenants are aware of the name of the contractor and the names of the supervisors and manager.

    If the contractor is replacing another one, make adequate changeover arrangements.

    Make suitable arrangements for timely payments.

    Assure that there is a suitable process communication and liaison. At the supervisory level in particular, set up a means of communicating complaints and a method for dealing with them. Set up a communications process that assures feedback to the complainer of how or whether the problem was resolved.

    Open lines of communication at the management or ownership level are also important. Meetings should be held regularly, not just in times of dissatisfaction or crisis.

A formal monitoring of the contractor's performance is recommended, both to determine that you are getting what you are paying for and to determine whether or not the contractor should be allowed to bid again for the servicing of this building or others in your management portfolio. There are several ways of monitoring performance:

1. Conduct regular inspections with the contractor of areas selected at random by yourself. Make notes about these inspections and give copies to the contractor. It should not all be of a negative nature; the inspection report should include favorable as well as unfavorable comments.
2. Solicit feedback from the tenants.
3. Develop a system of verifying the man-hours used by the contractor.

3.7 BEWARE OF TRAPS

Price Jacking

Contractors have been known to bid very low to get the contract, do a good job for a few months (at considerable expense), and then ask for a price increase on some pretext, such as a misunderstanding over specifications and standards, wanting to pay higher wages, or inflation.

Solution.   Check references carefully to uncover this type of activity. Normally your screening process would eliminate such a contractor.

Disputes over Additions to Contract

There are times when things that should have been included in the contract were missed, or something new was added to the contract. Disputes may arise over the price to be paid for these additions.

Solution.   Try to build into the original contract some formula for handling this type of situation when it arises.

The Squeaky-Wheel Contractor

This type of contractor usually bids low to get the job, and starts off by doing a good job for a month or two. As soon as the manager is lulled into believing that everything is fine, and the monitoring process starts to slip, the quality of the work being done by the contractor starts to slide. When the manager complains, the contractor puts on a "heroic effort" to bring the standards back up to where they should be. When the manager's attention is moved to other things, the quality again slides below standards, and the cycle repeats itself.

Solution.   Get rid of this contractor and select a successor.

3.8 SUMMING UP

Contractor turnover, like turnover of on-site staff, tenants, owners, or occupants is costly, inefficient, and ineffective. Property managers must place special emphasis on the process of carefully defining the contract conditions, the specifications related to the work being done, and the process of selecting the right contractor using the selective bidding process.

Define the standards and specifications as if you were the owner of the building or the tenant paying the highest rent. Watch the costs as if the money being spent were money right out of your own pocket. Define and assure the achievement of the image that you want to project to your present and future customers.

Set down in detail the terms of the contract that will provide these objectives.

- Draw up specifications and standards listing tasks to be performed. Be detailed, specific, and realistic. Do not over- or under-specify.
- Specify the initial term of the contract and the manner in which it will be renewed or continued. Specify clearly that you can terminate the contract at any time for nonperformance or poor performance of specs, and the amount of notice that you would give.
- State an escalation formula for increases in the contractor's labor rates or other labor-associated cost increases that are beyond the contractor's control.
- Define carefully the costs that you will pay and those that are the responsibility of the contractor.
- Require that bidders break down their labor and material costs.
- Specify the minimum insurance coverage you require.
- Define the payment terms.
- State your security requirements and the times that the contractor may have access to the building.
- Select only three bidders based on the following criteria:
    Their reputations
    Their financial stability
    The length of time that they have been in business
    The strength of their senior management team
    Their depth in terms of key personnel; recruiting, training, and upgrading programs; and their technical support expertise
    Their experience and performance record with other people

Management should spend adequate time with each bidder to ensure that there are no midunderstandings about what is expected.

- Invite the bidder to give you price and draft contracts incorporating the items you have spelled out.
- Make it clear that the major part of the selection process has already been accomplished by selecting those who will bid and that price will be a major factor in awarding the contract.

Help the contractor you choose succeed.

- Give adequate lead time.
- Set up clear communication and liaison arrangements.
- Notify the building occupants whenever hiring a contractor.
- Provide adequate on-site facilities for the contractor.
- Pay invoices on time, especially if the work is labor intensive.

Property managers must keep in mind that whenever they hire on-site staff or a contractor, they expect to get the right things done right efficiently and effectively. Do not accept from your management staff or your service contractors performance that is below your standards.

A services and suppliers guide should be used by on-site staff and people in management offices as a quick reference guide to the services and suppliers that are recommended by the company (Figure 3.1). It is an excellent way to organize the long list of services and suppliers that are needed by buildings.

Coordinating the myriad tasks that must be done in a building to make it function the way it was designed is not an easy job. This guide, along with written standards and specifications that should be developed and provided by management, helps the people involved decide what needs to be done to assure that building owners get full value for each dollar spent on maintenance and operations.

Management should be aware that all the services listed in the services and suppliers guide must be assigned to someone. In all cases, it is the responsibility of management to set the level of maintenance standards, to include the specifications requirements for the program in the master action plan, and to include in the budgets the costs for all the activities required by a building. It is also the responsibility of management to assure that the people on the management team are trained to recognize an abnormal condition; know whom to call to correct the situation; and are able to monitor the results of those providing services in each of the buildings in the management portfolio.

The services shown in the services and suppliers guide are listed in alphabetical order. It is not necessary that you use the account classifications illustrated in Chapter 5, but they are recommended as guidelines. You should use some kind of account classification (preferably a sequential one) to help you organize your information. The numbers are included so that you can automate the system; however, the program can be used without a computer.

Building Name _____
Building Address _____
Building Number _____
Date _____

Company Name And Address	Type of Contract or Service	Account No.(s)	Phone No(s).	Contact	Rates	Terms & Discounts
	Appliance Service					
	Building Hardware					
	Boiler Service					
	Burner Service					
	Brickwork					
	Cable Television Service					
	Carpet Cleaning					
	Carpet Repairs					
	Carpets New					
	Carpenter					
	Compactor Service					
	Caulking					
	Chiller Service					
	Cleaning Supplies					
	Cooling Tower Service					
	Communication System					
	Dom. Hot Water Tank Service					
	Doors					
	Draperies & Blinds					
	Electrician					
	Extinguisher Service					
	Elevator Service					
	Fan Coil Unit Service					
	Filters Supplies					
	Fire Protec. & Comm. System					
	Floor Service					
	Furnace & Fan Service					

70

Garbage Bin Service & Rental							
Garbage Bags							
Gardening Contractor							
Groundskeeping Supp. & Serv.							
Housekeeping Contractor							
Housekeeping Supplies							
Intercom System							
Light Bulbs & Fixtures							
Lighting (Emergency)							
Locksmith							
Painter & Paperhanger							
Paving							
Pest Control Service							
Plasterer							
Plumber							
Motor Service (Pumps & Fans)							
Pump Service							
Roofer							
Signage							
Security Guard Contractor							
Security System Service							
Snow Removal							
Swimming Pool Service							
Television Distribution System							
Tile Setters							
Wall & Ceiling Services							
Waste Disposal							
Water Treatment							
Window Cleaning							
Window Repairs							

Figure 3.1 All the possible service and suppliers that are needed by a building. It is important that building owners make decisions about what kind of service is needed, specifications and standards expected, and whether to use outside help or in-house or on-site staff. In a large organization it is important that everyone on the management team be aware of these decisions and the specifications for them. This form is used as a communication tool.

Inspection Techniques

Managers should be encouraged to measure progress toward objectives, and that these objectives should apply to every area where performance and results directly and vitally affect each building business unit. It is important that managers narrow the range of attention of each person on their management teams to focus on definite and measurable results that have a clear meaning for each individual. The selection of the proper factors to be measured is an important decision because usually that which is measured is that which receives attention.

One definition of *management* is "the achievement of agreed upon goals through other people, using a minimum of resources."* To be successful, management must have a maintenance management plan that assures that the right measurement system is in place, one that will allow managers to plan, organize, staff, direct, and control all aspects of each building's design, construction, management, operations, and maintenance activities. This plan must be such that it establishes a meaningful framework that unites all of the disciplines associated with leasing, sales, administration management, revenue management, and maintenance management under a common purpose and management plan.

*Dr. Harvey A. Silver at a Cadillac Fairview in-house management seminar, April 29–30, 1977.

4.1 THE MASTER ACTION PLAN

Management is "getting the right things done right through other people." This process involves the coordination of labor, equipment, tools, products, supplies, spare parts, materials, and money. It also involves delegating, motivating, communicating, evaluating, and improving ourselves and others on the management team.

To achieve all these goals and to assure that each building business unit is successful, it is necessary to develop a *master action plan* for each building that you manage. The best approach in preparing a plan is to start with a building profile for each building in your management portfolio. The information gathered will identify everything that needs maintenance or that will wear out and need replacement. This profile then becomes the basis for the strategic plan that will allow you to skillfully select the things that have to be done in each building.

Funds for renovations, retrofits, repair and maintenance, on-site staff salaries, fuel, electricity, and water should be built into the budgets by organizing the information. The most logical way of doing this is to match the information to a building's functional activities, components, and services. This information is gathered from observations made during inspections, from records kept of previous expenditures, and from the results of the previous year's plan.

The master action plan could be generalized in the following manner, but managers must be cautioned that the correct plan must be tailored to suit the needs of each individual building.

INCOME

- Set a market-based rental fee.
- Set a suitable, agreed-upon monthly maintenance fee for condominiums.
- Allow for sundry fees such as income from laundry machines.

MARKETING

- Survey the competition.
- Advertise.
- Arrange for an adequate sales presentation and leasing process.

ADMINISTRATION

- Maintain rent-roll records.
- Institute a suitable accounting and recordkeeping system.
- Develop a system for collecting rents or maintenance fees and for making deposits.
- Develop a system for handling delinquents.

- Develop a purchasing and bill-paying procedure.
- Develop a procedure for moving people in or out.
- Develop a system for controlling keys and parking.
- Develop a payroll system.
- Develop a procedure for handling the planning and budgeting process.

CONTROLLING MAINTENANCE AND OPERATIONS EXPENSES

- Conduct a building takeover inspection.
- Detail interior and exterior elements.
- Tag electrical-mechanical equipment.
- Detail equipment records.
- Prepare a building maintenance work load.
- Communicate to the on-site staff their responsibilities.
- Prepare responsibility lists for all management staff.
- Staff the building.
- Supply maintenance tools, equipment, spare parts, chemicals, and other inventory required by the building.
- Develop an emergency procedure.
- Follow up, if necessary, construction guarantees in a new building.
- Develop a suppliers and services guide that recommends the outside suppliers and services required by the building. Specify the workmanship and quality standards dictated by the policies of the building owners.
- Assure that service contracts are signed.
- Arrange for daily, weekly, monthly, and semiannual inspections and assign the responsibility for them. Property managers must establish an inspection plan for themselves and assure that they and other staff who have been assigned inspection routines carry them out.
- Prepare a zero-base budget for each building in your portfolio using repair and maintenance account classifications and the budget-builder working papers discussed in Chapter 5 as guides for keeping notes and assuring that all the maintenance activities outlined in your master action plan are included in the budget.
- Store all this information in a building profile manual.

STRUCTURAL SERVICES

- Develop an inspection schedule for walls, roofs, sidewalks, parking lots, building hardware, common area locks, security systems, and the general aesthetics of the building.
- Assess the needs for structural renovations and retrofits, specify and receive bids, award contracts, and supervise any work that is being done.

HOUSEKEEPING SERVICES

- Arrange to sweep the underground garages to suit the needs of the building.
- Arrange to clean the exteriors of all windows.
- Arrange to clean all the carpets in the building to suit the needs.
- Arrange to wash all common area walls to suit the needs.
- Set up a system that will control all housekeeping tools, equipment, supplies, chemicals, etc.

GROUNDSKEEPING SERVICES

- Depending on the building owner's policy, plan and schedule all gardening chores for either in-house staff or outside contractor: such things as servicing equipment; ordering and planting flowers; purchasing and applying fertilizers; ordering and using salt and sand in the winter; pruning; cultivating; replacing all dead trees and perennials; controlling inventory of parts, tools, chemicals, and other supplies.

ELECTRICAL-MECHANICAL SERVICES

- Assign the responsibility for conducting an annual preventive maintenance inspection of service panels and emergency power services and provide for responsive service when required.
- Assign the responsibility for light bulb replacements.
- Assign the responsibility for lubricating motors and the equipment they operate.
- Assign the responsibility for changing filters.
- Assign the responsibility for servicing pumps, fans, and motors.
- Arrange for a full maintenance contract for the elevators.

COOLING SYSTEM

- Arrange for full maintenance contract for chillers.
- Arrange for full maintenance contract for cooling towers.
- Arrange for testing the cooling system water and adding the right chemical treatment.
- Arrange service for incremental or fan-coil units (if applicable).
- Arrange service for all free-standing or roof-top units (if applicable).
- Develop a system for monitoring the efficiency of the chiller on a daily basis and assure that it is being done.

HEATING SYSTEM

- Arrange service for boiler controls.
- Arrange service for the boiler burners and assure combustion efficiency.
- Arrange to inspect boilers' interiors and exteriors and for service when needed.
- Arrange service for fan-coil units (if applicable).
- Arrange service for hot-air furnaces (if applicable).
- Arrange tests for heating-system water and assure that the right chemical is added.
- Monitor the water treatment program.
- Arrange for inspection and topping up of glycol in ramp and corridor air heat exchangers.
- Develop a system for monitoring the efficiency of the heating system on a daily basis and assure that someone is doing it.

PLUMBING AND DRAINAGE SYSTEMS

- Arrange to clean the sanitary drains as required.
- Arrange service for the domestic hot water storage tanks.
- Arrange service for the heat exchangers in those tanks.
- Arrange service for the heating boilers and burners used to heat the domestic water.
- Arrange service for pressure-reducing valves.
- Arrange service for all plumbing fixtures, especially those in each apartment unit.

VENTILATION SYSTEM

- Arrange to clean the fan housing. The frequency would be dictated by conditions in the area in which the building is located.
- Assign the responsibility for changing filters. The schedule of service would be dictated by conditions in the area in which the building is located.
- Assign the responsibility for inspecting, aligning, and replacing belts on all air-handling equipment.

SECURITY

- Assure that the security system suits the needs of the building.
- Assign the responsibility for testing the fire control and voice communication systems.

- Assure that there is suitable service for the video cameras, intercom system, and door hardware. Service and control all keys and locks.

RECREATIONAL FACILITIES

- Arrange for the opening, closing, operating, and maintenance of all recreational facilities.

4.2 SUPPLIERS AND SERVICES POLICY

Management has two policy decisions to make related to the maintenance of buildings. Is the maintenance program to be based on prevention of costly structural failures or electrical-mechanical breakdowns, or is it going to be responsive to them as they occur?

If it is to be responsive, then the people involved must decide about the problems that might arise and what to do about them. If it is to be preventive, then the people involved must know how to plan and assign responsibilities for daily, weekly, monthly, and semiannual inspections to people who are trained to recognize problems and to have them corrected while they are still minor. They must assure that they have both on-site staff and outside contractors who can support the on-site staff when it is confronted with problems beyond its ability to overcome.

Management's Maintenance Services Choices

Management is faced with three choices when deciding how best to handle the maintenance services of a building. These services may be routine maintenance activities, or responses to tenants' complaints and unforeseen maintenance requests (see Figures 4.1, 4.2, and 4.3).

1. Some minor problems can, and should be, handled by the on-site operator; however, managers should keep in mind that it is counterproductive to presume that the building superintendent can do all nonroutine tasks that managers sometimes assign to them, especially if these tasks interfere with the superintendent's daily schedule of assigned duties or they are not qualified to handle them.
2. Maintenance services that are beyond the ability of the on-site staff can be handled by in-house maintenance staff.
3. Maintenance services can be performed by an outside contractor.

It will be necessary to keep copies of all work orders and purchase orders for these accounts to assure that you have the information you need to prepare future budgets (Figures 4.4 and 4.5). Using the numbers makes the orders eas-

NAME OF MANAGEMENT COMPANY

MAINTENANCE REQUEST NO.

Building Address	Bldg. No.
Tenant's Name	Suite No.
Phones: Home	Office
Request Details:	
Received By	

CONSENT TO ENTER SUITE

I wish to have the above maintenance attended to and I herby authorize management personnel to enter my apartment. Should it be necessary to use an outside service company to correct the problem, or if it is necessary to make more than one visit, I also signify my consent.

Tenant's Signature _____   Date _____

Comments of on-site staff:

Investigated by: Date

Comments: If on-site staff unable to correct the problem.

√ *BELOW TO INDICATE WHETHER WORK OR PURCHASE ORDER*

√	Type Of Form	Supplier	Date	Cost	No.
	Work Order No.				
	Purchase Order No.				
	Insurance Claim No.	√ Tenant to be invoiced? ☐ Yes Invoice No.		☐ No	

Work authorized by:

This maintenance request was created so that the on-site staff and the management office would have some way of recording any tenant comment or maintenance request. It should be printed in duplicate so that one copy can be kept by the receiver of the request until the work is completed. It should be sized to fit in a person's pocket. In this way staff can be encouraged to carry a pad at all times. Other documents such as work or purchase orders are a follow-up to this document.

Figure 4.1 A maintenance request form. This form is both an information document and a training tool.

NAME OF THE COMPANY HERE

RAINWATER INFILTRATION MAINTENANCE REQUEST   NO.

Building Name	Address		Suite No.	Date
Tenant's Name			Phones: Res.	Bus.

Problem:	**TENANT'S CONSENT TO ENTER SUITE**	Tenant's Signature
	I hereby authorize management staff to enter my apartment to investigate and correct this problem. If an outside service technician is needed or more than one visit is required, I also signify my consent.	
Received by:		Date

Rainwater infiltration is a serious problem in buildings and the problem can be satisfactorily corrected only if its cause has been properly diagnosed. The use of this rainwater infiltration or leakage form was designed to organize the investigation of this sort of problem. It must be completed at the time of the leak.

CONDITIONS FOUND UPON INVESTIGATION

1. In which room did the leak occur?

2. Indicate with a √ where in the room the leak occurred.   At Floor Level ☐ Under window ☐   Above Window ☐   At Sides Of Window ☐

   If leak occurred in any other location indicate with a √:   In corner of the suite ☐   In Clothes Closet ☐   At Ceiling ☐

   On walls with no windows ☐   On Outside Wall ☐   Inside Wall ☐

3. Which area is leaking area facing?   East ☐   West ☐   North ☐   South ☐

4. Was there enough water to warrant using one of the following?   Wet vacuum ☐   Mop ☐   A Cloth ☐

5. If leaking under the radiator, did you check the piping?   Yes ☐ No ☐

6. Is this the first report of a leakage problem in this apartment?   Yes ☐ No ☐

7. Does it happen each time it rains?   Yes ☐ No ☐

OBSERVATIONS AND RECOMMENDATIONS

	Investigator's Signature

DETAILS ABOUT WORK TO BE DONE AND RECOMMENDATIONS OF SPECIALIST:

	Investigator's Signature

			ACTION TAKEN BY MANAGMENT OFFICE
Indicate by check mark document required			
√	Document Type	Date Issued	Contractors Name
	Work Order No.		
	Purchase Order No.		
	Insurance Claim No.,		

Figure 4.2   A form for keeping information about rain infiltration problems. This form is both an information document and a training tool. The use of a maintenance request, especially a heating maintenance request, assures that all incidents are documented, investigated, and corrected and that the manager's energy management program is not causing problems for the tenants.

ier to sort. The information on these forms also provides management with an accurate record of all previous maintenance problems. It is wise to sort this information into the various structural and electrical-mechanical functions. In this way the information is in a logical place for reviewing the problems that

NAME AND ADDRESS OF THE COMPANY HERE

HEATING MAINTENANCE REQUEST   NO.

Building Name	Address	Suite No.	Date
Tenant's Name		Phones: Res.	Bus.
Problem:	**TENANT'S CONSENT TO ENTER SUITE** I here by authorize management staff to enter my apartment to investigate and correct this problem. If an outside service technician is needed or more than one visit is required, I also signify my consent.	Tenant's Signature	
Received By:		Date	

Numerous calls may indicate that the problem is in the boiler room. If this is the case complete section B and list suites visited
If the problem is with the in-suite blend valve, complete section "A" - Part 1, and if problem persists, complete Part 2.

SECTION "A" - CONDITIONS IN SUITE

PART ONE	√ Yes No	PART 2	√ Yes No
1. Are the heating convector isolating valves fully open?	☐ ☐	8. Is the convector blocked by foil, paint, etc.?	☐ ☐
2. Is the in-suite blend valve free to turn?	☐ ☐	9. Is there a through-the-wall-sleeve in the suite?	☐ ☐
3. Does this valve operate on demand from the thermostat?	☐ ☐	10. Has weather strip been installed around entrance?	☐ ☐
4. What is the temp. on the tenant's thermometer? °F		11. Are the exhaust vents operating properly?	☐ ☐
5. The setting on the thermostat is °F		12. Is there a humidifier in use in the suite?	☐ ☐
6. The thermometer reading on the thermostat is °F		13. Is the heat from a lamp, T.V. near the thermostat?	☐ ☐
7. The dry bulb readings of the sling psychrometer are:		14. Are there drafts from windows or doors?	☐ ☐
		15. Are the convectors clear of window draperies?	☐ ☐

Living Room °F	Bedroom °F	Bedroom °F	Other °F

16. Are the convector fins free of dust or lint?	☐ ☐

B. CONDITIONS IN THE HEATING SYSTEM	OBSERVATIONS AND RECOMMENDATIONS
1. Boiler Pressure psig	
2. Boiler Supply Water Temperature to Header °F	
3. Boiler Return Water Temperature °F	
4. Blended Heating Water Supply Temperature °F	
5. Building Heating Water Return Temperature °F	Investigator's Signature
6. Outdoor Temperature °F °C	

C. ACTION TAKEN BY MANAGMENT OFFICE	DETAILS ABOUT WORK TO BE DONE:

√	Document Type	Supplier	Date Issued	
	Work Order No.			
	Purchase Order No.			

Figure 4.3 A form for keeping information about heating complaints. This form is both an information document and a training tool.

occurred during the year, their cost, what action was taken, and whether the problems were eliminated.

All relevant information should be fed back to the developer, designer, and builder. This information is invaluable when they are deciding about new projects; renovations; retrofits; repair and maintenance policies and standards;

NAME AND ADDRESS OF THE COMPANY

Date _____   Work Order Issued to: _____   No. ____

Left section:

Building Address

Suite No. _____ Tenant's Name _____

Building Phone _____ Tenant's Phone _____

Insp. Report No. _____ R.P. No. _____ Mtce. Req. No. _____

Is Tenant to Be Invoiced? ☐ No ☐ Yes   Inv.#/date paid _____

Building No. _____ Oper. Cost No. _____ Ins. Claim No. _____

Full Description of Work Requested:

_____

_____

☐ √ If Consent To Enter Received   Bldg. Oper. Day Off Is: _____

This work order was phoned in by _____ at _____
A copy was mailed to confirm the order on _____

Comments by the Person Doing the Job:

_____

Authorized by	Completed by

Right section:

DATE		WORK DONE BY IN-HOUSE STAFF			
Mon.	Day	By Whom	# of Hrs	Hrly. Rate	Labor Cost

TOTAL LABOR COSTS

MATERIAL FROM IN-HOUSE INVENTORY		
Qty.	Description	Cost

TOTAL IN-HOUSE MATERIAL COST

Date Pur. Order Issued	Name of Supplier or Contractor	Cost

TOTAL SUPPLIER/CONTRACTOR COST

Copies of P.O's
☐ Will Follow   TOTAL COST OF JOB

A work order is used to communicate to an in-house support service group about any problem that is beyond the ability of the on-site staff; or to requisition, supplies, parts, materials or equipment from a central supply source for use in a building. There should be four copies: One is for the cost file and serves as an internal invoice to the building involved; one should be sent to the building's management office to be used for planning and budgeting purposes; one is used in a follow-up file; and the fourth copy is sent to the building operator, who should be made aware of the order and who is to complete it.

Figure 4.4   A work order form.

81

PURCHASE ORDER TO:	PURCHASE ORDER NO. _____

Name of Supplier	NAME OF COMPANY ISSUING ORDER
Address of Supplier	Name of Building Ordering
	Addresss of Office Placing Order - Invoice Address
Attention of:	Attention: Phone:
Supplier's Phone:	
	Ship to:
	Attention of: Phone

Quantity	Description	Cost No.	Unit Price	Amount

Building Address	Ordered by:	Date Ordered
Tenant's Phone	Phone at Work	Suite No.

Maintenance Request #	R.P. #	Inspection Report #	Insurance Claim #	Tenant Invoice #	Date Tenant Paid

RECEIVING REPORT - TO BE COMPLETED AND SIGNED BY RECIPIENT OF GOODS OR SERVICES

Date Goods Received and/or Work Completed	Tradesman's Hours	
	In	Out
Comments:		
Total Hours Worked (allow for travel time)		

FOR PAYMENT OFFICE ONLY			DISTRIBUTION OF COSTS			
Invoiced Date	Invoice Number	Amount	Bldg.#	Ins./R.P.#	Cost #	Amount
	Totals				Totals	

Received by	Inv. Ext. Checked by	Information Check'd. by	Payment Approved by	Check No.

Date Invoice Received in Payment Office	Supplier's Code No.
Payment Due Date	Cash Discount Percentage and Terms

Purchase orders are used to order equipment, parts, supplies, materials, and services that are not available from on-site or in-house staff or for problems that are beyond their ability to correct. Maintenance requests are used for on-site staff, and work orders are used for in-house services. The form becomes an important communication tool when several copies are distributed as follows: A match-up document to verify an invoice; a copy for the cost or follow-up file that also becomes a back-up for budgeting; and a copy for the person who is expecting the delivery or service work - - this informs that an order has been placed - - it is then used as a verification document to indicate that goods or services have been received as ordered.

Figure 4.5   A purchase order form.

the on-site staff responsibilities; and the control of the fuel, electricity, and water used in each building. It is difficult for management to know whether the decisions that it makes about the maintenance and operations of a building are the right ones unless there are records that show the results achieved by various decisions.

The advantages enjoyed by management when using a fairly detailed and formal participative system of budgeting include improved communication; participation by everyone involved, including the building owners; and a means of comparing activities on a monthly basis with factual information about each one. The plan provides flexibility so that it can be easily adjusted to accommodate unforeseen circumstances.

Because managers must narrow the range of attention of each person on their management teams to focus on definite and measurable results, and because the selection of the proper factors to be measured is an important decision, management must have a system that includes all of the activities detailed on the master action plan.

4.3 INSPECTIONS AND STANDARDS

The quality of management is measured by its conformity to defined requirements. Many say that effective management is impossible without including an inspection process that starts with a daily "look, listen, and touch" inspection by the on-site operator and a follow-up inspection on a regular basis by the manager. Further, specific inspections are required by housekeeping, groundskeeping, and structural and electrical-mechanical specialists to analyze and recommend solutions to specific problems. These specialized inspections are especially required when building owners are intending to renovate or retrofit a building.

Inspections help management by assuring that the standard of management that is offered to their customers is being maintained and that they are not giving their customers cause to consider offering the management contract to a competitor. Inspections are also an ideal way of soliciting feedback from the on-site staff and the tenants who live in the building. Written inspection reports are the only way to assure that everything that was seen and heard is documented, followed up, and corrected. These inspections are valuable sources of reference material if notes are made on formal budget-builder working papers that match the maintenance and operations account classifications discussed in Chapter 5.

Everyone in the design, construction, and building management industry agrees that inspections are important, but few take the trouble to organize formal inspections, to detail them in writing, to properly follow up to assure that all problems uncovered are corrected, and to keep records of the results.

Learning to See

We must train ourselves to comprehend what we see. We must learn how to recognize and understand how the various building components are put together and how they operate and to comprehend the normal and abnormal aspects of building structures and their electrical-mechanical systems. Because we are creatures of habit, a problem may appear to be normal because we are accustomed to its appearance and sound when in fact a problem exists that requires attention.

Managers must also know

when to inspect;
how to inspect;
how often to inspect;
who should inspect;
what to inspect; and
where to inspect.

Most important, managers must know enough about structures and electrical-mechanical equipment to make the right decisions about what to do to correct problems uncovered during inspections.

4.4 INSPECTIONS AS COMMUNICATION TOOLS

Building management communication can be described as the dialogue between the customers, occupants, or owners; the on-site operating staff; the administrative staff; the support services; the tradespeople; the suppliers; and the property manager.

Harvey Silver, in one of his seminars, explained the importance of communication by commenting that "the effectiveness of management to make decisions depends on the quality of the ideas and the acceptance of the group that has to implement them. If either of these factors is low, then effectiveness will be low."

Communication can be briefly described as follows:

- Communication is the instruction that results in action.
- Communication is the ability to listen, ask, and understand.
- Communication should include recommendations for improvement in any area or task.
- Communication should include the cooperation of line and staff efforts that result in the formation of objectives and policies for an enterprise.

- Inspections and communication are vital to the successful management of buildings.

4.5 TYPES OF INSPECTIONS

Housekeeping

General housekeeping maintenance tasks can be organized into daily, periodic, and special task groupings. To organize and achieve the desired standard of cleanliness, the following must be considered:

- An appropriate program for the area being serviced.
- The need to avoid overcleaning as well as undercleaning.
- The standards of cleanliness must be based on the service being performed, the frequency of the service, the work skills of the people performing the service, and the habits of the building's occupants.

Good housekeeping is often the criterion in judging a building being used by the public. Dirty halls, odoriferous toilets, and a general state of untidiness are all negative influences. First impressions made on people visiting sales and rental offices, or guests visiting building occupants, could mean the difference between the success or failure of a building project. Management should be aware that first impressions are lasting ones.

To ensure that the housekeeping staff is performing a satisfactory job requires close supervision by management. This would include inspections, instruction, and correction of problems as soon as they are discovered. The philosophy behind inspections should be to help everyone do a better job in carrying out the management philosophy developed by the building owner.

Groundskeeping

There are many factors that must be considered when carrying out groundskeeping inspections. Management must bear in mind that it is quite easy to become accustomed to the general appearance of the grounds and other areas of a building and accept it as adequate when it is not. Because the grounds change during the year, it is a good idea to schedule formal inspections to match the seasons. In addition to the general curb appeal, it is important to pay close attention to the landscaping, the hard surface areas, and the general condition of the facade of the building.

Trees, shrubs, and lawns.   One area that needs particular attention is the trees, shrubs, and lawns. Look for dead trees, plants, and grass. Notice how the grass is being cut. Check out the need for pruning, edging, and other conditions that indicate neglect. These inspections should be done during the growing season so that the person doing the inspection can properly assess conditions.

Materials, supplies, tools, equipment, and inventory.   It is a good idea to carry a set of material and inventory lists so that management can prepare information that will help make decisions about next year's planting. In fact, all information that could be pertinent to preparing the budgets should be gathered and documented during inspections.

Physical Features

Regular inspections and observations by managers and building staff can un- cover structural, as well as groundskeeping, problems so that they can be cor- rected before they become major. Major problems can be averted if the people discipline themselves to look closely and observe any subtle change of condi- tions such as cracked pavement; sunken curbs; broken sidewalks; the condition of brickwork and caulking; doors that squeak, stick, or bind; loose hardware; closers that leak or do not close doors; and signs of moisture in plaster in the form of peeling paint or efflorescence.

Building owners and managers should realize that there are no permanent building materials but that their useful life can be greatly extended by inspec- tion and preventive maintenance. Waiting for obvious damage to occur is the most expensive and least efficient means of learning about building problems. Observation, reporting, and correction of structural problems before they be- come emergencies are essential if you expect to control maintenance expenses.

The Roof

There are many things that people should observe when walking through a building or during formal inspections. People are constantly going up to the roof for various reasons, especially because many equipment rooms are located on the roof. Whenever they do, they should look for any abnormal condition and listen for any unusual sound.

Conventional roof.   The conventional built-up roof with a weatherproof membrane on top provides the opportunity to visually observe many potential problems. Always look for signs of pressure ridges, blisters, movement, or shrinkage in the surface felts. Should the surface feel spongy under foot, it is usually a sign that moisture has penetrated the insulation below. Check for exposed felts, which can transmit water through the membrane into the insula- tion. On flooded areas of the roof, wind and wave action can scour away the gravel, reducing the protective qualities of the roof.

Upside-down, or inverted, roof.   In the upside-down roof, the waterproof membrane is under the insulation, so inspections will not uncover membrane problems. Inspectors should assure that the crushed stone is covering the insulation and that there are no flooded areas on the roof.

The Building Exterior

When making exterior inspections or just when visiting a building, it is a good idea for each person on the team to make a general observation of the condition of brickwork, walls, parapets, windows and frames, doors and their frames, balcony dividers, balcony railing anchorages, etc. The most critical areas are the meeting points of dissimilar materials, such as where masonry meets concrete or columns and where masonry meets metal, to assure that the caulking has not failed.

Inspecting Asphalt

The early detection and repair of minor defects is without doubt the most important work done by the person responsible for pavement maintenance. Cracks and other surface breaks, which in their first stages are almost unnoticeable, may develop into serious defects if not soon repaired. This may occur quickly in the case of an underdesigned pavement that is being used for heavy traffic. It is for this reason that management should keep a close watch on the condition of asphalt.

Electrical-Mechanical Inspections

One cannot envision a successful building without the efficient operation of the electrical-mechanical equipment. A successful program starts with the right action plan; assurance that the funds for carrying out the plan are included in the budget; and assurance that the program has been properly assigned to the on-site staff, the trades, and contractors who will carry it out.

The Look, Listen, and Touch Inspection

It is the responsibility of management to assure that the on-site staff is trained to conduct daily look, listen, and touch inspections. It is the responsibility of the person performing this inspection to carry out a daily walk through the building.

This type of inspection should include making entries on operation logs; checking housekeeping equipment and equipment rooms; lubricating motors, pumps, fans, and other equipment; changing filters and belts; and adjusting equipment to run more efficiently. It should also include listening to the sound of the equipment and touching it to determine if motors or bearings are over-heating, rumbling, or pulsating.

It is always a good idea to operate mechanical doors, to try the keys in entrance doors, and to report problems when they are small, without waiting for things to break down.

The on-site staff should understand why it is necessary to keep equipment and equipment rooms clean and dust free. One of the main reasons for painting mechanical rooms and keeping them clean is to overcome the problem of dust settling on motors and the equipment that they run. Dust settling on motors, housings, windings, and slip rings works its way into the bearings. Once inside bearings, dust can be as harmful as sandpaper to the highly polished bearing surfaces. If allowed to fill the open spaces in a motor winding, dust turns the entire wound section into a sponge for soaking up harmful soil, moisture, and acid fumes, shortening the life of the motor and leading to break-downs.

Successful managers believe in planning, organizing, directing, and controlling their maintenance programs through inspections, the right operational standards, and communication. This belief is one of the foundations upon which a positive management attitude is built. Managers should keep in mind that the people who carry out their maintenance programs, whether they are on-site staff or contractors, are being paid to do an adequate job. Do not accept standards of maintenance that are below those expected by the building owners.

5

The Planning and Budgeting Process

To establish a means of controlling a building's maintenance and energy expenses, it is necessary to have a system of recordkeeping that provides management with the information it needs for making the right decisions. The controlling function is the planning, organizing, staffing, directing, and monitoring of the results initiated by a planning process.

The system of recordkeeping that is recommended here begins with the takeover of a building and the gathering of information about it that is included in a building profile. Aside from the historical data about a building, its profile identifies all the components that require maintenance or that will wear out and need replacement. These maintenance requirements for a building are classified as recurring and nonrecurring maintenance needs. This information is then organized into repair and maintenance classifications such as those illustrated in Figures 5.1 to 5.5. These classifications are organized to match the structural and electrical-mechanical components found in buildings. They also include other controllable expenses such as on-site staff salaries and the cost of fuel, electricity, and water.

The information that is needed to develop budgets for these accounts is developed around the master action plan and suppliers and services guide discussed in Chapters 3 and 4. To help a manager build the budget and include myriad tasks that need funding and activating for a meaningful maintenance

Year	Building No.	Building Name			
Building Address					

Acc. Nos.	Description	Actual Year		Budget	
		Previous	Current	Present	Over or Under

CAPITALIZED EXPENDITURES

Acc. Nos.	Description	Previous	Current	Present	Over or Under
20	Building Additions				
21	Building Replacements				
22	Construction Deficiencies				
23	Equipment Additions				
24	Equipment Replacements				

HOUSEKEEPING SERVICES

Acc. Nos.	Description	Previous	Current	Present	Over or Under
25	Carpeting				
26	Cleaning Supplies				
27	Cleaning Contractors				
28	Interior Decorating				
29	Pest Control				
30	Signage				
31	Waste Disposal				
32	Window Cleaning				

GROUNDSKEEPING SERVICES

Acc. Nos.	Description	Previous	Current	Present	Over or Under
33	Gardening				
34	Snow Removal				
35	Vehicle Maintenance				

An example of the way the accounts are reported. In this example are shown the annual totals with comparisons against budgets and the previous year's results. This same format could be used to show quarterly results or actual year-to-year comparisons on a building-by-building basis for projects or for the total portfolio (see Figure 5.5). It follows that income and other repair and maintenance expenses, the cost of on-site staff salaries, the cost of fuel, electricity, and water, should all be a part of this information and reporting system. These accounts are further classified as structural, electrical-mechanical, and administrative services, each with its own set of budget-builder working papers that include, plumbing, heating, cooling, ventilation, fire safety, security, and all the structural components that need maintenance. Note that the organization of information matches the recommended organization of people.

Figure 5.1 Maintenance and operations expense account classifications for renovations and retrofits (capitalized expenditures), and housekeeping and groundskeeping services (From Mel A. Shear, *Handbook of Building Maintenance Management,* © 1983, p. 16 [A Reston Publication]. Adapted by permission of Prentice-Hall, Inc., Englewood Cliffs, New Jersey).

Year	Building No.	Building Name				
Building Address						

Acct. Nos.	Description	Actual Year		Budget	
		Previous	Current	Present	Over or Under

STRUCTURAL SERVICES

Acct. Nos.	Description	Previous	Current	Present	Over or Under
36	Brickwork & Concrete				
37	Building Hardware				
38	Caulking				
39	Counters & Cupboards				
40	Doors				
41	Exterior Painting				
42	Floors				
43	Paving (Concrete & Asphalt)				
44	Roofs				
45	Walls & Ceilings				
46	Windows				

ELECTRICAL SERVICES

Acct. Nos.	Description	Previous	Current	Present	Over or Under
47	Appliances				
48	Wiring Distribution				
49	Fire Protection				
50	Television System				

MECHANICAL SERVICES

Acct. Nos.	Description	Previous	Current	Present	Over or Under
51	Cooling System				
52	Elevators				
53	Heating Systems				
54	Plumbing & Drainage				
55	Pool Operations				
56	Ventilation System				

The information needs related to buildings should be value analyzed by asking the following questions: How should information be organized? What do we need to know? How can the information best be used to help the management process? What kind of maintenance programs does each building require? Who should be doing the work? How often? How much will it cost? What are the benefits? What will the results be?

Figure 5.2 Maintenance and operations expense account classifications for structural, electrical, and mechanical services (From Mel A. Shear, *Handbook of Building Maintenance Management,* © 1983, pp. 17–18 [A Reston Publication]. Adapted by permission of Prentice-Hall, Inc., Englewood Cliffs, New Jersey).

Year	Building No.	Building Name				
Building Address						

Acct. Nos.	Description	Actual Year		Budget	
		Previous	Current	Present	Over or Under

MISCELLANEOUS

Acct. Nos.	Description	Previous	Current	Present	Over or Under
57	On-Site Communications				
58	General				
59	Insurance Claims Deductible				
60	Recreation				
61	On-Site Telephones				

ON-SITE STAFF SALARIES

Acct. Nos.	Description	Previous	Current	Present	Over or Under
62	Building Operators				
63	Day Help				
64	Engineering				
65	Gardeners				
66	Recreation				
67	Leasing, Sales, & Administration				
68	Fringe Benefits				

Using a zero-base budget that is organized to match a building's systems and services allows the people on the management team to communicate with each other as they gather the information they need to prepare the budget. This planning process involves inspecting the building, knowing the labor costs and the materials for each job and the costs for all planned and responsive maintenance. These costs are then built into the budget and compared with actual results during the budgeted year.

This system allows management to identify each saving opportunity and to plan programs that drive up the performances of themselves, the structure, and the electrical-mechanical equipment to their highest levels and at the same time reduce the remaining saving potential to its lowest level. The program would not be considered a success until there are no more identifiable opportunities to save.

Figure 5.3 Maintenance and operations expense account classifications for miscellaneous expenses and the cost of on-site building staff salaries (From Mel A. Shear, *Handbook of Building Maintenance Management,* © 1983, p. 18 [A Reston Publication]. Adapted by permission of Prentice-Hall, Inc., Englewood Cliffs, New Jersey).

Year	Building No.	Building Name			
Building Address					

Acct. Nos.	Description	Actual Year		Budget	
		Previous	Current	Present	Over or Under

UTILITIES

Acct. Nos.	Description	Previous	Current	Present	Over or Under
69	Fuel Oil				
70	Electricity				
71	Water				
72	Natural gas				

SUMMARIES OF TOTALS OF RENOVATIONS, RETROFITS, & MAINTENANCE EXPENSES

Acct. Nos.	Description	Previous	Current	Present	Over or Under
20 to 24	Capitalized Expenditures				
25 to 32	Housekeeping Services				
33 to 35	Groundskeeping Services				
36 to 46	Structural Services				
47 to 50	Electrical Services				
51 to 56	Mechanical Services				
57 to 61	Miscellaneous				
62 to 68	On-Site Staff Salaries				
69 to 72	Utilities				
73	Security Services				
TOTALS					

These classifications are recommended for monthly and annual continuity and to provide management with a sensible organization of accounting information that is compatible with the budget-builder working papers, which are organized to match the services and components found in a building.

Figure 5.4 Maintenance and operations expense account classifications for fuel, electricity, and water and summaries of the totals for all maintenance and operations accounts (From Mel A. Shear, *Handbook of Building Maintenance Management*, © 1983, p. 18 [A Reston Publication]. Adapted by permission of Prentice-Hall, Inc., Englewood Cliffs, New Jersey).

Year	Building Number	Building Name
Building Address		

Acct. Nos.	Description	ACTUAL ANNUAL EXPENDITURES			
		1988	1989	1990	1991

RECURRING & NONRECURRING MAINTENANCE AND OPERATIONS EXPENSES

Acct. Nos.	TOTAL CAPITALIZED MAINTENANCE AND OPERATIONS EXPENDITURES				
20	Building Additions				
21	Building Replacements				
22	Construction Deficiencies				
23	Equipment Additions				
24	Equipment Replacements				
21 to 24	**Total Capitalized Expenses**				
14	Realty Taxes				
15	Legal & Audit				
16	Insurance				
17	Management Fees				
18	Sundry				
25 to 32	Housekeeping Services				
33 to 35	Groundskeeping Services				
36 to 46	Structural Services				
47 to 50	Electrical Services				
51 to 56	Mechanical Services				
57 to 61	Communications & Recreation Services				
73	Security Services				
14 to 73	**Total Repair & Mtce. Costs**				
62 to 68	**Total On-Site Staff Costs**				
69	Fuel				
70	Electricity				
71	Water				
72	Other Sources Of Energy				
69 to 72	**Total Energy Costs**				
	Totals for each year, as well as the total expenses for each classsification to assure a continuity of comparisons.				

Figure 5.5   A format for summarizing maintenance and operations expenses for a building. This allows building managers to list expenses on a monthly, quarterly, semiannual, or annual basis.

and energy management program, a set of working papers should be developed to detail all these activities. The planning process revolves around the budget-builder working papers illustrated in Figures 5.6 to 5.31, and organized to match the account classifications in Figures 5.1 to 5.5.

5.1 UNDERSTANDING MAINTENANCE

Most building management companies use a combination of on-site and in-house staff and outside contractors to carry out their maintenance programs. The decision as to which method to use can be made only after defining the maintenance needs for each building in the management portfolio. If a program is planned, management must decide how best to carry out that plan. If it is merely a program of responsive maintenance, then it is necessary to have contractors available only when needs arise.

Unless the needs are clearly defined, it is possible that many of the jobs that could be done by the in-house staff will be done by outside contractors. As an example, it would be unwise to call an electrician to change a fuse, or a plumber to replace a faucet washer, when the superintendent, who is already on the payroll, could quite easily—if properly trained—do this job. On the other hand, it would be unwise to expect that the on-site staff would be capable of doing the work of a carpenter, plumber, electrician, tile setter, or some other specialist.

To get a better idea of some of the contracts that may be required by a building, review the services and suppliers guide (Figure 3.1).

Types of Maintenance

When considering the maintenance needs of buildings and the philosophy of handling them, it is a good idea to understand the different types of maintenance. In general they can be classified as follows:

- *Breakdown Maintenance*—fixing things as they fail
- *Corrective Maintenance*—repairing conditions as they exist
- *Redesigning, Retrofitting, or Renovating*—improving existing conditions to eliminate failures, improve efficiency, to save maintenance and energy costs
- *Preventive Maintenance*—a system of periodic inspections of existing facilities to uncover conditions leading to breakdown or harmful depreciation, and the correction of them while they are still minor

Budget Year			Building No.	
Building Address				
Building Name				**TOTAL BUDGET**
CAPITALIZED EXPENDITURES Account Summary		Account Number	Account Totals	
Building Additions		20		
Building Replacements		21		
Construction Deficiencies		22		
Equipment Additions		23		
Equipment Replacements		24		

A capital expenditure is an expenditure for long-term additions or betterments, properly charged to a capital assets account. Building additions include any changes from the original design. These accounts would be used for any additions or improvements costing over an amount stipulated by your accountant or the tax department. In effect, when money is spent to change the original structure or a component in the electrical-mechanical equipment, the accountants add these amounts to the original cost of the building.

Building replacements are any expenditures required to replace components that failed after the first five years of a building's life, at a cost greater than an amount stipulated by your accountant. Some building replacements are piping, boiler tubes, roofs, ventilation system components, television distribution systems, paving, brickwork, and caulking.

Whether an expense is charged to a capitalized account is determined by the accounting policies of your company or by income tax rulings. If not charged to a capitalized account, the expense would be included in the repair and maintenance expenses for the building. In some public buildings these expenses are called nonrecurring expenses.

Equipment additions or replacements are also governed by the policies of your company or the tax department.

Any capitalized expense that is incurred in the first five years of a building's life is charged to the construction deficiency account.

Figure 5.6 A form for itemizing renovations and retrofits (capitalized accounts). Managers require details to support the account totals (see Figures 5.38 and 5.39 for schedule of proposals (From Mel A. Shear, *Handbook of Building Maintenance Management,* © 1983, p. 9 [A Reston Publication]. Adapted by permission of Prentice-Hall, Inc., Englewood Cliffs, New Jersey).

Budget Year			Building No.		
Building Address					
Building Name				**TOTAL BUDGET**	
HOUSEKEEPING SERVICES Account Summary		Account Numbers	Account Totals		
Carpeting		25			
Cleaning Supplies		26			
Contract Cleaners		27			
Interior Decorating		28			
Pest Control		29			
Signage		30			
Waste Disposal		31			
Window Cleaning		32			

To ensure above-average results and value for the dollars spent on housekeeping, management must be able to effectively plan, organize, staff, direct, and control housekeepers; what they do and how they do it; the time they take to do a job; the tools, equipment, supplies, and chemicals they use, and how they use them.

The decision about whether you contract the work or do it yourself should be made only after a manager clearly understands the needs, has prepared a work load for a building, and scheduled the responsibilities, as if it were the intention to do the work with in-house staff. This in effect sets the standards and specifications for the job. This is the only way to properly assess the people bidding for the contract.

Whether the decision is made to do the work in-house or through a contractor, the manager who is able to develop a housekeeping plan is best qualified to assess the performance of the people doing the job. Assessment would include inventory control; specifications for equipment, tools, supplies, materials, and chemicals; the square footage of areas being maintained; and schedules of duties for everyone responsible for housekeeping services.

Regular inspections by management are the basis for making decisions about performance and when preparing annual budgets.

Figure 5.7 An account summary for housekeeping expenses. The amounts shown are supported by detailed budget-builder working papers illustrated in Figures 5.8 and 5.9 (From Mel A. Shear, *Handbook of Building Maintenance Management,* © 1983, p. 10 [A Reston Publication]. Adapted by permission of Prentice-Hall, Inc., Englewood Cliffs, New Jersey).

Budget Year		Building Number	
Building Address			
Building Name	Account Numbers	Sub-totals	**TOTAL BUDGET**
HOUSEKEEPING SERVICES - 1	25 to 28		
CARPETING	25	Total	
Cleaning	251		
Repairs & Patching	252		
Walk-Off - Additions - Replacements	253		
CLEANING SUPPLIES	26	Total	
Equipment	261		
Materials	262		
Paper Products	263		
CONTRACT CLEANERS	27	Total	
Building	271		
Garage Sweeping	272		
INTERIOR DECORATING	28	TOTAL	
Draperies & Blinds	281		
Lobby	282		
Painting & Papering	283		
Wall & Ceiling Cleaning	284		

Figure 5.8 Budget-builder working paper for carpeting, cleaning supplies, contractors, and interior decorating (From Mel A. Shear, *Handbook of Building Maintenance Management,* © 1983, p. 180 [A Reston Publication]. Adapted by permission of Prentice-Hall, Inc., Englewood Cliffs, New Jersey).

Energy Consumption

Figures 5.32 to 5.35 illustrate the recommended format for keeping records of the consumption and cost of fuel, electricity, and water. When managers begin using the utility information forms recommended in this planning and budgeting system, the first thing they should do is gather three years' past bills for

Budget Year		Building Number		
Building Address				
Building Name	Account Numbers	Sub-totals		**TOTAL BUDGET**
HOUSEKEEPING SERVICES - 2	29 to 32			

PEST CONTROL	29	Total	

Contract Costs	291	
Extras To Contract	292	

SIGNAGE	30	Total	

Changes or Updates	301	
Directory Boards	302	

WASTE DISPOSAL	31	Total	

Bin Pick Up & Repair	311	
Garbage Chutes	312	
Compactors	313	
Incinerator (burner-fuel-repairs)	314	
Plastic Bags	315	

WINDOW CLEANING	32	Total	

Contract Costs	321	

Figure 5.9 Budget-builder working paper for pest control, signs, water disposal, and window cleaning (From Mel A. Shear, *Handbook of Building Maintenance Management,* © 1983, p. 181 [A Reston Publication]. Adapted by permission of Prentice-Hall, Inc., Englewood Cliffs, New Jersey).

each building and enter the information on the appropriate forms. The average of these three years will be the current budget for those buildings. The challenge is to reduce this consumption average by 20 percent.

Budget Year		Building Number	
Building Address			
Building Name			**TOTAL BUDGET**
GROUNDSKEEPING SERVICES Account Summary		Account Numbers	Account Total

Gardening	33	
Snow Removal	34	
Building-Owned Vehicle Maintenance	35	

If you asked tenants the reason they wanted to live in a particular building, other than the location and the amount of rent they paid, you would probably find that there was something about the building that attracted them. This something is sometimes called "curb appeal."

There is no doubt that the design and installation of the landscaping substanially contributed to this "curb appeal" and set the standards for the building. The manner in which the landscape is maintained assures that the right people are attracted to the building and that the tenants feel a sense of pride in their home or have a feeling of well-being in their working environment.

If you study the groundskeeping account classifications, you will agree that keeping the grounds in top shape involves more than just cutting the grass. Aside from dealing with the plant materials, soil, chemicals, fertilizers, tools, equipment, and watering, groundskeeping staff have to schedule, pick up litter, sweep sidewalks and parking lots, cut grass, edge the walks and flower beds, cultivate, plant, and prune.

Using a zero-base budget helps management plan and include the myriad things that need to be done to keep the grounds or the interior landscape at a high level of maintenance while reducing the costs to their lowest possible levels. To develop a meaningful budget managers need the following:

• Specifications for equipment, tools, supplies, materials, chemicals, parts, etc.
• Copies of contracts, work specifications, work loads, and schedules of duties.
• Inventory lists of all equipment, tools, supplies, materials, chemicals, etc.
• A plot plan showing water and gas mains, buried electrical cables, lighting, sewer lines, contours of land, all trees, shrubs, and flower beds.
• Lists of the annual and perennial plant materials that will be used.
• Lists of all fertilizers and chemicals required.
• Quantities and prices that management will pay before they can prepare a meaningful budget.

Figure 5.10   An account summary for groundskeeping expenses. The account totals are supported by the budget-builder working papers illustrated in Figure 5.11. (From Mel A. Shear, *Handbook of Building Maintenance Management*, © 1983, p. 10 [A Reston Publication]. Adapted by permission of Prentice-Hall, Inc., Englewood Cliffs, New Jersey).

Budget Year		Building Number		
Building Address				
Building Name	Account Numbers	Sub-totals	**TOTAL BUDGET**	
GROUNDSKEEPING SERVICES	33 to 35			

GARDENING	33	Total	
Accessories	331		
Architectural Changes	332		
Gardening Contractor	333		
Plant Materials	334		
Soils, Chemicals, & Fertilizers	335		
Tools & Equipment	336		
Watering Equipment	337		

SNOW REMOVAL	34	Total	
Contractor	341		
Fuel & Snow Removal Equipment	342		
Salt & Sand	343		
Tools	344		

BUILDING-OWNED-VEHICLE MAINTENANCE	35	Total	
Car Allowances	351		
Fuel	352		
Insurance	353		
Maintenance	354		
Tires	355		

Figure 5.11 Budget-builder working paper for gardening, snow removal, and for any building-owned vehicles. Inventories, plant material lists, and equipment lists support the totals (From Mel A. Shear, *Handbook of Building Maintenance Management,* © 1983, p. 217 [A Reston Publication]. Adapted by permission of Prentice-Hall, Inc., Englewood Cliffs, New Jersey).

Budget Year		Building Number	
Building Address			
Building Name			**TOTAL BUDGET**
STRUCTURAL SERVICES Account Summary	Account Numbers	Account Totals	
Brickwork & Structural Concrete	36		
Building Hardware	37		
Caulking	38		
Counter Tops & Cupboards	39		
Doors	40		
Exterior painting	41		
Floors	42		
Paving (Concrete & Paving)	43		
Roofs	44		
Walls & Ceilings	45		
Windows	46		

The structural account classifications are organized to allow management to logically think about all the things that have to be done to maintain a building. This format also provides management with a sensible way of organizing and inspecting each component to assure that it is not deteriorating and that the necessary funds to keep the building from being downgraded are included in the budget.

When building owners are considering an energy management program, the design of the building's skin becomes very important because it has a direct bearing on the thermal and seasonal efficiency of the energy consumed by the building.

Management usually has no control over the location, the design, or the way a building was built; the only thing that they can do is to keep proper records of energy use along with details of the costs of each building's maintenance program. In this way they monitor each building's progresss toward the energy and maintenance targets set by the manager. Tenant complaints should also be documented to assure that the tenants are not uncomfortable. No money should be spent on structural or electrical-mechanical retrofits until management is assured that the consumption of energy has been reduced to the lowest possible level, while the building remains in its as-built condition.

Figure 5.12 An account summary for structural components. The account totals are supported by the information developed by the budget-builder working papers illustrated in Figure 5.13–5.15. (From Mel A. Shear, *Handbook of Building Maintenance Management,* © 1983, p. 11 [A Reston Publication]. Adapted by permission of Prentice-Hall, Inc., Englewood Cliffs, New Jersey).

Budget Year	Building Number		
Building Address			
Building Name **STRUCTURAL SERVICES - 1**	Account Numbers	Sub-totals	**TOTAL BUDGET**

BRICKWORK & STRUCTURAL CONCRETE	36	Total	
Chimneys	361		
Garages	362		
Retaining Walls	363		
Slab Edges & Other Exterior Cladding	364		
Tuckpointing, Taping, & Grouting	365		

BUILDING HARDWARE	37	Total	
Ashtrays, Wall Urns, & Other Accessories	371		
Lock Cylinders	372		
Door Closers & Other Door Operators	373		
Door Handles	374		
Keys	375		
Locksets	376		
Padlocks	377		

CAULKING	38	Total	
Columns, Slab Edges, & Exterior Cladding	381		
Doors, Windows, & Balconies	382		

Figure 5.13 Budget-builder working paper for brickwork, structural concrete, building hardware, and caulking. Key control lists, building hardware information, and inspection reports support the totals (From Mel A. Shear, *Handbook of Building Maintenance Management,* © 1983, pp. 134, 282 [A Reston Publication]. Adapted by permission of Prentice-Hall, Inc., Englewood Cliffs, New Jersey).

Budget Year		Building Number	
Building Address			
Building Name	Account Numbers	Sub-total	**TOTAL BUDGET**
STRUCTURAL SERVICES - 2	39 to 42		
COUNTER TOPS AND CUPBOARDS	39	Total	
Counter Tops	391		
Cupboards	392		
DOORS	40	Total	
Balcony	401		
Garage	402		
Doors (Exterior & Interior)	403		
EXTERIOR PAINTING		Total	
Balconies (Panels - Dividers - Railings)	411		
Concrete & Masonry	412		
Galvanized Metal	413		
Prepainted Metal	414		
Windows, Doors, & Door Trim	415		
FLOORS	42	Total	
Tiles (Ceramic - Quarry - Others)	421		
Tiles (Hardwood)	422		
Tiles (Vinyl)	423		

Figure 5.14 Budget-builder working paper for kitchen countertops and cupboards, doors, exterior painting, and floors. Door schedules, exterior renderings, floor covering details, and inspection reports support the totals (From Mel A. Shear, *Handbook of Building Maintenance Management,* © 1983, p. 283 [A Reston Publication]. Adapted by permission of Prentice-Hall, Inc., Englewood Cliffs, New Jersey).

Budget Year		Building Number	
Building Address			
Building Name	Account Numbers	Sub-totals	**TOTAL BUDGET**
STRUCTURAL SERVICES - 3	43 to 46		

PAVING (ASPHALT, CONCRETE, & PAVERS)	43	Total	
Curbs	431		
Paving (Asphalt, Concrete, & Pavers)	432		
Ramps	433		
Sidewalks & Steps	434		
ROOFING	44	Total	
Eavestroughing & Flashing	441		
Patching & Repairing	442		
Replacing	443		
Scraping & Applying 3-Ply	444		
WALLS & CEILINGS	45	Total	
Ceilings (Plaster, Tiles, & Other Materials)	451		
Patching (Including Painting & Other Finishes)	452		
Tub Caulking	453		
Wall Tiles (Including Grout, Soap Dishes, etc.)	454		
WINDOWS	46	Total	
Reglazing	461		
Rescreening	462		
Other Maintenance	463		

Figure 5.15 Budget-builder working paper for paving, roofing, walls, ceilings, and windows. Window schedules, the building's plot plan, and inspection reports support the totals (From Mel A. Shear, *Handbook of Building Maintenance Management,* © 1983, p. 284 [A Reston Publication]. Adapted by permission of Prentice-Hall, Inc., Englewood Cliffs, New Jersey).

ELECTRICAL SERVICES Account Summary	Account Numbers	Account Totals	TOTAL BUDGET
Budget Year Building Number			
Building Address			
Building Name			
Appliances	47		
Electrical Wiring Distribution	48		
Fire Protection System	49		
Television Signal Distribution System	50		
Security Services System	73		

To properly plan, organize, direct, and control a successful maintenance and energy management program, managers need a means of organizing the myriad tasks that need to be done by the on-site staff, the in-house or outside consulting and contract services, and building these costs into a budget. These budget-builder working papers give management a way of doing just that. Using the same account classifications for keeping records of the actual expenditures will monitor the results against the plan.

Each of the classifications shown on this chart has a further breakdown (Figures 5.17 and 5.18) of the electrical components that may require maintenance.

Using the account classifications illustrated on those charts allows management to think about and analyze many electrical-mechanical energy measures and, where warranted, include the funds needed to implement them in the budgets - - such things as:

- Providing a pool cover for swimming pools
- Adding photocells to outside lighting and indoor windowed areas
- Adding timer clocks where needed and assuring that they are always correctly adjusted
- Programmable lighting
- Adjusting lighting to a reasonable level
- Painting all equipment rooms and underground garages white
- Replacing all incandescent bulbs in garages and equipment rooms with fluorescents
- Arranging lighting so that it will be feasible to group relamp

Figure 5.16 An account summary for electrical services. The account totals are supported by the information developed by the budget-builder working papers illustrated in Figures 5.17 and 5.18 (From Mel A. Shear, *Handbook of Building Maintenance Management,* © 1983, p. 12 [A Reston Publication]. Adapted by permission of Prentice-Hall, Inc., Englewood Cliffs, New Jersey).

Budget Year		Building Number	
Building Address			

Building Name	Account Numbers	Sub-totals	TOTAL BUDGET
ELECTRICAL SYSTEM - 1	47 - 48		

APPLIANCES	47	Total	
Dishwashers	471		
Dryers	472		
Floor Polishers	473		
Refrigerators	474		
Stoves	475		
Vacuum Cleaners	476		
Washing Machines	477		

ELECTRICAL WIRING DISTRIBUTION	48	Total	
Emergency Lighting	481		
F.M. Radio	482		
Fixtures & Light Bulbs	483		
Fuses, Electrical Panels, & Controls	484		
Wiring Distribution	485		

Any successful energy management program will reduce the cost of electrical energy by controlling manually or automatically the following:

- Lighting
- Power factor of motors
- Reuse of heat generated by people, lights, equipment, or appliances
- Controls to turn on or off energy users when they are not required; assure optimum use of electrical system; and warn management of problems

Figure 5.17 Budget-builder working paper for appliances and wiring. The information on this chart is supported by inventories showing serial numbers, models, manufacturers, suite numbers, and tag numbers of all appliances. Fixture and light bulb lists, typical wiring circuits, and anticipated life expectancy can also be used as support material (From Mel A. Shear, *Handbook of Building Maintenance Management,* © 1983, p. 503 [A Reston Publication]. Adapted by permission of Prentice-Hall, Inc., Englewood Cliffs, New Jersey).

Budget Year			Building Number	
Building Address				
Building Name	Account Numbers	Sub-totals	**TOTAL BUDGET**	
ELECTRICAL SYSTEM - 2	49 - 50 73	totals		

FIRE PROTECTION SYSTEM	49	Total	

Alarms	491	
Batteries	492	
Fire Hoses & Fire Extinguishers	493	
Motors & Pumps	494	
Piping, Valves, & Controls	495	
Sprinkler System	496	
Standby Generator	497	
Testing the System	498	

TELEVISION SIGNAL DISTRIBUTION SYSTEM	50	Total	

Cable Contract	501	
Signal Distribution System	502	

SECURITY SERVICES SYSTEM	73	Total	

Alarms, Cameras, & Wiring of System	731	
Contracted Security Guard Service	732	

Figure 5.18 Budget-builder working paper for fire protection, television, and security systems. The information is supported by inventories and equipment details showing serial numbers, models, manufacturers, tag numbers, and services performed on the equipment (From Mel A. Shear, *Handbook of Building Maintenance Management,* © 1983, pp. 134, 504 [A Reston Publication]. Adapted by permission of Prentice-Hall, Inc., Englewood Cliffs, New Jersey).

Budget Year	Building Number	
Building Address		
Building Name		**TOTAL BUDGET**

MECHANICAL SERVICES Account Summary	Account Numbers	Account Totals	
Cooling System	51		
Elevators	52		
Heating System	53		
Plumbing & Drainage System	54		
Swimming Pool & Fountain Operations	55		
Ventilation System	56		

The electrical and mechanical systems are the nerve centers of a building's energy management program. A successful program depends on combustion efficiency, heat transfer efficiency, thermal efficiency, and how effectively the operator controls the indoor comfort temperature.

All of these factors are critically important when considering the potential for savings available to building owners through an effective maintenance and energy management program. These budget-builder working papers allow management to assess everything that needs maintenance or that will wear out and need replacement and build the costs of recurring and nonrecurring maintenance into a logical place in the budget. This system also includes the cost of on-site staff, the cost of consulting and contract services, and the cost of fuel, electricity, and water. The accounting system that is used to record the actual expenses is also organized to match the account classifications in the budget-builder working papers. In this way, each building competes only against itself while management maximizes income and reduces the cost of management to its lowest possible level without downgrading the structure, the electrical-mechanical equipment, the building's ambience, or the comfort and sense of well-being of the occupants.

If this information, maintenance, and energy management system is accepted and used by by everyone in the construction and building management industry, it will provide the basis for a management plan that will allow the developers, designers, builders, managers, operators, or support service contractors to unite under a single workable system.

This systematic approach applies the concept of identifying problems, collecting pertinent information about them, and then assigning the responsibility and authority to the right people to solve them without creating new ones.

Figure 5.19 An account summary of mechanical systems. The totals are supported by the information found in Figures 5.20–5.25. The totals found in each of the budget-builder working papers are supported by information found on inventories, equipment lists, contract information, inspection reports, and records of services performed on the equipment (From Mel A. Shear, *Handbook of Building Maintenance Management,* © 1983, p. 12 [A Reston Publication]. Adapted by permission of Prentice-Hall, Inc., Englewood Cliffs, New Jersey).

Budget Year		Building Number			
Building Address					
Building Name		Account Numbers	Sub-totals	**TOTAL BUDGET**	
MECHANICAL SERVICES - 1 THE COOLING SYSTEM		51			
Chillers & Condensers		510			
Cooling Towers		511			
Compressors		512			
Evaporators		513			
Fan Coil Units		514			
Filters		515			
Motors & Pumps		516			
Packaged or Individual Room Units		517			
Piping, Valves, & Controls		518			
Water Treatment		519			

Using these account classifications allows building managers to build the costs of maintaining and operating cooling systems into budgets and then to monitor the results against the building's master action plan -- such things as the cost of

• Fully maintaining and servicing chillers
• Fully maintaining and servicing cooling towers
• Servicing all room units, free-standing units, and rooftop units
• Installing proper thermostats, guages, and other controls that may be necessary to assure efficient operation of the system
• Testing, adding, and monitoring of water treatment
• Servicing motors, pumps, and valves
• Changing of filters and the cost of buying replacements
• Handling all nonroutine repairs

Figure 5.20 Budget-builder working paper used to gather anticipated costs for maintaining and operating the cooling system (From Mel A. Shear, *Handbook of Building Maintenance Management,* © 1983, p. 448 [A Reston Publication]. Adapted by permission of Prentice-Hall, Inc., Englewood Cliffs, New Jersey).

Budget Year	Building Number		
Building Address			
Building Name	Account Numbers	Sub-totals	TOTAL BUDGET
MECHANICAL SERVICES - 2 **ELEVATORS**	52		

Inspections	521	
Licenses	522	
Overtime Labor Costs	523	
Repairs Not Covered by Service Contract	524	
Service Contract	525	

It is not unreasonable to expect that elevators installed in buildings should last for the life of the building (50 years). This makes the choice of the elevator a critical one. Before the right design decision can be made about an elevator, it must be understood that the elevator must satisfy the traffic and height needs of the building and that the quality of the elevator can be determined only by researching the reputation of the manufacturer and the effectiveness of its service department.

An examination of the elevator equipment room reveals many electrical cabinets filled with relays, timers, resistence tubes, plug-in boards, motors, and machines. Without purchasing a service contract that includes the replacement of the parts that wear out, we would need many pages of components that would need to be priced and included in the budget-builder working paper shown on this chart.

It is for this reason that it is recommended that management purchase a full maintenance contract. Approximately 60 to 70% of elevator parts are subject to wear, and all of them will wear out and need replacement over a period of 22.5 years. When management buys a full maintenance contract, it amortizes the cost of these replacements over the life of the contract. Reputable contractors replace them before they break down, others don't.

When building owners find that their elevators are continually breaking down, they usually change service contractors in the hope that the next one will be better. When they buy a full maintenance contract, the cost of all parts that wear out and need replacement are included in the cost of the contract. Investigation will probably determine that the reason for the breakdown is because the service contractor did not replace the parts before they failed. Management should understand that these parts were already paid for in the full maintenance contract, and they should not have to be purchased and paid for again.

When buying elevators, don't sacrifice quality for price of either the elevator or the service contract.

Figure 5.21 Budget-builder working paper used to gather anticipated costs for maintaining and operating the elevators (From Mel A. Shear, *Handbook of Building Maintenance Management,* © 1983, p. 523 [A Reston Publication]. Adapted by permission of Prentice-Hall, Inc., Englewood Cliffs, New Jersey).

Budget Year		Building Number		
Building Address				
Building Name	Account Numbers	Sub-totals	TOTAL BUDGET	
MECHANICAL SERVICES - 3 **THE HEATING SYSTEM**	53			

	Account Numbers	Sub-totals
Boilers, Heaters, or Furnaces	531	
Burners	532	
Fan Coil or Other Unit Heaters	533	
Filters	534	
Humidifiers	535	
Individual Room Units	536	
Motors & Pumps	537	
Piping, Valves, & Controls	538	
Water Treatment	539	

Using these account classifications allows building managers to build the costs of maintaining and operating a building's heating systems into the budgets and then to monitor the results against the building's master action plan - - such things as the cost of

• Servicing and calibrating the outdoor reset and blend-valve controls
• Servicing burners and monitoring combustion efficiency
• Servicing both the fire and waterside of boilers
• Cleaning the interior and exterior of heat exchangers
• Testing and topping up, when necessary, glycol in heat exchangers
• Cleaning direct heaters used for heating domestic water or swimming pools
• Cleaning heat exchangers on boilers with atmospheric burners
• Servicing hot air furnaces
• Testing, adding, and monitoring water treatment in heating, and cooling
  systems, swimming pools, and fountains
• Servicing motor, pumps, and valves
• Installing proper thermostats and guages
• Servicing other heating system components to assure efficiency of operation
• Effectively handling nonroutine repairs

Figure 5.22 Budget-builder working paper used to gather anticipated costs for maintaining and operating the heating system (From Mel A. Shear, *Handbook of Building Maintenance Management,* © 1983, p. 393 [A Reston Publication]. Adapted by permission of Prentice-Hall, Inc., Englewood Cliffs, New Jersey).

Budget Year		Building Number		
Building Address				
Building Name		Account Numbers	Sub-totals	**TOTAL BUDGET**
MECHANICAL SERVICES - 4 PLUMBING & DRAINAGE		54		

	Account Numbers	
Domestic Hot Water Storage Tanks	541	
Drain Cleaning & Drain Repairs	542	
Motors & Pumps	543	
Piping, Valves, & Controls	544	
Plumbing Fixtures & Parts	545	

Using these account classifications allows building managers to build the costs of maintaining the plumbing and drainage system into the budgets; when the actual expense classifications match the classifications listed on the budget-builder working papers, management can monitor the results against each building's master action plan - - such things as the cost of

• Cleaning sanitary drains and catch basins
• Servicing the tanks that store the domestic hot water
• Servicing the heat exchangers in these tanks or the individual heaters used to
    heat the water
• Servicing the motors, pumps, and valves
• Installing the proper thermostats, guages, and thermometers
• Installing and maintaining piping and replacing equipment and parts
• Installing and maintaining insulation where economically feasible
• Handling of nonroutine repairs

Figure 5.23   Budget-builder working paper used to gather anticipated costs for maintaining the plumbing and drainage system (From Mel A. Shear, *Handbook of Building Maintenance Management,* © 1983, p. 322 [A Reston Publication]. Adapted by permission of Prentice-Hall, Inc., Englewood Cliffs, New Jersey).

Information Needs for a Building Project

Figure 5.36 illustrates the information that is needed by someone developing, designing, building, managing, operating, or servicing a building. Traditionally much of the development, design, and building information is never

Budget Year			Building Number		
Building Address					
Building Name		Account Numbers	Sub-totals	TOTAL BUDGET	
MECHANICAL SERVICES - 5 SWIMMING POOL AND FOUNTAIN OPERATIONS		55			

Chemicals & Other Accessories	551	
Contractor Costs	552	
Electrical Services	553	
Housekeeping Supplies	554	
Opening & Closing	555	
Plumbing & Drainage, Including Filters & Pipes	556	
Structural Repairs to Shell, Deck, Fence, etc.	557	

Decorative fountains and swimming pools have become very common in apartment buildings, hotels, motels, and schools. Decorative fountains can also be found in many office buildings, institutions, and shopping centers. Maintaining and operating these pools presents a big problem for management.

The complexity of this management challenge can readily be understood by reviewing the major components: the pool shell; the pumps; motors; piping; filter; ladders; surface skimmers; vacuums; brushes; materials; supplies and chemicals; and the training needed by the people who act as lifeguards, who are responsible for the safety of the swimmers, the filtering and backwashing, and the water treatment.

To assure that the funds for all of these activities are included in the budgets and properly allocated, all the account classifications shown on this chart must be supported by inventory lists of tools, supplies, chemicals, parts, and other things that are needed to effectively operate and maintain the pools or the fountains in buildings.

Figure 5.24 Budget-builder working paper used to gather anticipated costs for maintaining and operating swimming pools or fountains (From Mel A. Shear, *Handbook of Building Maintenance Management,* © 1983, p. 322 [A Reston Pulication]. Adapted by permission of Prentice-Hall, Inc., Englewood Cliffs, New Jersey).

Budget Year	Building Number		
Building Address			
Building Name	Account Numbers	Sub-totals	**TOTAL BUDGET**
MECHANICAL SERVICES - 6 THE VENTILATION SYSTEM	56		

Belts, Pulleys, & Sheaves	561	
Housing, Ductwork, & Louvers	562	
Filters	563	
Heat Recovery Equipment	564	
Motors, Fans, & Controls	565	

Using these account classifications allows building managers to build into the budgets the costs of maintaining and operating the ventilation systems. If the actual account classifications match the budget-builder working papers, it is not too difficult to monitor the results against a building's master action plan - - such things as

• Balancing the system
• Cleaning the fans and the fan housing
• Installing time clocks or other equipment
• Servicing back-draft dampers
• Installing carbon monoxide sensors in the garages that control the exhaust fans
• Installing humidity controls in high humidity areas
• Cleaning all air intakes and exhausts
• Replacing filters
• Servicing V-belt drives, sheaves, bearings, and motors
• Handling nonroutine repairs effectively

Figure 5.25 Budget-builder working paper used to gather anticipated costs for maintaining and operating the ventilation system (From Mel A. Shear, *Handbook of Building Maintenance Management,* © 1983, p. 448 [A Reston Publication]. Adapted by permission of Prentice-Hall, Inc., Englewood Cliffs, New Jersey).

seen by the property manager. It may be filed in the developer's, the designer's, or the builder's files and never seen by the people who are managing the building. On the other hand, the information gathered by management about the cost and specifications for renovations, retrofits, repair, and mainte-

Budget Year		Building Number		
Building Address				
Building Name				**TOTAL BUDGET**
MISCELLANEOUS EXPENSES Account Summary		Account Numbers	Account Totals	
Communication Material		57		
General		58		
Insurance Claims Deductible		59		
Recreation		60		
Telephone Services		61		

Because buildings today have so many uses and because some operations expenses do not fit into the structural and electrical-mechanical expense classifications, management must have somewhere else to charge them. Most buildings have a need for the account classifications illustrated on this form. If they do not, or if they require different classifications, the account titles can be changed to suit the needs of any building.

Communication materials are anything that is used to communicate with the tenants of a building, for example, notices. General is for any unusual expense that does not occur too often and as such would not require a specific classification. Recreation is for any expense incurred for a card room, library, tennis court, etc. Telephone services are for any on-site telephone, including a phone used by an on-site building operator.

Figure 5.26 An account summary of miscellaneous expenses. The information in this summary is supported by the amounts found in Figures 5.27–5.30 (From Mel A. Shear, *Handbook of Building Maintenance Management*, © 1983, p. 13 [A Reston Publication]. Adapted by permission of Prentice-Hall, Inc., Englewood Cliffs, New Jersey).

nance; on-site staff salaries; or the utility costs is probably filed in the management office and not fed back to the designers and builders of the structure.

Figure 5.37 shows how this information can flow and be used by building owners and managers to make important management decisions. It is easy for

Budget Year		Building Number	
Building Address			
Building Name	Account Numbers	Sub-totals	**TOTAL BUDGET**
MISCELLANEOUS - 1 **COMMUNICATION**	57		

	Account Numbers	Sub-totals
Delivery Costs	571	
Membership Cards	572	
Office Supplies	573	
Pictures	574	
Postage	575	
Printing	576	
Stationery	577	

Today there are many buildings that have on site some common management office or recreation area that requires communication materials. The typical expenses incurred for these purposes are included in this set of account classifications. Condominium corporations and senior citizens buildings would be good examples of buildings that would spend money on these kinds of things.

When developing a budget for these expenses, it is a good idea to encourage participation from the tenants. It is also recommended that someone representing the condominium board participate in developing the budget-builder working paper classifications and the account classifications for repair and maintenance expenses, the cost of on-site salaries, the cost of fuel, electricity, and water, and the cost of all major renovations or retrofits. Condominium board representatives should participate in any inspections that are made during budget preparation.

Figure 5.27   Budget-builder working paper used to gather anticipated costs for communicating with the building's occupants.

managers to improve the way they plan, organize, staff, direct, and control the management process if they have the information they need to make the right decisions. Feedback helps improve the management process by communicating relevant information to the developers, designers, and builders.

Budget Year		Building Number		
Building Address				
Building Name	Account Numbers	Sub-totals		**TOTAL BUDGET**
MISCELLANEOUS - 2 GENERAL & INSURANCE DEDUCTIBLES	58 & 59			

GENERAL	58	Totals	
Advertising for On-Site Staff	581		
Credit Bureau (new tenant and prospective on-site staff checks)	582		
Memberships in Trade Assocations	583		
Nuisance Claims by Tenants	584		
Moving Building Staff	585		
Publicity	586		
Other	587		

INSURANCE CLAIMS DEDUCTIBLE	59	Totals	
Deductible Only	591		
Less Than the Deductible	592		

The costs for checking out prospective tenants and employees is borne by the building and charged to account 582.

When management value analyzes the premiums paid for insurance against the cost to repair or replace things that have been physically damaged, the cost of liability claims, and the cost of crime, there comes a point when it makes sense to pay a deductible fee or to self-insure. It is difficult to determine what the cost for this will be unless you keep records. Account numbers 591 and 592 are used for just that purpose.

The other expense classifications illustrated are self-explantory.

If management of a particular building finds that the accounts listed here do not suit their needs, they can be changed to suit any situation, or other account classifications can be added.

Figure 5.28 Budget-builder working paper used to gather anticipated general expenses and information about insurance claim deductibles. (From Mel A. Shear, *Handbook of Building Maintenance Management,* © 1983, p. 13 [A Reston Publication]. Adapted by permission of Prentice-Hall, Inc., Englewood Cliffs, New Jersey).

Budget Year	Building Number		
Building Address			
Building Name	Account Numbers	Sub-totals	TOTAL BUDGET
MISCELLANEOUS - 3 RECREATION	60		

	Account Numbers	Sub-totals
Arts & Crafts Supplies	601	
Entertainment	602	
Equipment Rental	603	
Equipment Repairs	604	
Equipment New (and costing under $500)	605	
Nursery Supplies	606	
Playground Expense	607	
Refreshments	608	
Saunas	609	
Tennis Courts	610	
Towels & Linens	611	

The above account classifications were established to allow management to build in recurring expenses related to the recreational amenities that are part of a building project. Depending on the design of the building, all or some of these accounts should fit.

In some buildings, it may be necessary to design a special set of accounts for a particular project.

Figure 5.29 Budget-builder working paper used to gather anticipated costs for recreational activities. (From Mel A. Shear, *Handbook of Building Maintenance Management*, © 1983, p. 14 [A Reston Publication]. Adapted by permission of Prentice-Hall, Inc., Englewood Cliffs, New Jersey).

Budget Year			Building Number	
Building Address				
Building Name	Account Numbers			TOTAL BUDGET
MISCELLANEOUS - 4 TELEPHONES & NUMBERS	61	Sub-totals		

	Telephone Numbers		
Answering Service		612	
Building Operator		613	
Extensions		614	
Long-Distance Calls		615	
Paging Devices		616	
Management Office		617	
Rental Office		618	
Security Desk		619	

It is easy to understand that the number of phones and the expenses incurred by them can significantly add to the operating costs for a building. It is especially important to control long-distance calls. Anyone on the management staff who makes long-distance calls should make a record of the call and submit the information to the management office.

Some of the phones are used only for temporary periods, such as the phone that is used at an outside pool in the summer. Having a special account classification helps you organize the information about phones and allows you to properly plan for installation and removal of the temporary phone.

It is important to know what phone equipment is installed in a building to assure that any phones purchased or rented match the descriptions on the phone bill. It is not uncommon to find that you are being charged for a service that you don't require or for something that you do not have.

Figure 5.30 Budget-builder working paper used to gather anticipated telephone expenses (From Mel A. Shear, *Handbook of Building Maintenance Management,* © 1983, p. 14 [A Reston Publication]. Adapted by permission of Prentice-Hall, Inc., Englewood Cliffs, New Jersey).

Budget Year	Building Number
Building Address	
Building Name	

ON-SITE STAFF SALARIES

Employees Name	Hours Wrkd.	Current Salary			No. of Pays	Total Annual Salary
		Rate	Per	Total		
1.						
BUILDING OPERATOR		Total Account Number			62	
1.						
2.						
HOUSEKEEPERS		Total Account Number			63	
1.						
2.						
ENGINEERS		Total Account Number			64	
1.						
2.						
GARDENERS		Total Account Number			65	
1.						
2.						
RECREATION		Total Account Number			66	
1.						
2.						
LEASING, SALES, & ADMINISTRATION		Total Account Number			67	
TOTAL BUDGET FOR ON-SITE STAFF - ACCOUNTS 62 TO 67						

This form is a planning tool that allows building managers to build into a building's budget the cost of on-site staff salaries. This chart is designed to show you how to organize the various on-site staff's salary information. You could eliminate the classifications that do not fit the needs of a particular building, or you could have a separate page for each type of employee for a large project.

Figure 5.31 Budget-builder working paper used to gather anticipated costs for on-site staff. Summaries of the people involved in each occupation support the information on this chart. Schedules of duties also support the need for each person included on the building's payroll (From Mel A. Shear, *Handbook of Building Maintenance Management,* © 1983, p. 15 [A Reston Publication]. Adapted by permission of Prentice-Hall, Inc., Englewood Cliffs, New Jersey).

Building Number	Account Number	Building Name		

Building Address		Township		

No. of Suites	Meter Number
	Utility Account Number

Rate Classification	Rate Increase Dates

Date Contract Expires	Minimum Consumption

If there is no separate meter for the domestic water - use fuel used in summer as the fuel used to heat the water. • The average fuel used to heat water is: MCF

Name of Utility Company	Phone	Contact

Phone to Call for Degree-Day Information	Glazing?	Single ☐ Double ☐

* The consumption figures are adjusted by the utility compny for pressure & temperature to determine the volume of fuel that is used.

Year	Energy Used in Thousands of Cubic Feet (MCF)					Total Cost Per Month	Elapsed Degree-Days Celcius
Date Meter Read	No. of Reading Days	*Volume Used	Less Fuel for Dom. Water	Equals Fuel Used to Heat Bldg.	Rate		
Annual Totals							

For accurate year-to-year comparisons, divide the annual fuel used to heat the building by the annual degree-days for the area in which the building is located. A degree-day is the average daily temperature that drops below 18°C or 65°F; each degree below these levels would be one degree-day. Elapsed degree-days are the degree-days that are calculated between the meter reading days shown on column two.

Figure 5.32 Monthly fuel use and cost. Elapsed degree-days are the degree-days calculated between reading dates in column 2 (From Mel A. Shear, *Handbook of Building Maintenance Management*, © 1983, p. 601 [A Reston Publication]. Adapted by permission of Prentice-Hall, Inc., Englewood Cliffs, New Jersey).

122

Building Number	Building Name

Building Address	Township

Number of Suites	Meter Number
	Utility Account Number

Dates of Rate Increases

How Is Building Heated?	Cooled?

How Is Domestic Water Heated?	Domestic Water Consumption per Day

Utility Company Phone No.	Glazing?	Single ☐ Double ☐

Year		Kilowatt	Hour	Consumption	
Date Meter Read	No. of Read. Days	Demand	First 100 kWh	Second 100 kWh	Remainder	Total
Totals						

Figure 5.33 Monthly electrical energy consumption (From Mel A. Shear, *Handbook of Building Maintenance Management*, © 1983, p. 589 [A Reston Publication]. Adapted by permission of Prentice-Hall, Inc., Englewood Cliffs, New Jersey).

Building Number	Account Number	Building Name		
Building Address			Township	
Number of Suites	Meter Number			
	Utility Account Number			
Dates of Rate Increases			Current Rates	
How Is Building Heated? Cooled?			Demand	
			First	
How Is Domestic Water Heated?			Second	
Utility Company Phone No.			Remainder	

Year		MONTHLY	ELECTRICAL	ENERGY	COST	
Date Meter Read	No. of Read. Days	Demand Charge	First Charge	Second Charge	Remainder	Total Cost
Totals						

Figure 5.34   Monthly electrical energy cost.

5.2 A POSITIVE TAKEOVER APPROACH

Managers take over buildings whenever they start a new job or take over any building that is added to their management portfolios. Whether it is a new building or not, the basis for a sound maintenance management program is

Building Number	Account Number	Building Name		
Building Address			Township	
Number of Suites		Meter Number		
		Utility Account Number		
Dates of Rate Increases			How Is Water Heated?	
Daily Amount of Fuel Used to Heat Water			Summer	
Storage Capacity		How Is Piping Zoned?	Winter	
Utility Company Phone No.			Comments	

Year								
Date Meter Read	No. of Reading Days	First Meter Reading	Second Meter Reading	Monthly Consump.	Rate	Cost	Water Used Each Day	
Totals								

Figure 5.35 Monthly water consumption and cost (From Mel A. Shear, *Handbook of Building Maintenance Management,* © 1983, p. 594 [A Reston Publication]. Adapted by permission of Prentice-Hall, Inc., Englewood Cliffs, New Jersey).

ADMINISTRATIVE INFORMATION	CONCEPT & DESIGN INFORMATION
Office Procedures Standard Forms & Charts Contract Management Lease Management Auditing Risk Management Human Resources Management	Drawings Specifications Contracts Installation Manuals Feasibility Studies Site Development Structure Exterior Finishes Interior Finishes Electrical Systems Mechanical Systems Special Systems

CONSTRUCTION, RENOVATION OR RETROFIT INFORMATION

MANAGEMENT CONTROL	DOCUMENTS	ELEMENTS
Scope and Feasibility of Project Cost Analysis Planning and Budgeting Accounting Cash Flow Statements Life-Cycle Projections Value Analysis Element and Quality Control Performance Controls Materials Scheduling Guarantee Control	Quantities Estimating Costing Tendering Contracts Procurement	Supervision Installations Trial Testing As-Built Changes and Revisions Problems

COMMISSIONING INFORMATION

BUILDING PROFILE	DOCUMENTS	ELEMENTS
Documenting, Tagging, and Color Coding Equipment Inventory Developing Work Loads Scheduling of Duties	Guarantees Acceptance Operations Manuals Take-over Procedure	Testing Overcoming Deficiencies Completion Procedure Approvals Inventory Acceptance Process

OPERATIONS AND MAINTENANCE MANAGEMENT INFORMATION

Electrical System Control Mechanical System Control Monitoring of Operations Structural Element Control Housekeeping Contract Renovation Management	Specifications and Contract Management Energy Management Support Service Management Planning, Budgeting, and Expense Control Groundskeeping Control Retrofit Management

Figure 5.36 Information needed, sources of material, and documents required by a building during its development, design, construction, management, and operation stages.

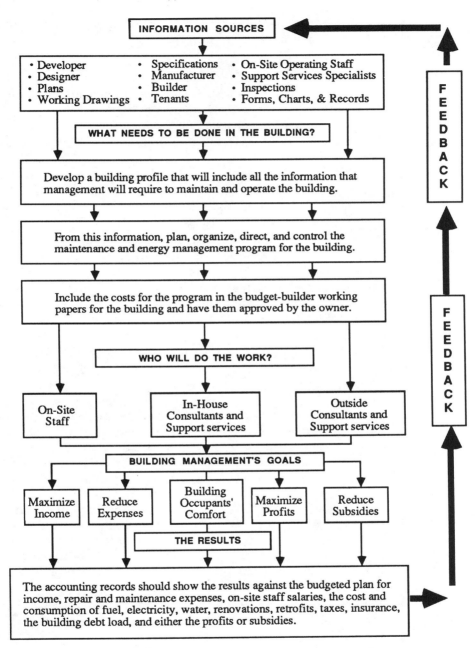

Figure 5.37 The flow of information needed to plan, organize, staff, direct, and control a building project over its life span.

dependent upon a manager's becoming thoroughly familiar with the building. There are several things that must be kept in mind when taking over a building.

1. The completion of a new structure should be considered as the beginning of the building's life, not the end of the project.

2. The transition from construction to management of the structure and electrical-mechanical systems should be formalized and executed professionally.

3. The architect and engineer should participate in the turnover and should ensure that adequate instructions and information are available for future management personnel. If necessary, factory experts should be available to explain more sophisticated equipment.

4. Project managers, on-site construction staff, property managers, on-site operating staff, and office staff should be trained to handle the responsibilities assigned to them.

5. Management should receive the necessary drawings and operations manuals soon after the structure is built and the electrical-mechanical equipment is installed.

6. Management should develop a system of preventive maintenance inspections that will uncover conditions leading to breakdown or harmful depreciation and correct these conditions while they are still minor.

7. This preventive maintenance inspection and service plan is supported by the on-site staff, contractors, support-service trades, consultants, and the manager who carry out these inspections on a daily, weekly, monthly, semiannual or annual basis as discussed in Chapter 4. To assure that the on-site staff clearly understand their responsibilities, the manager should develop work loads, establish duty schedules, and assure that the standards and expectations are communicated to the people responsible.

    Managers should be involved in the process of recruiting, hiring, training, assessing performance of, and upgrading the on-site and any in-house support-service staff. Managers and their staffs must also be qualified to monitor the work done by outside contractors, and to help them do a better job conforming to the specifications and standards that are set for the buildings.

8. The on-site operating staff should be provided with all the necessary equipment, tools, spare parts, materials, and chemicals they require to handle the jobs that are assigned to them.

9. All electrical-mechanical equipment that requires maintenance or that will wear out and need replacement should be tagged and color coded, as

should be all shut-off valves. The information about them should be detailed in the building profile manual that is developed for each building. On-site staff must be trained to valve-off pipe risers or shut down electrical-mechanical equipment in cases of floods or other emergencies.

10. Logs to monitor operations, maintenance, and energy consumption should be developed. The maintaining of these logs is one of the ways that management can be assured that the on-site operator is visiting the electrical-mechanical rooms every day. Keeping formal records of energy consumption is one of the ways that management can be assured that the energy program initiated for each building is meeting expectations.

11. The on-site operating staff should be taught how to recognize anything that would be considered abnormal and what to do when these conditions are discovered.

12. Management should develop a system of communicating to its staff the standards that are expected in the building and the suppliers and services that are recommended for services and supplies. This would include copies of all the service contracts that have been signed with outside contractors to carry out the services that are beyond the expertise of on-site staff and included in the master action plan for their buildings (see Chapter 4).

13. All planned expenditures for renovations, retrofits, repair and maintenance expenses, on-site staff salaries, the cost and consumption of fuel, electricity, and water should be included in the zero-base budgets prepared for each building in a management portfolio.

5.3 THE BUDGET

The most commonly used mechanism in management control is the budget, an integral tool of the management planning process. Once the plan is activated, the budget becomes the control point of the system. Its function is to monitor results initiated by the planning process. This manner of budgeting allows management to measure maintenance activities and compare their values against predetermined standards and prices. The purpose is to ensure that the goals and objectives that are set by the building owners for the maintenance and operations of the buildings in a management portfolio are being attained or have been accomplished.

A suitable system allows management to plan actions that, when completed, assure the building owner a reasonable chance of success in achieving these agreed-upon goals and objectives. Everyone, including the on-site staff, should be involved in the planning process. This is the only way that they can be made aware of the plan.

5.4 BUDGET-BUILDER WORKING PAPERS

The budgets are built around the master action plan, inspections, and the results of the previous year's building operational expenses.

The repair and maintenance account classifications shown (Figures 5.1 to 5.4) and the breakdown of these classifications into the activities that match the structural and electrical-mechanical components that are found in buildings is the recordkeeping system recommended.

Detailing all the maintenance activities into a set of budget-builder working papers (Figures 5.6 to 5.31) allows management the opportunity to build in the expenses for the myriad tasks, supplies, tools, equipment, spare parts, chemicals, etc., that are used to maintain and operate a building. In this way, specific preventive maintenance programs can be translated into detailed work schedules. A set of these working papers should be prepared for each building in the management portfolio, and they should be ready to use at the beginning of the building's fiscal year. During the year, notes and information are documented on these forms from inspections, work and purchase orders and from the actual costs of the previous year's operations.

Not all aspects of this program can be foreseen nor are they always the same from one year to the next. This is especially true when management is considering costly renovations and retrofits. These major expenses must receive special attention, and where necessary specialized consultants should be used to help identify problems; to set specifications; to obtain quotations; and to recommend solutions. Building owners should always be given the opportunity to approve or reject a proposed expenditure unless it is for an emergency.

5.5 RENOVATION AND RETROFIT PLANNING PROCEDURE

All expenditures that are above an amount specified by the accounting policies set by the company must receive special attention during the planning and budgeting process and when the actual work is being bid on or contracts are being signed. Whether for an emergency or when the work is completed, all the details concerning these expenditures should become a part of the history of the building and included in the building profile.

Procedure

During an operational year and no later than six months before a year end, property managers should prepare an income and expense budget for each building they manage. The expense budget, aside from the expenses for taxes (except in condominiums, where they are paid by each owner), insurance, management fees, principal and interest payments, and so forth should place special emphasis on repair and maintenance expenses, on-site staff salaries, and the cost of fuel, electricity, and water, as these are the controllable expenses.

Initially, all major renovations, equipment replacements or additions, or any major retrofit measures, should be included in the budget-builder working papers. Each of these nonrecurring expenses of over a predetermined amount (depending on the policy of the company) is removed from the original budget and listed on a schedule of renovations and retrofit proposals (Figure 5.38).

When the renovation lists are prepared (a separate list is made for each building in the management portfolio), they are submitted to the owner for approval. The property manager should be prepared to explain to the owner the rationale for the recommendation or answer questions about what is being recommended. Once these items are approved, they are added to the budgets for the coming year. Any that are not approved would be reassessed, and if they still appear to make economic sense, they would be added to the renovations lists for the following year.

Approval Process

During the budget year and at the appropriate time (e.g., energy retrofit measures to hearing systems would have to be completed while the heat is off), the person recommending the renovation initiates the activities required to complete the job.

A renovation proposal form (see Figure 5.39) is prepared and should include the specifications and standards expected for the job, estimates of the cost to complete the work, and reasons for and benefits expected from the proposed renovation. This form is sent to the building owner for approval before the job goes out to tender. In this way, the owner has a second opportunity (the first was during the planning and budgeting stage) to study and approve the actual proposal before the money is spent. Once the owner has approved the actual proposal, the contracts are awarded and the job is completed.

Supervision

The manager or someone delegated that responsibility should closely supervise the work being done to assure that the work is completed to their complete satisfaction. In some cases, progressive payments may have to be made if the job involves a lengthy time span. All payments and the final payment will be made only if the work is completed according to contract specifications.

Building Name	Building Number
Building Address	Budget Year
Presented by	Date
Approved by	Date

Approved	R.P. No.	Description of proposal -- if more detail is needed, add further comments and attach to this listing.	Account Numbers	Anticipated Cost
	1			
	2			
	3			
	4			
	5			
	6			

RENOVATIONS OR RETROFITS NOT APPROVED

R.P. No.	Description	Account Numbers	Cost

These renovation and retrofit schedules are for all budgeted expenditures of over $_____, other than recurring maintenance expenses that may be more than this amount. As each building should be considered its own business unit, or profit center, each would have its own set of budget-builder working papers, and all recurring and nonrecurring expenses would be initially detailed on these forms. Any expenditure that would be considered a renovation or retrofit would be included on these R.P. lists and removed from the working papers. They would be identified on the working paper with the R.P. No. If the portfolio has several buildings, each building would have a separate list.

Figure 5.38 A form used to list all major renovations and retrofit proposals that are projected for the coming year. These are approved before they are included in the budget.

132

The R.P. number must appear on all purchase and work orders and on contrators' or suppliers' invoices. If there is a variance from the approved amount of tender, an explanation must be sent to the person who approved the R.P. Copies of all R.P.s should be filed in the building profile, and all as-built drawings should be amended to reflect any changes.

Building Name	Recommended by			
Building Address		Building Number	Acct. Class. Number	R.P. No.
Date				
Budget Year	Amount Budgeted ————		Not Budgeted ☐	

REASON FOR THE RETROFIT/PROPOSAL OR PROBLEM TO BE CORRECTED

DESCRIPTION OF THE WORK TO BE DONE
(Attach all specifications and quotes to this tendering form.)

Names of Contractors & Suppliers Recommended	Estimated Cost	Invoice Date	Actual Cost
1.			
2.			
3.			
4.			

COMMENTS AND AUTHORIZATION TO PROCEED

Approved by	Date

All renovations and retrofits, unless emergencies, must be detailed on this tendering form and approved before the work is commenced. Emergencies are responded to before this form is prepared.

Figure 5.39 A form used to detail each renovation and retrofit proposal submitted to the owner for approval before the work is completed. The information on this form becomes a permanent record of every renovation and retrofit and should be kept for future reference (From Mel A. Shear, *Handbook of Building Maintenance Management*, © 1983, p. 88 [A Reston Publication]. Adapted by permission of Prentice-Hall, Inc., Englewood Cliffs, New Jersey).

5.6 ADVANTAGES OF THIS BUDGETING SYSTEM

A PLANNING TOOL

- It specifies objectives and reflects management's basic policies.
- It specifies courses of action to accomplish management's objectives.
- It reflects plans and includes all preventive maintenance activities.
- It allows management to look ahead.

A CONTROL TOOL

- It provides management with a basis for comparison with the master action plan.
- It provides a means whereby variances with the plan can be pinpointed.
- It motivates those who are involved in using the system.

A COMMUNICATIONS TOOL

- It plans ahead and thus requires participation of and communication between the building owner, the property manager, the building on-site staff, and the support-service consultants, contractors, and tradespeople.
- Its reports compare budgets with actual performance and thus provide a basis for communication concerning all the activities included in the master action plan.
- Its reports provide the opportunity for communication about possible revisions to the master action plan activities that are detailed in the budget-builder working papers for each building in the management portfolio.

SUMMING-UP

- It allows for planning activities in detail.
- It promotes communication concerning long- and short-range plans for each building in the management portfolio.
- It promotes participation by all the people involved in managing and operating a building.
- It provides a means of analyzing the renovations, retrofits, repair and maintenance activities, and their costs on a systematic basis for each building in the management portfolio.
- It provides a means of gathering factual information about the performance of the structural and electrical-mechancial equipment in the building. The inspections and detailed records of expenditures will provide a means of value analyzing the money spent to buy, install, and operate each component. Feeding back this information to the developer, de-

signer, and builder will certainly help them to get the best value for the dollars they spend on buildings in the future.

- It helps identify the need for, and promotes efficient allocation of, support service resources. This assures that only the needed services are provided.
- It helps provide better planning and control over expenditures by presenting information in an understandable and organized manner.
- It provides a flexibility that allows problem areas to be pinpointed.
- The organization of the information and an analysis of the problems will lead to the development of specialists who will be trained to overcome the problems.
- Once the master action plan is executed, costs and stopgap solutions to problems decrease drastically.
- Once the master action plan has been active for a few years, the budgeted plan closely matches the actual expenses—year after year. This results in very few surprises for the building owner. The process leads to establishment of a continuity of care for each building being managed.
- Once this management process is initiated and used by everyone on the management team, it gets better and better, as each year passes. It just naturally leads to improved communication and feedback from the people involved and when their suggestions for improving the process are acted upon it results in continual improvements in the system.

5.7 DIFFICULTIES IMPLEMENTING THIS BUDGETING SYSTEM

- It is difficult to sell because it appears easier to average the previous year's total maintenance and operations expenditures and adjust the expenses to reflect inflation than to prepare a detailed budget such as the one recommended here.
- It is difficult to sell because people resist change.
- It is difficult to sell because people do not understand that the needs of the structure and the electrical-mechanical equipment require that someone must inspect, housekeep, lubricate, and attend to the little preventive maintenance things on a daily basis and that responsive maintenance is uncontrollable and very costly.
- Building owners are reluctant to implement all the preventive maintenance activities and to spend money on the renovations and retrofit programs that may be necessary to overcome built-in problems that have not been dealt with in the past because they appear costly.
- If, in the past, management policy has been to defer maintenance, it will appear costly to catch up when you suddenly start spending money on problems that were not corrected in the past.

- It creates human relations problems when it is implemented, not understood, and not accepted by everyone involved. Unless the management staff understand the reasons for changing the traditional planning process, they can literally cause the system to fail.

The effectiveness of any plan depends on the quality of the idea and the acceptance by the group that has to implement it. If either of these factors is low, effectiveness will be low.

5.8 ACHIEVEMENTS OF THIS BUDGETING SYSTEM

Experience has shown that the use of this planning and budgeting system produces the following results:

- Problems are constantly being identified, attacked, and eliminated.
- People are assigned the jobs that best suit them, whether the on-site staff, in-house support services staff, or outside contractors.
- The need for specialized people is identified. When outside specialists are not available, in-house people can be trained for specialized on-site and support service roles that fill the identified needs.
- It can trigger a more formal human resources program that would include recruiting, hiring, assigning, assessment, and upgrading for management staff. People should be encouraged to overcome their weaknesses by training. This training should be a constantly ongoing activity, conducted one-on-one during building inspections and supported with in-class and on-site special clinics. The results can be monitored by comparing the actual results achieved at each building against the budgeted plan.
- This system of planning, budgeting, and activating the master action plan for each building establishes a meaningful framework that assures that all the needs of the building and the people involved are satisfied.
- The ultimate goal of this budgeting system is to identify every opportunity to improve the staff, the building, and the comfort of the occupants. The activity generated as a result of this management process allows every potential for savings to be activated without allowing the structure and the electrical-mechanical equipment to deteriorate.

5.9 MAKING THIS MANAGEMENT APPROACH WORK

To assure that the system is properly planned, organized, and implemented, management needs the total support of everyone on the management team from the chief executive officer to the on-site staff, from the service contractors, and, especially, from the administrative and accounting departments.

Complete success will be achieved only when no further opportunities to save are evident. The goal is to maximize income while reducing the costs of maintenance and operations to their lowest possible levels without downgrading the structure, the electrical-mechanical equipment, the comfort, and sense of well-being of the occupants.

If the management system outlined in this book is implemented, it makes available to management the right decision-making information. The information leads to the development of the right consulting and support services and helps support the need for the right training program. To make the system work requires not only support but the development of people with the right skills working within the right organizational climate. That climate emerges when people are organized by functions.

The right management program must include a process that will effectively manage renovations, retrofits, repair and maintenance expenses, the on-site staff costs, and the cost of fuel, electricity, and water. Once it has been properly implemented, building owners will enjoy the following benefits:

- This management approach helps the people involved to plan ahead.
- Even if building owners or managers have implemented an energy management program, further savings can be conservatively guaranteed if the recommendations in this book are implemented.*
- The planning stage of this management system allows everyone involved to communicate as they inspect and plan and include costs in the budgets for each building.
- This system isolates all major expenses (renovations and retrofits) and keeps a detailed record of what was done, why it was done, and the costs. As-built drawings should be constantly updated to reflect any major changes.
- This system provides a means of pinpointing items at variance to the plan and shows exactly where all the controllable expenses occurred. Even when an activity is deferred, the specific amount for that activity is removed, not an unspecific amount of money. It thus allows for deferring a specific item at the request of the owner or manager.
- This system provides a basis for monthly, quarterly, semiannual, or annual comparisons for any specific item as long as the account classifications are not changed.

---

*This system of managing the maintenance and energy expenses for Cadillac Fairview's 17,000-suite apartment portfolio saved the company $3 million in maintenance and operations expenses and $2 million in energy expenses in 1980.

- This system can provide accurate lists of supplies, parts, tools, chemicals, inventory, and services for each building. If these lists are combined with the specifications and standards established by management, they can be used to negotiate purchases of these items and as a means of value analyzing the decision against actual performance costs on a monthly, quarterly, semiannual, and annual basis.

- It provides a basis for communication concerning every activity in the master action plan because it is detailed in a logical place within the budget-builder working papers. Communication is with all the people who are involved in the planning process, even outside service contractors.

- It promotes participation by everyone involved as they inspect the building, analyze previous records, and meet to develop the budget for each building.

- This system of planning and budgeting provides a means of analyzing all the activities detailed in the master action plan and the budget-builder working papers, and their costs, on a systematic basis.

- This planning and budgeting process provides a system of management that could link all the disciplines involved in development, design, construction, management, operations, and support services under a single workable system.

- This management approach identifies problems, collects pertinent information about them, and assigns the responsibility and authority to the right people to solve them without creating new ones.

- The development of this management system provides the basis for decisions about the need for specialists in housekeeping, groundskeeping, structural services, and electrical-mechanical systems.

- The development of this system provides the basis upon which decisions are made about the effective allocation of on-site and outside support service technicians and what their responsibilities should be.

- This system of management helps satisfy the emotional needs of the people involved.

- The organizational climate within which the people involved function keeps improving as the program develops and grows.

Human Resources Management

6.1 THE IMPORTANCE OF PEOPLE

Most companies measure their success or failure by the bottom line of their financial statements. The only problem with this approach is that by the time the bottom-line figures are available, the decisions that dictated management's actions are history. Although we can learn from our past mistakes, people in our industry must stop managing *yesterday* and start managing *tomorrow*.

If management is getting the right things done right—through other people, then knowing how to manage human resources is one of the keys to success. There are two basic problems faced by people who manage any enterprise. One is the problem of economics—problems of competition, adjusting the organization to meet changing markets, and so forth. The other is the problem of "internal equilibrium"—maintaining a social organization in which individuals and groups can satisfy their own emotional needs and desires through working together (see Figure 6.1).

These problems are interdependent: The social organization within a concern is related intimately to the effectiveness of the whole organization; likewise, the success with which the concern maintains external balance is related directly to its internal organization.

To be effective, property managers must be able to motivate their employees positively and satisfy the building owners and tenants (Figure 6.2).

EMOTIONAL NEEDS

SATISFACTION	- by achievement
BELONGING	- by being a part of a team
RECOGNITION	- in positions that enable employees to maintain their self-respect
EMOTIONAL SECURITY	- needed on the job and understood
OPPORTUNITY FOR ADVANCEMENT	- through training, upgrading and development
FINANCIAL SECURITY	- through pay and other benefits

The management plan explained in this book establishes a meaningful framework that unites the disciplines associated with development, design, construction, management, operations, and support services under a common purpose and, at the same time, allows all those involved to satisfy their own individual needs, as well as the needs of their professions.

Figure 6.1 Emotional needs in order of importance.

Successful managers must be endowed with the correct balance of human, conceptual, and technical skills if they expect to manage buildings, information, and a broad spectrum of people: the people who occupy residential, commercial, industrial, or institutional buildings as well as the people who develop, design, build, manage, operate, and service them (Figure 6.3).

	POSITIVE MOTIVATION	NEGATIVE MOTIVATION
GENERAL	• Clear lines of responsibility and authority • Flexible organization structure • Decision making officials available • Teamwork among line staff	• Overlapping authority • Overly complex organizational structure • Frequent communication breakdowns • Decision makers unavailable when needed
POLICIES	• Good rapport among managers • Agreements are honored • Employees and managers know where they stand and how they are doing • Policies clearly and quickly communicated • Fair and current reward systems	• Too much paperwork • Managers try to "beat the system" • Excessive intradepartmental rivalry • Deadlines mean nothing • Information is difficult to get • New ideas are allowed to die

DECISIONS	• Decisions tie in well with plans
	  and policies
	• Managers and their staffs participate
	  in decisions
	• Delegation is adequate
	• Bad decisions are withdrawn
	• Clear lines of accountability are evident
		• Decisions are slow to be made
		• Subordinates do not participate in
		  making decisions
		• Meager delegation
		• Real issues are evaded
		• Decisions are motivated by fear

LEADERSHIP	• Staff meetings produce results
	• Meetings are well planned and
	  have a definite purpose
	• Subordinates are well informed
	• Employees know the full scope
	  of their responsibilities
	• Boss shows dignity and fairness
		• Assignments and orders are unclear
		• Unreasonable deadlines
		• High degree of regimentation
		• Tendency to lower standards
		• Policies and lines of responsibility
		  unclear

ATTITUDES	• Pride in team performance • Managers and their staffs support each other • Goals and standards are high • Management hears grievances • Overall group output is high	• Large number of cliques • Favoritism is shown • Productivity is inadequate • Griping is common • Recurring rule violations is evident • Goals and professional standards are low

JOB CONDITIONS	• Managers are highly challenged
	• Employees talents and skills
	  are well utilized
	• Employee feedback encouraged
	• Performance standards are realistic
	• Achievements are recognized
		• Difficult to get jobs done
		• Ideas put aside too often, too fast
		• Rules broken, ethics sacrificed
		  to get jobs done
		• Restlessness and boredom are obvious
		• Pay scales are not realistic

STATUS	• Job privileges are reasonable • Association with company yields a high community status • Management is open minded	• Favored few get recognition • Criticism exceeds compliments • Many jobs are dead end • Individuals look out for themselves

Figure 6.2 Clues to positive and negative motivation.

KEY MANAGEMENT SKILLS

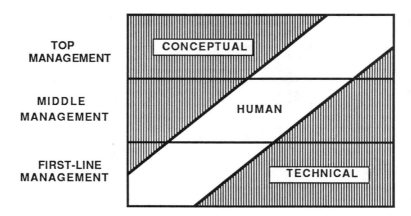

This chart shows the proportion of management skills required by each level of a
management team. The head of a construction an building management business
unit or profit center (a building project) must have an abundance of conceptual skills,
while the on-site staff, must be highly skilled in each of their functional skills of
housekeeping, groundskeeping, and structural, electrical, and mechanical services.

To be successful, managers must be able to operate within the right organizational
climate, and everyone on the management team must be linked by a common purpose
and have the common goal of maximizing income while reducing the cost of management
services to its lowest possible level without downgrading the structure and the electrical-
mechanical systems, the ambience, comfort, or sense of well-being of the building's
occupants.

Figure 6.3   Human, conceptual, and technical skills.

The Human Resource Challenge

The challenge is being able to create a social organization in which people can
satisfy their own desires through working together and at the same time satisfy the needs of the people who occupy the buildings being managed and those
of the owner of the property. This is not easy, and that is why the design,

construction, and building management industry has not been able to come to grips with the problems faced by the industry.

One true measure of a company's success or failure is the strength of its management team. In the past 85 years, several people have made significant contributions to improving the way we manage human resources. Fredrick W. Taylor developed a scientific management approach in 1900; Henri Fayol made observations of management principles in 1921; behavioral school studies in a Western Electric plant were completed in 1932, and in 1947, Max Weber developed an organization structure for management teams.*

The people involved in the design, construction, and building management industry have never really studied the best way to overcome the problems of economics or organizational equilibrium. The industry is constantly facing periods of highs and lows and the problems left over from people who use buildings for short-term rather than long-term rewards. If you ask people who develop, design, build, or manage buildings what business they are in, you get many strange answers.

Developers believe they are in the development business. Builders believe they are in the building industry. Managers believe they are in the property management industry. There are some people who use buildings as financial objects, who trade or flip them, inflating the debt load and skimming off the extra money for themselves.

Because buildings provide shelter, a basic necessity of life, and because they should have a life span of 50 years, everyone involved with buildings should have the same long-term goal of making each building business unit a long-term success. That is the economic side; let's look at the human side of the situation.

The Human Side of the Equation

When we consider the human element, we refer to the relationship between success and the feelings of satisfaction, comfort, and well-being of the building occupants, and the feelings of satisfaction of the people involved with developing, designing, building, managing, operating, and servicing a building. Human resources management deserves very special attention if we expect to overcome the problems faced by our industry. People who own and occupy buildings will pay a premium for excellence.

Cadillac Fairview's residential maintenance and operations department discovered the importance of people and did something about improving the caliber of those that operated and serviced the apartment buildings. The pro-

---

*This information is taken from K. R. Blowatt, *Project Management Theory* (Brock University, 1976), p. 22.

gram explained in this chapter was developed over a 20-year period and proved quite successful.

Although the people involved managed and operated residential buildings, the program will also work in commercial, industrial, or institutional buildings. As the program was being developed, the company continued to look for ways to improve the way it managed buildings, people, and information. The more people adopt this system and attitude, the better it will become as new ideas are incorporated into the plan. When you encourage the right people to do the right things, the management team will contribute substantially to the growth and profitability of your business and to the satisfaction of your customers.

6.2 A HUMAN RESOURCES MANAGEMENT PHILOSOPHY

The first thing that you need in any human resources management program is a philosophy—one that is more than words on paper, one that you are dedicated to put into practice and make work. The following outline the human resources philosophy that Cadillac Fairview used:

- Treat human resources with respect and dignity.
- Develop a code of ethics in business activities, and teach the people involved to respect it.
- Cooperate with and support others as knowledge and expertise is shared throughout a company and in the industry.
- As succession and career planning are vital to the efforts of the company, depend on formal organization planning and the development of a pool of people to meet new demands for expertise in the company.
- Give a high priority to training and development of people.
- Identify a career path for as many people as possible on the management team.
- To attract and keep people, design jobs that provide opportunities for effective contribution and growth.
- Achieve strength by matching the right people with the right jobs.
- Wherever possible seek candidates for jobs from within the company.
- Provide equal opportunity and consistency of treatment for all employees.
- Provide a sense of involvement by encouraging participation and communication.
- Welcome suggestions for improvement or change and encourage appropriate feedback.

6.3 CHARTER OF ACCOUNTABILITY MANAGEMENT CONCEPT

Overview

The charter-of-accountability concept was developed between 1961 and 1965 by a group of managers at a large United States aircraft factory.* In 1961, it became apparent to the managers of that firm that there was something wrong in their management organization. To their top management, it seemed that many middle managers lacked initiative; they were not demonstrating the responsibility and imagination necessary to do an outstanding job. Other managers seemed to practice brinksmanship; they were somewhat reckless and irresponsible, often taking actions far beyond their authority, apparently to test how far they could go before being stopped by top management. Throughout the organization there seemed to be a lack of teamwork. There was obvious confusion and a certain amount of bickering over the responsibilities and authorities inherent in the various management positions, particularly where the staff managers' functions overlapped those of the line managers.

As seen by the middle managers, the major problems were somewhat different. They saw a lack of direction from the top: They didn't know exactly where the company or its departments were going. They complained of conflicting assignments: It was not clear to them how the responsibilities and authority of the staff and line groups should mesh. They felt that there was too much interference from the top: Senior managers became involved in day-to-day operations, as if middle managers needed help to handle the simplest details.

Management Development Program

The first step toward solving these problems was to institute a management development program that was attended by all middle managers. Among the topics covered were the following:

Span of control.   From a study of this management concept, they concluded that for most effective management, only a moderate number of people should report directly to any one manager.

Communications.   From the study of this topic they came to two conclusions:

1. The key to improved skill in communications is the ability to listen, ask questions, and understand the other person's point of view.

*This history of the development of the charter of accountability management concept was provided by Harbridge House, management consultants hired in 1967 by Cadillac Development.

2. Too many vertical levels between the executive and the personnel in key jobs would impede internal communications.

Delegation.   They concluded that high-caliber managers delegate to others all routine tasks and decisions, thus obtaining for themselves the time to plan and evaluate results.

One worker–one supervisor.   They accepted the old truism that "no one can serve two masters" and concluded that they needed to be more explicit as to who worked for whom in their organization.

Motivation.   They studied the factors that motivate people on the job and concluded that *participation, involvement, opportunity for personal growth,* and similar "higher-level" factors are powerful motivators for managers to offer their people. Today it is known that profit sharing is also an important motivator. (See Figure 6.2.)

Results

The results of this program were a greater awareness by the managers of the complexity of the management function, the broad scope of their responsibilities as managers, and the need for improved skills in applying some effective management techniques.

The next step was to begin to develop a new method of job description and design based on their own experiences, what they learned in their seminars, and the basic writings of important management thinkers.

From their own experience, they had learned that the term *responsibility* was a confusing one. It could refer, for example, to a function or objective, such as the marketing director's responsibility for sales or the president's responsibility for achieving a profit. Or it could mean a trait of character, the need for the manager to be a responsible person of integrity. Therefore, they decided to use the term *responsibility* only in the latter sense: a desirable trait of character, a willingness and ability to make decisions, to take action, and to accept the consequences of action.

For delegated functions or objectives, they decided to use the term *accountability*. They found that people easily understood that accountability means a person is held accountable *to* someone *by* someone for doing a specific thing.

From the writings of the scientific managers, Taylor and others, dating back to the early part of the century, they learned that

- For delegation to succeed, authority to take necessary action must be delegated along with the accountability for performing a specific function.
- Delegated functions can be isolated and studied individually, thus a manager's performance can be objectively measured.

From the behavioral scientists, who analyzed the ways in which people's motivations affect the way they act on the job, they learned that

- If people set their own goals, they set them higher than others would normally set them.
- People react much more positively to being evaluated on how well they have achieved specific goals than on such nebulous factors as "personality," "cooperation," and "initiative."

From the revisionist group of management writers, they learned that

- Because managers know more than anyone else about their own jobs, they are the best equipped to set realistic and meaningful goals for themselves.
- People work harder toward achievement of goals that they set for themselves.

From the management scientists, who are now applying the mathematical concepts of operations research and systems analysis to business management, they learned that

- It is possible to have a system of management that is highly effective and efficient and, at the same time, very human and satisfying to the individuals involved.
- It is possible to devise a system of management that will improve itself as it grows and develops.

Essentials of the Charter of Accountability Concept

From the above study and research, the group developed the charter-of-accountability concept. They found that there are three essentials required to make this approach succeed.

1. The terms of the charter must be written, not oral, and should be in a clear, simple format.

2. There must be mutual and objective understanding between the two individuals who sign it, the superior and the subordinate.
3. The charter must be implemented and used, not merely put away in a drawer.

To satisfy the requirement for mutual understanding between the superior and subordinate, it is essential that both participate in preparing a charter. The basic accountability for preparing the charter, however, remains with the individual who must live up to the terms, the person being chartered. Thus, even if much of the preparation is done by someone else, the person whose job is being chartered must review it, discuss it with his or her superior, and if necessary change it until both feel that they can live with it.

Basis for the Structure of the Organization

The charters of accountability become the basis for the structure of an organization, the ruling documents describing the relationships between individuals, and the measuring stick against which performance of individuals, departments, and industries is measured. They also become the means whereby training programs are developed to help people live up to the terms of their charter and to help them overcome their weaknesses so that they can develop and grow.

6.4 CHARTERS OF ACCOUNTABILITY

The charters that follow were developed in 1968 after a series of seminars and workshops conducted by Cadillac Property Management. These charters have been revised many times since then. In 1968 the charter was developed for property managers only. Then, as today, property managers were responsible for buildings only after they were built, even though the role of the manager should be that of "head of a building business unit."

In many cases, property managers spend most of their time leasing, collecting rents, and administering an office. Their original charter detailed these responsibilities and delegated to them responsibility for renovations; retrofits; repair and maintenance expenses; and the costs of on-site staff salaries, fuel, electricity, and water using specialized resource support staff to provide professional advise because of the managers' weaknesses in these areas.

The concept of giving property managers total responsibility led to overlapping and conflict within the group.

There are few things that must be kept in mind when trying to develop a suitable management organization of the construction and building management industry.

1. The industry is involved in only one product—a building.
2. Each building should be considered as an individual business unit, and as such, all decisions made during the development, design, construction, management, and servicing stages of its life must be based on the long-term goal of making each business unit a success.
3. There are only three stages to a building's life:—the development, design, construction stage (the project management stage)—the marketing, leasing, sales, or rental stage (the sales or rental stage)—and the maintenance and operations stage (the maintenance management stage).
All these stages have to be professionally and effectively executed.

To achieve this goal of making building business units successful, a manager or head of a management group must be qualified to manage the development, design, construction, management, and operations stages of a building's life, not just the marketing, leasing and, sales stages. It was with this concept in mind that the following charters were developed.

6.5 CHARTER FOR A PROPERTY MANAGER

Purpose of the Charter

1. To define the development, marketing, leasing, administrative, and maintenance services accountabilities of the head of a construction and building management business unit or profit center.
2. To set objectives and standards against which performance can be measured.

Purpose of the Manager

1. To successfully develop, design, build or buy, manage, or operate a building or buildings by maximizing profits for a privately owned building and reducing subsidies for buildings that are owned publicly.
2. To assure that the comfort and safety of the occupants and the ambience of the building are better than can be obtained elsewhere.
3. To protect the owner's reputation for quality and integrity and the investment in the property.
4. To achieve agreed-upon goals using a minimum of time, dollars, tools, equipment, ideas, people, and space.
5. To achieve predetermined objectives through other people by coordinating labor, machinery, time, and materials. To get the right things done by

delegating, motivating, communicating, and evaluating and by improving themselves and others.

Objectives of the Manager

1. To identify the people needed on the management team, their goals and functional accountabilities.
2. To satisfy the emotional needs of the people on the team and those of the occupants of the buildings being managed.
3. To provide, today and tomorrow, all the qualified people needed to develop, design, build, manage, and operate buildings in the portfolio.
4. To assure the safety, security, and comfort of the occupants of the buildings being managed and of the members of the management team.
5. To maximize profits for the privately owned buildings and reduce subsidies for publicly owned buildings.

Management Intent

A building owner should delegate to the manager a large measure of initiative and self-direction, should clearly define accountabilities and responsibilities, and give the manager the full authority to carry them out.

A building owner should expect a manager to manage a property as carefully as he or she would if it were the manager's own business, to control expenditures as if all the money were coming from his or her own pocket.

An owner should expect a manager to be as critical of any flaw in courtesy, friendliness, and service in a building as would the tenant paying the highest rent.

To accomplish this, the manager must be qualified to carefully apportion time between improving tenant relations; controlling expenditures for renovations, retrofits, repair and maintenance, on-site staff salaries, fuel, electricity, and water; and assuring that someone qualified is personally inspecting the buildings.

The manager must resist giving too much time to any one of these functions—usually the one in which he or she is most experienced and interested. In fact, the manager and members of the team should place the greatest emphasis on those functions in which they are least experienced.

With the assistance of qualified support service specialists in development, design, and construction; housekeeping, groundskeeping, and structural and electrical-mechanical services; marketing and sales; administration, finance, and management; and through other construction and building management industry–recognized educational institutions, managers should be continually expanding their skills—human, conceptual, and technical to become competent managers.

Accountability

To adequately manage the services needed to develop, design, build or buy, manage, or operate a building, managers need to know about all the services listed in the building management services and suppliers chart (Figure 6.4) and detailed as functional accountabilities and forming a part of the charter described in Chapter 4.

FUNCTIONAL

1. Develop a management team that suits the business of the owner.
2. Define functional accountabilities for the middle- and first-line managers identified by that organizational hierarchy.
3. Recruit, hire, motivate, train, develop, assess performance of, and upgrade people to professionally and adequately fill the roles identified by that organizational hierarchy.
4. Develop policies and standards and assure that they are achieved.
5. When required, set up suitable management or field offices.
6. Establish short- and long-term maintenance and energy management goals.
7. Develop a system of preparing income and expense budgets for each building in the management portfolio.
8. Analyze the results of the management program and report information and suggestions to the owner on a regular basis.

FINANCE AND ADMINISTRATION

1. Assure that there is an administrative and finance system that adequately supports and value analyzes the feasibility of new ventures, acquisitions, renovations, or retrofits.
2. Assure that there is an administrative system that controls revenue received from leasing and other sources, as well as expenditures for renovations, retrofits, staff salaries, repair and maintenance, fuel, water, electricity, taxes, insurance, legal fees, and other management expenses.
3. Assure that there are adequate legal, tax, insurance, personnel, sales, marketing, leasing, and other operational services for the portfolio being managed.
4. Arrange bridge, mortgage, and other financing when required.

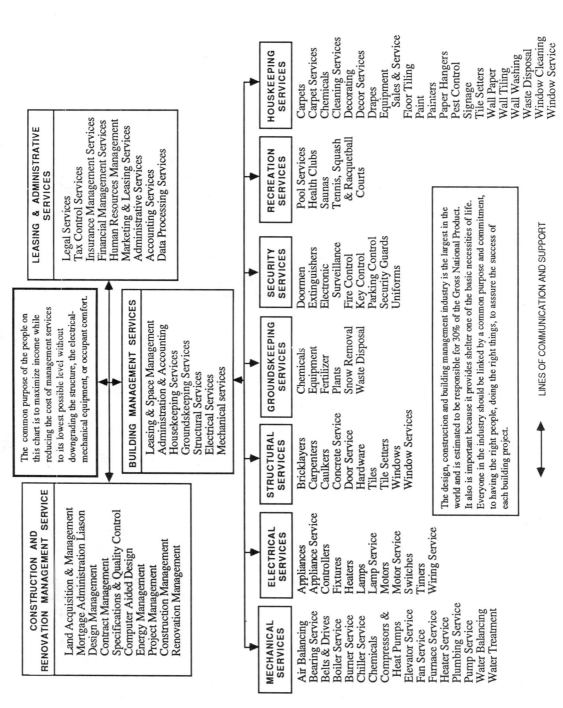

CONSTRUCTION AND RENOVATION MANAGEMENT SERVICE

Land Acquisition & Management
Mortgage Administration Liason
Design Management
Contract Management
Specifications & Quality Control
Computer Aided Design
Energy Management
Project Management
Construction Management
Renovation Management

LEASING & ADMINISTRATIVE SERVICES

Legal Services
Tax Control Services
Insurance Management Services
Financial Management Services
Human Resources Management
Marketing & Leasing Services
Administrative Services
Accounting Services
Data Processing Services

The common purpose of the people on this chart is to maximize income while reducing the cost of management services to its lowest possible level without downgrading the structure, the electrical-mechanical equipment, or occupant comfort.

BUILDING MANAGEMENT SERVICES

Leasing & Space Management
Administration & Accounting
Housekeeping Services
Groundskeeping Services
Structural Services
Electrical Services
Mechanical services

MECHANICAL SERVICES

Air Balancing
Bearing Service
Belts & Drives
Boiler Service
Burner Service
Chiller Service
Chemicals
Compressors & Heat Pumps
Elevator Service
Fan Service
Furnace Service
Heater Service
Plumbing Service
Pump Service
Water Balancing
Water Treatment

ELECTRICAL SERVICES

Appliances
Appliance Service
Controllers
Fixtures
Heaters
Lamps
Lamp Service
Motors
Motor Service
Switches
Timers
Wiring Service

STRUCTURAL SERVICES

Bricklayers
Carpenters
Caulkers
Concrete Service
Door Service
Hardware
Tiles
Tile Setters
Windows
Window Services

GROUNDSKEEPING SERVICES

Chemicals
Equipment
Fertilizer
Plants
Snow Removal
Waste Disposal

SECURITY SERVICES

Doormen
Extinguishers
Electronic Surveillance
Fire Control
Key Control
Parking Control
Security Guards
Uniforms

RECREATION SERVICES

Pool Services
Health Clubs
Saunas
Tennis, Squash & Racquetball Courts

HOUSEKEEPING SERVICES

Carpets
Carpet Services
Chemicals
Cleaning Services
Decorating
Decor Services
Drapes
Equipment
Sales & Service
Floor Tiling
Paint
Painters
Paper Hangers
Pest Control
Signage
Tile Setters
Wall Paper
Wall Tiling
Wall Washing
Waste Disposal
Window Cleaning
Window Service

The design, construction and building management industry is the largest in the world and is estimated to be responsible for 30% of the Gross National Product. It also is important because it provides shelter one of the basic necessities of life. Everyone in the industry should be linked by a common purpose and commitment, to having the right people, doing the right things, to assure the success of each building project.

LINES OF COMMUNICATION AND SUPPORT

Figure 6.4 The functional accountabilities of the people involved in the design, construction, and building management business. The head of each building business unit should have these support services available.

5. Provide financial audits and other management controls through an adequate information system.

NEW BUILDING DEVELOPMENT AND ACQUISITION

1. Assure that there is adequate design, specifications, project management, construction management, and maintenance services expertise to value analyze the acquisition of an existing property, to complete a renovation or retrofit, or to build a new building.
2. Identify major building components that will require maintenance or that will wear out and need replacement, and establish and maintain a current price list to monitor the initial and ongoing costs for these components over their life span.
3. Acquire land or new properties to satisfy the goals and future needs of the enterprise.
4. Liaise with design, construction, and maintenance support services about built-in problems and be aware of the costs to correct them.
5. Develop pro forma financial projections for the department and for any new projects.
6. Seek municipal approvals for projects when required.
7. Assume responsibility for a building until the building is occupied.
8. Assure that qualified on-site and in-house staff and outside maintenance services specialists participate during formal turnover of a new property and that they prepare a building profile.
9. Provide as-built drawings and microfilm files for them for all properties in the management portfolio.
10. At regular management meetings or by written reports, keep everyone on the management team informed about plans for developments, acquisitions, renovations, or retrofits.

MAINTENANCE SERVICES

1. Develop maintenance services standards and specifications for each building being managed and assure that they are maintained.
2. Define the on-site and in-house staff and outside suppliers and services required to maintain each building in the portfolio. Publish and keep an up-to-date services and suppliers guide.
3. Develop a system of budgeting that is suitable for each building in the portfolio and that includes projections for renovations, retrofits, repair and maintenance, on-site staff salaries, and the consumption and cost of fuel, electricity, and water.

4. Provide a system of keeping statistical data required for short- and long-term maintenance and energy management planning.
5. Develop, implement, and monitor a planned maintenance and energy management program.
6. Define, specify, document, obtain quotations for, and complete all the required renovations or retrofits in the buildings being managed.
7. Formally take over all new buildings that are added to the management portfolio.
8. Develop a building profile that includes an energy audit for all new and existing buildings being managed.
9. Keep up to date all as-built plans and microfilm files for them.
10. Prepare at least one annual written inspection report for each building being managed that would include an inspection of the structure, the housekeeping and groundskeeping conditions and an inspection of the electrical-mechanical systems.
11. Define the on-site, in-house, and outside suppliers and services for each building being managed. Set job specifications for the in-house staff. Recruit, hire, train, motivate, assess performance of, and upgrade on-site and in-house staff.
12. Keep the building owner and members of the management team informed about maintenance and operations activities, either at management meetings or by regularly submitting written reports.

MARKETING, LEASING, SALES, AND ADMINISTRATIVE

1. Define and provide marketing, leasing, sales, and administrative services that would satisfy the needs of the owner and the occupants of the buildings being managed.
2. Manage all leasing and sales functions. Set rent rolls or management fees for condominiums, document all move-ins and move-outs, manage any rent subsidies or other special leasing programs that may be needed for some buildings.
3. Formulate policies in relation to occupant eligibility criteria.
4. Liaise orally and in writing with building owners about plans for renovations, retrofits, repair and maintenance programs, the hiring of on-site staff, and energy management programs that involve the control of the use of fuel, electricity, and water.
5. Recruit, hire, train, motivate, assess performance of, and upgrade all people on the management staff.
6. Develop an income and expense budget for the management offices and for the staffs that work in them.
7. Develop and maintain an administrative system that will assure that the

building owner and the management staff have the records they need to effectively manage buildings.

8. Develop and maintain a directory of all the present tenants and an up-to-date client profile of all applicants on a waiting list. Maintain vacancy and availability records.

9. Prepare a revenue budget for each building being managed and maintain statistical data for long- and short-term planning.

10. Never argue with a tenant. Maintain a high level of public relations.

11. Cooperate and participate with any government ministry or other institution or agency that is involved with developing, designing, building, managing, and operating, and those providing supplies and services to the construction and building management industry.

6.6 TRAINING FOR A PROPERTY MANAGER

People in the industry spend a lot of money, and they should be taught how to spend it wisely. As many as half the buildings being designed, built, managed, and operated are owned or financed by the government. Because of this, and because governments are paying for shelter for people who cannot afford to live in the buildings that the industry has built, it is imperative that money be spent to train the people involved in building management. Knowing how to do the right things right could save a lot of maintenance and energy expense and tax dollars. A research study prepared in July 1986 for the Ontario Housing Corporation comparing the cost of operating a private-sector project with that of a public-sector project showed that the government spent 30 percent more than the private sector.

The suggested training program for someone who is managing a portfolio of building business units, or perhaps a one-building business-unit project, is aware that architects and engineers are not trained to be business managers and that most people involved in construction and management learn on the job. If their teachers are qualified, they learn the right things, but from those less qualified, they learn the wrong things. They cannot afford to leave their jobs to go to school full time, so a training program must be such that while still working at their jobs they can avail themselves of the training modules that they need to improve their weaknesses.

The following course is recommended to satisfy the needs dictated by the property manager's charter of accountability.*

---

*This book and Mel A. Shear, *Handbook of Building Maintenance Management* (Englewood Cliffs, N.J.: Reston Publishing Company, a division of Prentice-Hall, 1983) will provide the texts for the maintenance training program detailed in parts 1–3 of the course.

PART 1—BUSINESS MANAGEMENT

1. The Role of the Manager
2. Management Theory
3. Human Resources Management
4. Time Management
5. Information Management
6. Planning and Financial Management
7. Insurance and Risk Management
8. Tax Control
9. Communicating Orally and in Writing
10. The Tenant and Landlord Act
11. The Condominium Act
12. Legal Services

PART 2—MARKETING, SALES, LEASING, AND ADMINISTRATION

1. Administration and Recordkeeping
2. Marketing and Selling
3. Leasing and Space Management
4. Public Relations

PART 3—BUILDING OPERATION AND MAINTENANCE

1. Introduction
2. A Building as a Business Unit
3. Specifications Standards, and Contract Management
4. Inspection Techniques
5. Structure
6. Housekeeping
7. Groundskeeping
8. Plumbing and Drainage
9. Heating Systems
10. Cooling and Ventilation Systems
11. Mechanical Services
12. Security and Safety
13. Fire Protection and Control
14. Electrical Services
15. Energy Management
16. The Planning and Budgeting Process
17. Human Resources Management

PART 4—DESIGN, CONSTRUCTION, AND RENOVATION MANAGEMENT

1. Land Acquisition and Management
2. Mortgage Administration Liaison
3. Design Management
4. Specifications and Quality Control
5. Computer-Aided Design
6. Energy Management
7. Project Management
8. Contract Management
9. Construction Management
10. Renovation and Retrofit Management
11. Risk and Insurance Management
12. Human Resources Management
13. Administration and Recordkeeping
14. Communicating Orally and in Writing
15. Security and Safety
16. Life-Cycle Projections and Replacement-Cost Analysis
17. Inspection Techniques

Training Modules

Each of the training sessions could be further broken down into individual training modules. Some suggested modules for the program follow.

Business Management (Part 1)

THE ROLE OF THE MANAGER

The Nature, Philosophy, and Functions of Management
The Role of the Manager of Design, Construction, and Building Management and Others on the Management Team

MANAGEMENT THEORY

Development of Theories
Managerial Functions
Specialization and Departmentalization
Span of Management
Authority and Responsibility
Delegation

Unity of Command
Line and Staff Concepts
Centralization and Decentralization

HUMAN RESOURCES MANAGEMENT

Task Identification
Identifying Weaknesses and Upgrading
Resource Allocation
Labor Negotiations
Compensation
Pursuing Excellence
Encouraging Creativity
Labor Contracts
Compensation
Career Planning
Staffing
Recruiting and Hiring
Evaluating Performance
Training and Development
Firing Techniques
Organizational Behavior
Hierarchy of Need
Developing Negotiating Skills
Labor, Markets, Contracts, and Insurance

TIME MANAGEMENT

Managing Change
Achieving a Greater Return on Time Investment
Time Management Tools
Verbal and Nonverbal Techniques

INFORMATION MANAGEMENT

Developing Information Systems
Effectively Using Information

PLANNING AND FINANCIAL MANAGEMENT

Understanding Basic Accounting
    General Ledger, Accounts Receivable, and Accounts Payable
    Balance Sheets

Planning and Decision Making

Decision-Making Aids

Setting Financial Goals

Banking and Money Management
   Analyzing Financial Risks
   Arranging Mortgages
   Financial Planning

Planning Financial Strategies
   Budgeting
   Estimating
   Monitoring

Understanding Financial Statements

Monitoring Construction Costs

Understanding the Bid Process

How to Include Renovations and Retrofits, Maintenance, On-Site Staff
   Costs, The Cost of Fuel, Electricity, and Water, in the Plan

Monitoring the Results

Payroll Records
   Employee Benefit Plans

Controlling Rent Collections

Developing a Revenue System

Developing a Vendor's System
   Vendor's Lists
   Developing Standards and Specifications
   Audits
   Appraisal and Monitoring

Providing Support Information System
   Storing and Retrieval Data

Taxes and Assessments

Amortization and Depreciation

Basic Mathematics

INSURANCE AND RISK MANAGEMENT

Negotiating Policies

General Liability

Physical Damage
   Fire Damage
   Boiler and Machinery
   Structure

Fidelity Bonds

Crime

Claims and Claims Handling

COMMUNICATING ORALLY AND IN WRITING

Language, Manuals, Industrial Relations, and Word Processing

Social Skills in Management

Creating and Maintaining Good Customer Relations

Organizing and Running Meetings, Conferences, Seminars, and Workshops

Report Writing

Liaising with the Owner; Developer; Finance, Marketing, or Leasing Services; Administration; On-Site and In-House Maintenance Services; Consulting and Outside Support Services

Encouraging Feedback

THE TENANT AND LANDLORD ACT

Management's Responsibilities

Tenant's Responsibilities

THE CONDOMINIUM ACT

Management's Responsibilities

Owner's Responsibilities

LEGAL SERVICES

Management Agreements

The Powers Assumed by Managers

Obligations of Managers

Risks of Management

Design Management Course

(This course would also include Business Management Part 1)

URBAN PLANNING

Appraisal

Zoning By-laws

Regulations—Government, Industrial, and Professional

Planning and Feasibility Studies

Risk Identification and Control

Specification Writing

Mortgage Types and How to Value Analyze Them

BUILDING TECHNOLOGY

Structures

Electrical-Mechanical Systems

STANDARDS, SPECIFICATIONS, AND QUALITY MANAGEMENT

Value Analysis

Standards and Specifications Management

Construction Management Course (New Construction, Renovations, and Retrofits)

BUSINESS MANAGEMENT

(This course would also include Business Management Part 1)

Planning and Scheduling the Construction Process

Managing Renovations and Retrofits

Awarding Contracts

Negotiating

Controlling the Project

Managing the Job Site

COMMISSIONING

Inspections

As-Built Plans

Microfilming

Preparing Building Profiles and Operations Manuals

Property Management Course

MARKETING, SALES, AND LEASING (RESEARCH, STUDIES, STRATEGY, AND PLAN DEVELOPMENT)

(This course would also include Business Management Part 1)

Advertising

Surveying the Competition and District Amenities

Setting Policies
Signage
Taking Over a Building
Setting a Rent Roll
Tenant and Landlord Act
Condominium Act
Setting Up, Staffing, and Running a Sales and Rental Field Office
Selling Condominiums
Leasing a Unit
   Completing an Application to Lease or Buy
   Checking the Application
   Showing the Unit
   Moving Tenants In or Out
   Inspecting a Unit
Taking Deposits, Collecting Rents, and Following Up a Delinquent

THE BUILDING PROFILE

Taking Over a Building
Gathering and Maintaining Equipment Records
Tagging and Color-Coding Equipment
Tools and Inventory Control
Recognizing and Identifying Building Components
Life Safety Procedures and Drills
Understanding the Electrical-Mechanical Systems

ENERGY MANAGEMENT

Preparing an Energy Audit
Analyzing the Potential
Setting Energy Goals
Carrying Out the Program
Evaluating the Retrofit Potential
Initiating and Completing Retrofit Measures
Monitoring the Results

MAINTENANCE MANAGEMENT

Human Resources Management
Preparing Maintenance Work Loads

Planning and Scheduling Maintenance

Inspections Techniques
  House and Grounds Inspections
  Structural Inspections
  Electrical-Mechanical Inspections
  Look, Listen, and Touch Inspections

Managing Renovations and Retrofits

Standards, Specifications, and Contract Management

Ordering and Controlling Materials, Tools, Parts, Chemicals, and
  Supplies

Lubrication and Filter Changing

Belt-Driven Equipment

Preparing and Monitoring Operational Logs

Handling Housekeeping Services

Handling Groundskeeping Services

Understanding How a Building Is Put Together—Structural Services

Understanding the Electrical-Mechanical Systems—How They Work and
  Recognizing Components
  Electrical Services
  Mechanical Services
  Plumbing and Drainage Systems
  Heating Systems
  Cooling Systems
  Fire Control and Communication Systems
  Security Systems
  Recreational Facilities

NONROUTINE REPAIRS

Identifying On-Site, In-House, and Outside Support Services' Functional
  Responsibilities

Troubleshooting Complaints
  Heating Systems
  Cooling Systems
  Fire-Control Systems
  Plumbing and Drainage Systems
  Electrical Systems
  Structural Problems

Handling Maintenance Requests and Purchase Orders

Managing Renovations, Retrofits, Consulting Services, and the Outside
  Support Service Trades

6.7 CHARTER FOR AN ON-SITE BUILDING OPERATOR

Purpose of the Charter

1. To define the leasing, administrative, and maintenance services accountabilities of the on-site building operator.
2. To set objectives and standards against which performance can be measured.

Purpose of the On-Site Building Operator

1. To operate and maintain the assigned building and its electrical-mechanical equipment to the standards established by the owner.
2. To direct and supervise any other on-site or outside contracting staff performing maintenance work in the assigned building.

Objectives of the On-Site Building Operator

1. To help provide safety, security, and comfort for the tenants in the assigned building.
2. To always maintain the assigned building to the owner's standards.
3. To expand his or her skills, especially those in which he or she is least experienced, to become a more competent building operator.
4. To provide professional and prompt service to tenants who report problems.
5. To assist in protecting the owner's investment in the building by carrying out regularly scheduled inspections, routine maintenance, custodial care, and nonroutine repairs in a professional manner.

Accountability

1. To adequately perform services required by tenants of either residential, commercial, industrial, or institutional buildings, on-site building operators need to know how to perform the functions listed as leasing, administrative, and maintenance services and attached to this charter.
2. To adequately operate the building's electrical-mechanical equipment and maintain the interior and exterior of the building in accordance with the maintenance services tasks detailed and attached to this charter.
3. To adequately provide for the safety and security of the tenants.

Functional Performance Tasks

LEASING AND ADMINISTRATIVE

1. Obtain and maintain current and future rental vacancy information and keep up-to-date availability signs, including those for sublets, in accordance with information received from the owner or manager.
2. Have on hand a current price list for the leased space in the building.
3. Maintain a harmonious but formal relationship with occupants and visitors in the building.
4. Be aware of existing policies, the lease, and rules and regulations—such things as rental policies, electricity or heat included in rental fee, adult or family building, adult-only floors, and assisted-rental policies.
5. Be prepared to show available units, and be aware of rental features such as size of suites, amenities, and location of nearby schools, churches, shopping, and bus stops.
6. Complete applications to rent and accept deposits from prospective tenants.
7. Maintain key, parking, and locker control in accordance with the policies set by the owner.
8. If delegated the responsibility, collect rents and postdated checks from the tenants, give receipts for cash, and ensure safe delivery of all funds to the owner or to people authorized to receive them.
9. Control move-in and move-out of tenants, and prepare accurate incoming and outgoing inspection reports within the guidelines set by the owner.
10. Maintain files of all maintenance requests and work and purchase orders until the work is completed. Follow up on incomplete orders, and keep files up-to-date by verifying the time and material entries on contractor work orders or delivery slips. Send all completed orders to the owner or the property manager.
11. Report to the owner or the manager any unusual activities in the building, including an illegal removal.

MAINTENANCE SERVICES

1. Carry out, within the guidelines set by the owner and attached to this charter, daily, weekly, and scheduled inspections and maintenance on all the electrical-mechanical equipment installed in the building. Monitor the efficiency of the equipment by recording the readings on heating and cooling system logs.
2. Carry out daily, weekly, and scheduled housekeeping and, if requested, groundskeeping duties within the schedules set out by the owner and attached to this charter.

3. Hire and train all on-site building support staff that may be required to assist you with your work load. Prepare time cards and schedules of duties for all these people.

4. Clean and maintain vacant space in a rentable condition or to the standards set by the owner.

5. Know how to use, care for, and maintain all equipment, tools, supplies, chemicals, and materials assigned to the building. Maintain inventory lists and order replenishments as directed by the owner or property manager.

6. Document all tenant maintenance requests, follow up and correct problems where possible; if not possible, arrange to have problems corrected by sending the maintenance request to the owner or property manager.

7. Supervise all work done by support-service trades by observation and by recording on your copy of the purchase order their in and out times and the materials they used.

8. Make reports in writing, especially those of any deficiencies in the building that you may observe or that are brought to your attention.

SECURITY, SAFETY, AND EMERGENCIES

1. Respond to all emergencies, such as fire, flood, lack of heat, power failure, and other problems that could be considered emergencies.

2. Be aware of all valves and controls and their purposes so that they can be properly activated in event of an emergency.

3. Maintain, close to the phone, a list of all emergency numbers and the names of those persons to call for additional support.

4. Always post a notice of your whereabouts on the door of your office or apartment whenever it is vacant or locked.

5. During the winter season, the walks should be inspected on a regular basis so that any hazardous condition can be corrected as soon as possible.

6. Understand and know how to test the fire control systems.

7. Be qualified to use fire extinguishers.

8. Inspect the fire safety equipment and maintain information in the log books as required by the local fire codes.

9. Carry out a fire drill when requested.

10. Practice first aid when necessary.

ACCEPTANCE

The conditions and functional performance tasks detailed in this charter are mutually accepted by the undersigned.

Dated at _____this____day of_____19_____
Building Operator_____
Building Name_____
Building Address_____
Building Owner or Manager_____

6.8 TRAINING AN ON-SITE BUILDING OPERATOR

The charter of accountability for the on-site building operator defines all the functional responsibilities assigned. For the operator to perform his or her duties in a professional and effective manner requires training. The curriculum for the training program can be best developed once it is known what is expected of an operator as a condition of employment. The charter clearly defines these responsibilities and accountabilities and forms an excellent basis for developing a suitable training program.

The following courses are suggested as being suited to the needs identified in the charter for the on-site building operator.

PART ONE—THE BUILDING PROFILE

1. Building Takeover
2. Identifying Building Components
3. Gathering and Maintaining Equipment Records
4. Tagging and Color Coding Equipment
5. Knowing How to Use and Maintain Tools
6. Controlling Inventory and Ordering Supplies, Spare Parts, Chemicals, Products, etc.

PART TWO—THE STRUCTURE AND THE ELECTRICAL-MECHANICAL EQUIPMENT

1. Recognizing the Structural and Electrical-Mechanical Components
2. Understanding How a Building Is Put Together
3. Understanding the Purpose of Structural Components
4. Understanding the Electrical-Mechanical Systems
5. Understanding an Energy Audit and Monitoring an Energy Management Program

PART THREE—MAINTENANCE SERVICES

1. Preparing a Maintenance Work Load
2. Scheduling the Work Load
3. Carrying Out Look, Listen, and Touch Inspections

4. Maintaining Belt-Driven Equipment
5. Lubrication and Filter Changing
6. Troubleshooting Problems
7. Preparing and Monitoring Operational Logs
8. Handling Housekeeping Services
9. Handling Groundskeeping Services

PART FOUR—LEASING AND ADMINISTRATION (PAPERWORK)

1. Understanding the Leasing Process
    Completing an Application
    Showing the Space
    Moving Tenants In or Out
    Inspecting a Unit
2. Taking Deposits, Collecting Rents, and Following Up on Delinquents
3. Handling the Paperwork
4. Communicating Orally and in Writing
5. Maintaining Human Relations
6. Understanding an Income and Expense Budget
7. Parking and Key Control
8. Handling Tenant Complaints, Preparing Maintenance Requests, Ordering Supplies, Parts, Tools, Chemicals, and Outside Maintenance Services

6.9 A TRAINING PROGRAM FOR ON-SITE BUILDING OPERATORS

In 1974 Cadillac Fairview's residential division allowed each of its 13 property managers to independently recruit, hire and assign on-site building operators to the buildings for which they were responsible. In that year the managers turned over 75 operators in more than 100 buildings, and it was decided to centralize this function under one person who was given the responsibility for both recruiting and training operators. The following information was used to convince the company of the benefits of this centralized approach, the objectives, the when, why, what, where, and who, and how the program was planned, organized, staffed, directed, and controlled. By 1981 the turnovers were reduced to 12.

Why Train?

In 1975 the company spent $11 million on maintenance and operations for its residential portfolio. Because of inflation and the growth of the portfolio, these expenses rose by $2.5 million in the following year. The need to know how to control the expenditure of this amount of money was quite evident. One of the better ways to assure that maintenance and operations expense money was spent wisely was to upgrade the knowledge of the property managers, the on-site building operators, the in-house staff, and outside contractors who provided the support services to the buildings. The need to invest funds for recruiting and training management personnel was quite obvious. In 1970 Cadillac's residential maintenance and operations department had promised the company that it would save at least 10 percent on maintenance expenses and 20 percent on energy bills with a planned maintenance and energy-management program.

We pointed out to the company that to successfully achieve these goals we needed on the management team workers who knew what they were doing.

The Business Is Management, Not Development

We tried to convince the company that any money spent for recruiting and training should be considered an investment rather than an expense; that the investment in people might be more important than the investment in buildings; and that because we retained the buildings that we developed and built, Cadillac was in the management business and not in the development business, as most of the senior executives believed.

Although the company spent a lot of money developing a personnel department, that department did not appreciate the need to develop training programs for the management staff in the commercial, residential, industrial, and shopping center divisions of Cadillac Fairview. Training should have been its top priority, but it wasn't. All property managers in all divisions of the company were invited to attend our maintenance classes, but very few took advantage of this offer.

It was not made a condition of employment for the property managers to attend training sessions, even in the residential division. The senior executives in Cadillac's residential division felt that the on-site operators needed training, but not themselves.

Objectives of the Program

The following objectives were agreed upon for the training program:

1. To recognize, maintain, and develop attitudes necessary to professionally execute the responsibilities identified in the charters of accountability for everyone on the property management staff.
2. To develop the human, conceptual, and technical skills needed to effectively manage, maintain, and operate buildings assigned to the property management team.

3. To teach people to be self-directed learners by using our training manual as a textbook and reference, and to provide hands-on training with the assistance of the in-house support service specialists on the management team.

4. To help management assess the qualifications of the management staff and to help upgrade their weaknesses.

5. To set up a modular concept of training so that personnel can function at their assigned roles while learning and improving their human, conceptual, and technical skills.

6. To develop a training program that could be used to help recruit people identified on management's organizational hierarchy as well as those already doing those jobs.

7. To help maintain Cadillac Fairview's principle that its fine reputation was one of its more valuable assets and that the physical condition of the buildings owned by the company and the services provided to their tenants were major contributing factors in preserving that reputation. All training programs would teach this guiding principle so that over a period of time the management team would be staffed with people who were knowledgeable and dedicated to and able to fulfill this goal.

Who Needs Training?

Cadillac's residential maintenance and operations department recommended that training programs be developed for all construction and building management personnel. It was felt that everyone needed business management, marketing, sales, leasing and administration, design, construction and renovation management, and maintenance and operations training. When the idea was proposed to the chief executive officer in 1975, his first reaction was negative: He maintained that the company was in the development business, not in management. So in our on-site operator's course, we taught only operations and maintenance services: instruction in housekeeping, groundskeeping, structural and electrical-mechanical services, and how to plan, organize, staff, direct, and control these functions using the support information and technical expertise provided by Cadillac Fairview's residential maintenance and operations department.

Where to Train

We recommended that training combine full- or part-time, in-class, hands-on, or correspondence courses; seminars; workshops; audio-visual and computer aids; or specialized programs tailor-made to suit the needs of top, middle, and first-line management. The school was established, and the training program proceeded without support or encouragement from the company. We just did it!

Some spare space was found in one of Cadillac's apartment buildings, which was unfinished because the township said the building violated its density bylaws. The ceilings and walls were left open so that the students could see the piping, valves, and structure of each unit. The block walls were painted, and several types of floor covering, carpets, wall tiles were added. Hands-on components were provided so that the students could operate them.

When to Train

The department believed that training should commence on the first day of employment and continue until retirement. Unless people in the construction and building management industry improve their knowledge by at least 10 percent each year, they will not keep up with the specialized human, conceptual, and technical skills needed to manage, operate, and provide the support services required by owners of buildings.

Whom to Train

A training program should include all new employees, employees not performing to standards agreed to in their charters of accountability, employees preparing for a special assignment, and employees training for advancement. We recommended that Cadillac develop people from within the organization, as there were few schools available to train the staff to perform the functions outlined in an on-site operator's charter of accountability. The people developed through the training program would eventually have the specialized skills needed for future leaders.

Although the school was used primarily to train on-site building operators, it was felt that a company as large as Cadillac Fairview ($3 billion in real estate assets and $1 billion in income in 1980) needed training programs for everyone, from the chief executive officer to the housekeepers and gardeners, if it expected to achieve its corporate objectives.

Organization

The building operator's training program was separated into six phases as follows:

1. Interviewing, hiring, and orientation
2. Classroom training using the maintenance management handbook
3. Assignment to a building or in-house support services department

4. Job orientation and on-site training in the assigned building
5. Performance assessment through inspections by support service specialists and evaluation by reviewing, at least annually and more often if needed, the duties, functions, and tasks detailed in the charters of accountability
6. Upgrading and reassignment to overcome weaknesses or to broaden knowledge and experiences

Interviewing, Hiring, and Orientation

From the beginning it was felt that the training program would need to train students to carry out effectively the responsibilities outlined in their charters of accountability.

To make the program successful, Cadillac would have to become more professional in the way we interviewed, hired, and trained a new person. To assure that the on-site person was compatible with the building and the tenants, we felt that it was necessary to put more effort into the assessment and placement process. Management should not be spending money to advertise, recruit, hire, and train the wrong people.

Using the charter of accountability as a basis for recruiting, hiring, and training made a lot of sense. Yet except for the maintenance and operations department no one in the residential division or in the other divisions of the company used them.

We in the residential division felt that after hiring a new on-site candidate it would be wise to put him or her in a building to make sure that this was indeed the kind of job that he or she wanted or could handle. We selected several of our better on-site operators in various types of properties to act as on-site teachers. This hands-on orientation stage helped assure that there was no misunderstanding about the job before a new operator was assigned a building and moved in.

As you can see, phase one was as important to the employee as it was for the company. If either of them made a mistake, it could easily be resolved before the company spent a lot of time and money training the wrong person for the wrong job. The wrong staff doing the wrong things can quickly deteriorate a building. Once this happens it takes years to rectify, and there are many instances when such problems were never overcome.

Classroom Training

To provide the right atmosphere for learning and to motivate people to concentrate on the lessons being taught, it was felt that both classroom and hands-on training was necessary.

Training Records

Employees kept records of their progress in the training program on charts showing all the training modules and the dates they attended either in an on-site or in-class session. A training report was signed only if the teacher was satisfied that the student had understood the lesson. It was not the intention of the program to award points or percentages, but to assist employees by helping them to understand what was taught. A copy of the training record was kept by the employee and the trainer.

Link the Training Program to the Wage Scales

It was recommended that the training program be linked to the wage scale guidelines that were developed as an incentive for employees to improve their skills. Although this was never implemented at Cadillac Fairview, it is something that should be encouraged. Suitable accreditation for all people on the design, construction, and building management teams should be encouraged by the industry.

Orientation Phase

In the first week of orientation the new operator began a four-week orientation period by working with an experienced on-site building operator in one of Cadillac Fairview's apartment buildings. It was the company's policy to hire inexperienced people, so this phase was important. Several of the better operators were specially trained to help new employees become familiar with their responsibilities. After the first week the new operator was brought in for another interview to determine if he or she would be happy working in an apartment building. Those who wouldn't left at that time; the others carried on with the rest of the orientation program.

The following three weeks were divided between in-class and on-site training. The only on-site training recorded on the operators' training records was the hands-on sessions held in their permanently assigned building with the specialized support service technicians from Cadillac Fairview's residential maintenance and operations department. The specialists verified that the operators understood what they were doing and that they were actually performing well in their own buildings.

During the four-week orientation period both the trainer-operator and the recruiting and training director assessed the operators personally before it was decided about the kind of property that would best suit the new employee. An ideal situation would evolve when the trainer had several suitable candidates in the orientation program. This gave a property manager a choice from among several newly trained operators. The company always tried to have someone in training, even if there was no building available. One of the candidates could always fill in for an operator who was sick or cover for someone on vacation. When you have a large portfolio you can always use an extra person.

Assignment to a Building

When an operator is hired and moved into a building, the property manager should do the following:

1. Review with the operator the on-site operator's charter of accountability, which includes a schedule of duties for the operator and any other on-site staff. Have the operator sign it.
2. Introduce the operator to any other staff in the management office or to those who may be working in the building.
3. Formally inspect the building, pointing out the location of shut-off valves, explaining emergency procedures and the inventory of parts, equipment, and materials, and reviewing the procedure for handling tenant problems. At this point the operator should formally sign for tools, equipment, spare parts, supplies, chemicals, and keys.
4. Review and turn over to the operator the current rent roll, the rules and regulations for the building; rental features, applications to rent, deposit requirements, parking and locker records, move-in and move-out schedules, the keys and key-control policy, the schedules of duties for the operator as well as for other people who work in the building, and outstanding work and purchase orders.

The operator's charter, schedules of duties, inventories and other relevant information about the building now become a part of the building profile and is added to a binder containing the other profile information for that building.

Assigned Building Orientation

It is important, particularly for a newly hired person, that a support-service specialist help the operator become familiar with the structure and the electrical-mechanical equipment in the building. This can be done by visiting the building and inspecting the building with the new operator. At that time the support service specialist can answer any questions asked by the new employee particularly those about the structure, the equipment, or the systems. These questions can be answered by a review of the building's profile, a copy of which should be left with the operator.

As soon as possible, someone with housekeeping expertise and someone with groundskeeping expertise should visit the new employee to inspect the common areas and the grounds. In this way, the operator becomes aware of the building owner's standards of cleanliness and other conditions that the operator is expected to maintain.

Performance Assessment

Once the property manager and an on-site operator had agreed with and signed the charter of accountability, it becomes the basis for his performance evaluation. At least once a year, and more often if there were problems, the property manager and the on-site operator should meet to evaluate the operator's performance. This practice not only affords the opportunity for evaluation but also is a very important way of opening up and maintaining a line of communication between the manager and operator. This exercise also helps to ensure that there are no problems developing and that the operator is kept motivated to achieve the goals set forth in the charter and assures that the operator maintains a proper attitude. Working together during inspections and while developing a maintenance and operations expense budget provides the manager and operator with excellent opportunities for communication.

Feedback as a Channel for Communication

Often individuals may have unclear views of their strengths and weaknesses. When meeting with them on a regular basis to formally review their charter, during inspections, and while developing budgets and when meeting with them at other times, there are four things that property managers must keep in mind.

1. Employees should feel free to express true feelings and perceptions without fear of retribution.
2. Informal communication should be encouraged.
3. A habit of attentively listening should be developed.
4. The habit of correcting weaknesses by training is encouraged if one makes a point of giving out facts and straightforward answers when communicating with other members of the management team. Knowing how to carry out assigned responsibilities in an effective and professional manner helps everyone on the management team maintain a feeling of confidence and satisfaction through achievement. Overcoming weaknesses by seeking training should be encouraged during feedback sessions.

Inspection—Performance Assessment Tools

Inspections are excellent performance assessment tools if the manager uses them as an opportunity for dialogue with the on-site operator. Inspections are the surest way of becoming familiar with the building and assuring that the structure and the electrical-mechanical equipment are in acceptable condition. The operator should inspect daily, completing the daily operating log information, and making out maintenance requests for any problems that require correcting.

Property managers should inspect their properties every month, if possible; if not, they should inspect at least every two months. Support service specialists in housekeeping, groundskeeping, structural services, and electrical-mechanical systems should inspect at least once a year. Ideally they should inspect quarterly. Such inspections are a very important part of the hands-on training program.

Work Measurement Standards

To determine the on-site maintenance and operations staff requirements for a building, property managers must know how to calculate a work load and the time they need to handle the load they identify. This planning exercise helps managers in many ways.

- It assures that each building is properly staffed.
- It assures that each building has the tools, inventory, and equipment needed to perform the job functions identified in the staff's charters of accountabilities.
- It helps managers identify the training needs for their staffs.
- By identifying all the job functions, it allows managers to accurately include in their annual maintenance and operations expense budgets the cost for on-site staff.
- The information generated by this exercise and the actual results shown on the maintenance and operations chart of accounts allows managers to monitor the results of their maintenance programs.

Overcoming Waste by Positive Direction

Everyone should know in advance what to do; when to do it; how it should be done; how long it should take to do it; how to use the tools, equipment, materials, supplies, and parts; and what the end results will be.

Schedules of duties that are determined from each building's work load help management assure that the on-site staff know exactly what is expected of them as a condition of employment. Experience has shown that people respond best to strong and positive direction. Using this type of systematic approach to management assures the building owner, the manager, the operator, and the support service technicians that everything that needs to be done in a building is actually planned for and has a reasonable chance of getting done.

Learning and Teaching

Everyone was encouraged to help each other improve by the interchange of ideas and information, not only to help peers but also to help improve the performance of any subordinate who was given the responsibility of handling some of the supervisor's work load. To help motivate the staff, Cadillac taught the basic principles of communication and the fundamentals of learning and teaching.

Learning Sequence

Each training module was developed according to four facts about learning.

1. The purpose of instruction is to learn.
2. If management expects people to learn, employees must be motivated.
3. If management expects people to understand, employees must practice.
4. Management must understand that the purpose of practice is to learn by doing.

To make a learning sequence effective, a teacher must clarify the objective of each lesson, motivate students to open their minds, and create a desire to learn. In return, the students must apply themselves both physically and mentally to the instruction received. This learning must be accomplished in a short time and is best done by associating the subject with practical applications and examples. Audio-visual training aids and hands-on training are two excellent ways to teach and to instill the right attitudes for learning.

Audio-visual training modules are very useful for combining seeing, hearing, and doing if they are properly developed and combined with a work book. They are also excellent ways of repeating a message as often as necessary to encourage people to pay attention to what is being taught and to help assure that they understand what is meant. Most of all, those being taught must remember the message.

People understand more easily what they can both hear and see. We create clear mental images when we use visuals to aid oral messages. In effect, students really "see what you mean."

It is hoped that the information included in this book will encourage the initiation of training programs for everyone on design, construction, and building management teams. Aside from the formal training, each day everyone should read information about housekeeping, groundskeeping, structure, and electrical-mechanical systems, especially the manufacturers' manuals explaining the equipment installed in the buildings being managed.

Methods of Instruction

The following teaching guidelines were developed:

1. Lectures did not exceed one hour.
2. Conferences or workshops included time for questions and answers to assure that any misunderstandings were cleared up.
3. Demonstrations were well prepared, and we had either visual aids or hands-on equipment in the classroom. Because the school was located in a building, the students could actually participate in its operations and maintenance.
4. Classes were small so that everyone could learn by doing and become proficient by repetition.

In the instruction program, 15 percent of the time was spent telling; 25 percent, showing; and 60 percent, doing. To help assess whether the students understood what they were being taught, they were tested orally, by performance and by written test.

Corrosion and Water Treatment

7.1 FACTORS INFLUENCING CORROSION

The principal factors influencing the corrosion of metals in water systems are the types and concentrations of impurities in the water, plus the temperature and rate of water flow. If the rate of flow is restricted by scale or other substances generally found in domestic hot-water return lines, the corrosion will accelerate as the impurities have a better chance to attack the metal. Proper rate of flow moves the impurities before they can cause a problem. These may be periodically flushed out of the domestic hot-water lines through a blow-down bypass at the return line to the domestic hot-water storage tank (see Figure 10.8).

The chief chemical variables controlling the characteristics of water are

- Dissolved oxygen concentration
- Carbon dioxide content

This chapter is from Mel A. Shear, *Handbook of Building Maintenance Management*, © 1983, pp. 40–51 (A Reston Publication). Adapted by permission of Prentice-Hall, Inc., Englewood Cliffs, New Jersey. The illustrations and portions of the text were taken, with permission, from a paper presented in the 1930s to the Southern Ontario Committee on Electrolysis by T. R. B. Watson, a board member of Corrosion Service Company Limited, 369 Rimrock Road, Downsview, Ontario, M3J 3G2.

- pH
- Dissolved solids
- Presence of free mineral acid
- Sulphide
- Sulphur dioxide

Increased dissolved solids, particularly chloride and sulphate, enhance the corrosive effect of oxygen and carbon dioxide.

There are basically three types of corrosion: (1) physical corrosion, (2) chemical corrosion, and (3) electrochemical corrosion. It is important that you acquire a basic knowledge of these types of corrosion so you will understand the problem and know how to control the situation. Chemical salespeople may be selling you a chemical that is not suited to the solution of your problem. In many cases it may even make it worse.

Physical Corrosion

In discussing corrosion, it is unfortunately necessary to use technical terms. One can almost say that corrosion has a language of its own. These terms will be explained in as simple a form as possible.

Unfortunately, many people often accept corrosion as inevitable. Actually, something can and should be done to prolong the life of many metals exposed to corrosive environments. It costs money to replace deteriorated material. Thus corrosion control becomes a very important factor in the very important area of "dollars and cents." The cost, in terms of dollars, for corrosion and corrosion control in the United States in 1975 was estimated to be in excess of $10–15 billion per year. Inflation will compound these figures dramatically, and the costs in 1985 could easily be doubled.

In 1986 the Ontario Research Foundation* reported that Canadian industry loses an estimated $8 billion a year to corrosion and that about $2 billion of this is considered preventable if proper care is taken in the design and use of materials.

To combat this, large companies generally monitor corrosion rates and replace affected parts, equipment, or systems on a scheduled basis. Many firms, however, give little consideration to opportunities for cost savings that could result from research and development studies of their corrosion problems, or simply from better engineering design.

Most people are familiar with corrosion, particularly the rusting of an iron fence or a tin can, and the corrosion of steel pilings or boats.

*The Ontario Research Foundation is a nonprofit independent research organization governed by prominent businesspeople and scientists. They are located in the Sheridan Park Research Community, Mississauga, Ontario, Canada L5K 1B3.

When undertaking a study of corrosion it may be natural to think that corrosion is a simple single reaction and that it can be turned off like a spigot. Unfortunately, this is not the case.

Corrosion is the deterioration of a substance (usually a metal) or its properties because of a reaction with its environment. The deterioration of wood, ceramics, plastics, and other substances must also be included in a study of corrosion.

Chemical Corrosion

The action of oxygen increases corrosion. Furthermore, if iron is placed in two similar flasks filled with water and nitrogen is added to one and oxygen to the other, the iron in the flask with the oxygen will begin to rust, but the iron in the flask saturated with nitrogen, which helps eliminate the dissolved oxygen, remains bright.

This is significant because in domestic water and cooling systems we continually evaporate or use the water (H_2O) in the system and thus are continually adding fresh water, which perpetuates the corrosion problem by adding fresh oxygen.

Electrochemical Corrosion

There are many theories regarding the cause and mechanism of corrosion. The electrochemical theory is the most widely accepted and states that a potential must exist between two or more points, and current must flow for corrosion of metals to occur.

Metal corrosion is caused by electrochemical reactions in which metal at one location (the anode) corrodes while, at another location (the cathode), hydrogen ions are reduced or discharged. The cathode and anode can be miles apart, or can be so close together that they may be considered to be coincident, but at any one moment, oxidation is taking place at one spot while reduction is progressing at another. There are millions of both kinds of reactive areas operating simultaneously on a piece of metal. This action requires four components: anode, cathode, electrolyte, and a metallic path for electrons. Anodes and cathodes are caused by differences in the surfaces of metals, which are created by metallic inclusions, metallographic discontinuities, different grain orientation, different stress, or different temperature.

If two different metals are in electrical contact in an aqueous environment, a large difference in electrolytic potential is established, resulting in severe corrosion of the more anodic metals. For example, the combination of copper and steel is a bad one for steel. The electrolyte (water) influences the severity of the corrosive processes. The more dissolved salts water contains, the better the conductor it is, and the greater will be the corrosion. The quantity of dissolved oxygen is most important because it is oxygen that keeps the cathodes functioning. A completely deaerated water with a neutral or slightly alkaline pH is almost noncorrosive—as in a heating system in which the oxygen has been all used up by superficial corrosion. If one area has access to dissolved oxygen while another is shielded, corrosion of the metal under a deposit can occur.

In heating and cooling systems there are two causes of electrochemical corrosion:

1. Difference in the concentration of dissolved oxygen at one point compared with another
2. The use of dissimilar metal.

Bimetallic corrosion can occur when two dissimilar metals are brought into electrical contact in the presence of an electrolyte such as the water in the system.

Corrosion of metals in aqueous media, such as the water in heating systems, occurs by a combination of both anodic and cathodic reactions.

This corrosion does not happen in heating systems unless there is a leak or air is sucked into the system at the pumps. When needed chemicals are introduced into the water and controlled, the pH balance of the system can be maintained, and the corrosive electrochemical action can be stopped. To maintain this balance all leaks *must* be corrected immediately. The water in the heating and cooling systems must be regularly tested and chemically maintained by correcting any imbalance noted as soon as possible.

7.2 WHY METALS CORRODE

Metals corrode through sheer cussedness. They want to corrode. This stems from the fact that it is more natural for a metal to exist in the form of a compound, because compounds such as oxides contain less energy than metals and are therefore more stable.

In steelmaking, when iron is divorced from its associated oxygen in the blast furnace, a lot of energy is added in the form of heat. As long as it remains metallic, a piece of steel retains a portion of this energy, bound up within itself, always urging the metal to corrode back to the ore from which it was unwillingly derived. This energy supplies the power to drive the various corrosion reactions and provides the incentive to corrode. When steel rusts the latent energy is released, the metal, relieved of its uneasy hypertension, reverts to a stable oxide, and the cycle is complete. (See Figure 7.1.)

When steel rusts, the union with oxygen does not take place directly but by a rather roundabout series of reactions in which the passage of an electric current plays an important part. It is often stated that corrosion is caused by

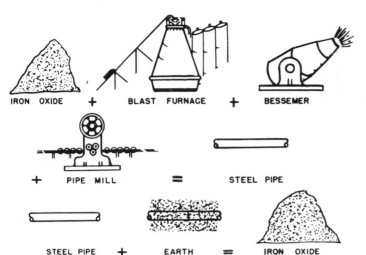

Figure 7.1 Why metals corrode. (Courtesy of T.R.B. Watson, Corrosion Services Company Limited, Downsview, Ontario, Canada.)

electric currents. It is perhaps more accurate to say that in most cases the electric current is caused by the corrosion, but the two forces are as interdependent as the chicken and the egg.

Corrosion Cell (Galvanic Activity)

Battery action (galvanic cell).   A good example of the way current is generated by corrosion is the galvanic cell. The ordinary dry cell battery, which consists of a zinc can holding a moist paste that constitutes the electrolyte, has a graphite rod in its center that acts as the cathode of the cell. Because the zinc has more stored-up energy than the graphite and is thus more eager to corrode, a potential of about 1.5 volts exists between the zinc and the graphite, and if the external terminals are joined with a wire, current will flow in the cell from the surface of the zinc, through the electrolyte, to the cathode, and back again through the wire. If a flashlight bulb is put in the external circuit, it will light. It is interesting that the electrical energy that lights it is the energy of corrosion of the zinc, the same energy that was put into the zinc when it was refined from its ore. As the zinc corrodes, it releases into the electrolyte small charged particles of itself, called ions, and these charged particles travel across the cell to the cathode where they discharge. The passage of ions constitutes an electric current. The more current flowing in a cell, the more the zinc is corroded. After the battery has been used for some time, corrosion will eat a hole in it, and the cell will leak. Many people have had the experience of having a flashlight battery leak inside the case. (See Figure 7.2.)

If the wire is disconnected from the external terminals, the current is

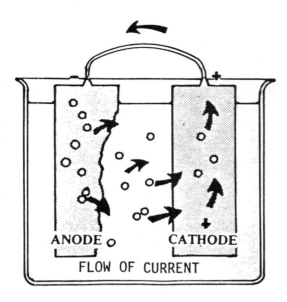

Figure 7.2 Corrosion cell (galvanic activity). The term *anode* is used to describe that portion of the metal surface that is corroded and from which current leaves the metal to enter the solution. The term *cathode* is used to describe the metal from which current leaves the solution and returns to the metal and on which a chemical reaction takes place. (Courtesy of T.R.B. Watson, Corrosion Services Company Limited, Downsview, Ontario, Canada.)

interrupted, and the ions released at the surface of the zinc, having nowhere to go, accumulate in such numbers that corrosion is virtually stopped. This demonstrates that for corrosion to take place there must be a complete circuit (Figure 7.3).

Note that only the anode is attacked in every electrolytic cell. The anode is the place where current leaves the metal to go into the electrolyte. The cathode is the place where the current flows back out of the electrolyte.

For every anode there is always, somewhere, a cathode. *Anodes corrode; cathodes do not.*

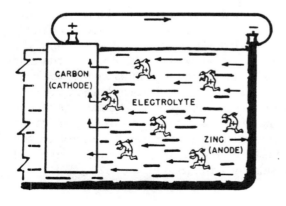

Figure 7.3 Battery action (galvanic cell). For corrosion to take place, there must be a complete circuit. (Courtesy of T.R.B. Watson, Corrosion Services Company Limited, Downsview, Ontario, Canada.)

7.3 CORROSION PROBLEMS IN BUILDINGS

In buildings, iron piping is the major source of corrosion. Heating pipes, domestic hot-water pipes, underground piping, and heating pipes for ramps give the most trouble. Corrosion in boilers and in reinforcing steel rods in underground garage slabs also contribute to the problem.

The costs to correct the corrosion problems are staggering because walls or concrete usually must be broken to replace galvanized pipe with copper or plastic pipes.

Corrosion Due to Dissimilar Metals

In actual practice, the behavior of a bimetallic combination, such as a brass or bronze valve or copper convector in an iron pipeline, usually does not result in rapid failure of the pipe. Corrosion undoubtedly takes place, but the ratio of the amount of iron to that of brass, bronze, or copper appears to be the governing factor. Corrosion is distributed over the surface of the iron to such an extent that penetration is generally negligible. If for some reason, such as turbulence, temperature, or oxygen distribution, corrosion of the iron is confined to a small area near the more noble metal, the attack will be serious and rapid, resulting in perforation.

A bimetallic galvanic cell is always established when two different metals in electrical contact with each other are buried adjacent to each other. In a home supplied by a steel gas service line and a copper water service, the metallic circuit between the two metals is completed through the water heater. The steel in this case will be corroded by the influence of the copper pipe, which acts as a cathode (see Figure 7.4).

For every ampere-year of current, 20 pounds of metal are dissolved, and the rate of penetration depends on the area from which this metal is taken. If the pipe is coated and subject to electrolysis from stray currents, the coating can, in some cases, cause more rapid penetration of the pipe because the areas from which metal can be taken are confined to pinholes or cracks in the coating (see Figures 7.5 and 7.6).

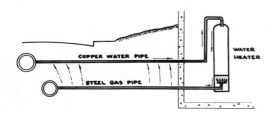

Figure 7.4   Corrosion resulting from dissimilar metals. (Courtesy of T.R.B. Watson, Corrosion Services Company Limited, Downsview, Ontario, Canada.)

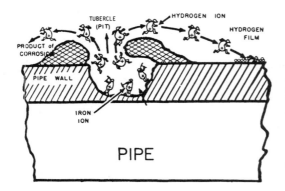

Figure 7.5 Pit action. A well-advanced corrosion cell in which the anode is corroded to form a pit. The corrosion product has built up over the top of the pit to form a tubercle. This rust deposit is soft and quite permeable and offers no resistance to the passage of the current through it; in fact, it aggravates the situation. Once a pit is started, the voltage of the corrosion cell goes up, and the action is intensified.

Problems Caused by New and Old Pipes

In the battery, the voltage was set up by the fact that the anode and cathode were made of different materials. In fact, it is always some difference of metal or soil that causes current flow and its associated corrosion. The greater the difference, the more severe the attack will be. Pipeliners say that pipes today are not as good as they used to be. The example is often cited of the line that last many years until one short section had to be replaced. The new pipe lasted only a few years before it had to be replaced again. The trouble was not a defective new pipe, but that in coupling new and old pipe, a cell of different materials was set up, in which the new clean pipe was strongly anodic to the old rusty pipe, and it corroded as a result of the currents. (See Figure 7.7.)

Corrosion Caused by the Nature of Soil

Take the case of a bare steel pipe buried in moist earth. Because of slight differences in metal composition or surface condition, and because of slight differences in the nature of the soil touching the pipe, small potentials, or voltages, are set up between some areas of the pipe surface and other adjacent areas. (This is analogous to the battery action described earlier.) From the more negative areas, current will flow into the soil (which acts as the electrolyte) and through it to the more positive, or cathodic, areas and back again through the metal of the pipe. At the negative, or anodic, area metal will dissolve. At the adjacent cathodes no corrosion will take place. This accounts for the common action of pitting: The pits are anodes where the metal is corroding, and the unaffected areas around the pits have been acting as cathodes and thus have been protected. Nevertheless, because every anode needs a cathode, the uncorroded areas were necessary to the reaction. (See Figures 7.8 and 7.9.)

Current is conducted through the moist earth by a stream of hydrogen ions. Where these ions arrive at the cathode areas they are discharged and result in a film of hydrogen. This usually reacts with oxygen dissolved in the

The results of corrosion of a building's buried main water line. It is not known whether a magnesium anode was ever attached to this pipe when it was originally buried in the ground. However, even if it was, there was no record available about the size and location of the anode or its expected life.

To protect buried iron pipes, anodes should be attached and checked periodically to assure replacement before they disappear. The location and life expectancy should be recorded on a plot plan.

Figure 7.6 A pitted supply water main.

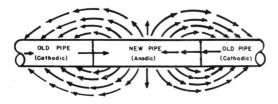

Figure 7.7 Corrosion resulting from dissimilar metals. It is always a difference of metal or soil that causes current flow and its associated corrosion. (Courtesy of T.R.B. Watson, Corrosion Services Company Limited, Downsview, Ontario, Canada.)

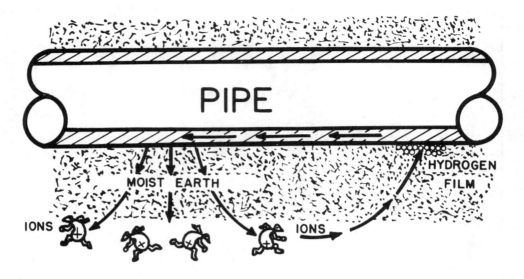

IONS in motion constitute an electric current

Figure 7.8   The hydrogen ion. (Courtesy of T.R.B. Watson, Corrosion Services Company Limited, Downsview, Ontario, Canada.)

soil and is not evolved as a gas. This little corrosion cell is representative of millions of similar ions on the surface of any pipe. The length of the current path may be anywhere from a millimeter or smaller to several miles, but the strength of the current is always proportional to the corrosion rate. *One ampere, flowing for one year, will dissolve 20 pounds of steel.*

Corrosion Caused by Aeration of Soil

If one surface of the pipe has more access to oxygen than has another surface, a similar cell will be set up. This accounts for a familiar condition when the bottom of the pipe, in contact with undisturbed, poorly aerated soil at the bot-

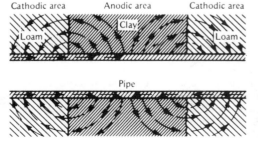

Figure 7.9   Corrosion caused by dissimilar soils. Differences in the nature of the soil in contact with a metal pipe can form galvanic cells. The lighter, more porous soils are most likely to become cathodes. The metal in contact with the more impervious clay will suffer. (Courtesy of T.R.B. Watson, Corrosion Services Limited, Downsview, Ontario, Canada.)

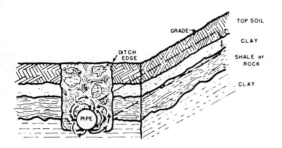

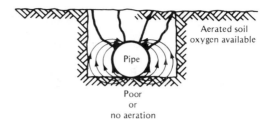

Figure 7.10 Corrosion caused by a mixture of soils. Such a condition exists when a trench is backfilled with a mixture of lumps of different kinds of soils. (Courtesy of T.R.B. Watson, Corrosion Services Company Limited, Downsview, Ontario, Canada.)

Figure 7.11 Corrosion caused by aeration of soil. (Courtesy of T.R.B. Watson, Corrosion Services Limited, Downsview, Ontario Canada.)

tom of the trench, is subject to more corrosion than is the top of the pipe, which has an ample oxygen supply through permeation into the loose backfill. (See Figures 7.10 and 7.11.)

7.4 CATHODIC PROTECTION

Magnesium Anodes

A current may just as easily be produced by galvanic action from the energy of corrosion of a magnesium anode. In this instance a piece of magnesium is connected to the pipe with a wire and buried some 10 feet away from it. Because the magnesium is much more active than the steel, a considerable voltage is established between the two metals, and protective current will flow from the magnesium through the earth to the pipe and back again through the wire. The magnesium, being the anode, will corrode in proportion to the current that it generates. In fact, the corrosion of the pipeline is transferred to the magnesium. Wherever these protective anodes are used they should be inspected and replaced before they disappear. Management must know where they are located so that they can be replaced before they disappear. (See Figure 7.12.)

Pipe Protection with Coating and Anodes

Fewer magnesium anodes are necessary to protect a coated structure than are necessary to protect a bare one, because the available current has only to go to the breaks in the coating instead of having to cover a large bare area. The current at the pinholes, although very small, causes a high protective current density at the minute breaks in the coating. (See Figure 7.13.)

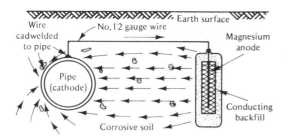

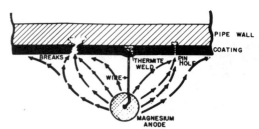

Figure 7.12 Cathodic protection magnesium anodes. A current may be produced by galvanic action from the energy of corrosion of a magnesium anode. (Courtesy of T.R.B. Watson, Corrosion Services Company Limited, Downsview, Ontario, Canada.)

Figure 7.13 Pipe protection with coating and anodes. The current at the pinholes, although they are small, causes a high protective current density at the minute breaks in the coating. (Courtesy of T.R.B. Watson, Corrosion Services Company Limited, Downsview, Ontario, Canada.)

Today, the majority of long-buried pipelines are coated with an organic coating, because experience has shown that corrosion can be controlled more cheaply on a coated structure. Corrosion may be stopped in two ways: (1) by maintaining a perfect coating, and (2) by impressing a protective cathodic current density on a bare line. The first measure is impossible because there is no such thing as a perfect coating; the second is unduly expensive because of the high current demand. Somewhere between the extremes of coating perfection and prodigal power demand lies the optimum economic combination of a good coating supplemented by a little cathodic protection to look after the inevitable pinholes. It can be said that corrosion is being controlled by the cathodic protection, and the coating is applied to make the cathodic protection cheaper.

Corrosion control is an economic measure and the cheapest way to achieve it is the best. The choice is easier if you know why metals corrode. (See Figures 7.14 and 7.15.)

7.5 CONTROLLING BIOLOGICAL FOULING

An Overview

Biological fouling is the result of excessive growth and development of different members of the lower forms of plant life, namely algae, bacteria (slime), and fungi. The main function of these microscopic life forms is to restore the natural balance of life cycles when they are disrupted. As long as the microscopic life forms remain isolated as single cells, they present no problem. However, when the balance of nature is disturbed by constructing systems to store and conserve water, an ideal breeding place for microbiological growths is pro-

A recurring maintenance task during the summer is to test the heating pipes for underground parking garage ramps to assure that they are not leaking.

You can imagine the surprise of the maintenance crew when they put a water test on this ramp.

Figure 7.14   Testing ramp heating pipes.

vided. Examples of breeding places are cooling towers and swimming pools. These growths can foul pipelines and interfere with heat transfer, cause corrosion of metal, and the disintegration of wood, and could possibly be the cause of Legionnaire's disease.

Figure 7.15 An extreme example of pipe corrosion. This piece of corroded pipe was cut from the piping used to heat a ramp for an underground garage.

Algae

Algae are defined as a group of water plants that make their own food and that have chlorophyll but not true stems, roots, or leaves. Algae are able to accomplish this because they contain the green pigment chlorophyll and thus use a process known as photosynthesis. Algae cannot survive without air, sunlight, or water. When pools and cooling towers are exposed to direct sunlight, they are plagued with the problem of algae growths.

Bacteria

Bacteria can be defined as very tiny and simple plants, so small that they can usually be seen only through a microscope. Bacteria consist of single cells, have no chlorophyll, and multiply by fission (splitting apart). In general they are unicellular, rod shaped, coccid, or spiral in form. Bacteria cause diseases such as pneumonia and typhoid fever, among others.

Slime-forming bacteria are the most common bacteria found in recirculating cooling water systems. The basic function of these bacteria is to form a gelatinous capsule that entraps other materials and protects the bacteria against the action of chemical and physical agents.

Legionnaire's Disease

In 1979, a University of Toronto research chemist, Dr. Dmyto Buchnea, conducted experiments that showed that corroded coils in a lab's air-conditioning system were blowing fine particles of aluminum through the air and actually interfering with other experiments.

Dr. Buchnea reported that the substance in the air could have degenerative effects on the human brain, and recent cases of nausea and dizziness linked to ventilation systems convinced him that he was right. Electrical-mechanical engineers have another theory that claims that this problem could be linked to the fact that building owners are cutting off the ventilation system or reducing the volume of air to save energy. Both problems are very serious, and owners and building managers must be aware of and take steps to correct them.

In the late 1970s there was growing evidence linking air conditioners with the dreaded Legionnaire's disease, which was suspected in four deaths in Toronto. This Toronto outbreak of the illness followed a 1976 incident in which 29 people died after 180 were stricken by a mysterious ailment while attending an American Legion convention in Philidelphia. Since then an organism linked to the disease has been found in air, soil, water, at building sites, and in air conditioners.

In 1978 in the United States, two separate outbreaks were traced to faulty air conditioners. At about that time Dr. Santu Toma, chief bacteriologist for the Ontario Health Ministry and a leading Canadian authority on the disease, placed the possibility of blame, not on home air conditioners but on badly maintained industrial air-conditioning systems equipped with cooling towers. If the cooling towers are not properly treated and cared for, a layer of wet slime can build up in the towers, providing conditions where bacteria can grow.

In May 1985 a similar outbreak occurred in Stafford, England. One hundred twenty-two people were affected, and 30 people died. The disease produces symptoms like those of pneumonia and is particularly dangerous for old or weak people. Public health authorities in England confirmed that they had tentatively traced the source of the infection to the air-conditioning cooling towers on the roof of the district hospital, which only opened 11 months before the outbreak.

This unfortunate problem is mentioned to reinforce the need for water treatment, the importance of knowing what the problems are before you attempt to treat them, and the importance of using experienced support-service specialists to assure that the water treatment does indeed control the biological fouling in cooling towers, pools, saunas, whirlpools, and in any other area that may be a source of trouble.

Problems Caused by Bacteria

Slime deposits on processing equipment retard heat transfer on cooling equipment and thus cause a serious loss of efficiency. Slime deposits on metal surfaces create local cell action and aggravate pitting tendencies.

Aerobic sulphur bacteria oxidize sulphur or sulphides to sulphuric acid. Some species of sulphur bacteria are commonly present in water containing dissolved hydrogen sulphide. These specific colored (red or purple) sulphur bacteria are similar to the chlorophyll-bearing plants in their ability to manufacture their food photosynthetically and to develop only in sunlight.

Iron bacteria precipitate ferric hydroxide (rust).

7.6 WATER TREATMENT

An Overview

The need for water treatment and cathodic protection becomes evident as one researches and develops a maintenance program. Problems such as corrosion, biological fouling, algae, bacteria, and other pollutants can be overcome only by introducing chemicals and using cathodic protection.

There is no such thing as a universal corrosion inhibitor, but each blend of inhibitor must be tailored to the type of equipment or cooling water that it is designed to protect. An inhibitor that may provide excellent protection for one system may fail to protect another system and may even aggravate the corrosion. In buildings, water treatment is required in heating systems, cooling systems, swimming pools, and decorative fountains.

pH—A Measure of Hydrogen Ion

As mentioned previously, water treatment must be tailored to the type of equipment it is designed to protect. One important factor that must be understood when treating and testing water is the pH measure of a sample. This is defined as the measure of hydrogen ion concentration (activity) of the sample.

The pH of the water must be accurately determined because the adjustment of pH is usually very important in the control of biological fouling and corrosion in heating and cooling systems, as well as in swimming pools and fountains.

A simple definition of pH is that it is a number between 1 and 14, denoting the intensity of acidity or alkalinity of a water (see Figure 7.16).

The pH number of water or of any solution indicates whether the liquid has an acid or an alkaline reaction. A neutral liquid, such as pure water, is neither acid nor alkaline and has a pH value of 7.

When water or any aqueous solution contains a surplus of hydrogen ions,

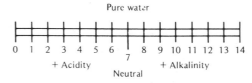

Figure 7.16   The pH scale of hydrogen-ion concentration. By measuring the hydrogen-ion concentration in a sample of water, it is possible to determine what corrective measures to take to counteract the corrosive characteristics of the water (From Mel A. Shear, *Handbook of Building Maintenance Management,* © 1983, p. 40 [A Reston Publication]. Adapted by permission of Prentice-Hall, Inc., Englewood Cliffs, New Jersey).

it has an acid reaction. Conversely, an excess of OH^- ions will produce a basic, or alkaline, condition. The H^+ ions liberated by the dissociation of the solution attack metal, causing it to dissolve. The greater the hydrogen ion concentration, the more rapid the attack and vice versa.

A neutral liquid such as pure water is neither alkaline nor acid and has a pH of 7. Water treatment must achieve this neutrality if it is to be effective. A good example of this water treatment would be in swimming pools. To maintain a proper pH balance, the lifeguards are constantly testing the water and introducing chlorine and other chemicals to control algae and to maintain the water chemistry. Sunshine and heavy use of the pool constantly upset this balance.

The heating- and cooling-system water must also be kept in balance chemically if corrosion of the boilers and the heating piping or biological fouling of the condenser tubes is to be overcome.

Water is a chemical combination of hydrogen and oxygen—two atoms of hydrogen to one of oxygen. Actually, one of the hydrogen atoms associates itself with the oxygen, and their combination, OH^- (hydroxyl ion), has a negative charge. The other hydrogen H^+, has a positive charge. If these ions are present in the same number, they neutralize each other, so the water has no charge. When the concentration of hydrogen ions exceeds that of hydroxyl ions, however, the water has an acid reaction, and if hydroxyl ions are in greater concentration than hydrogen ions, the reaction is alkaline, or basic.

In general, acid solutions are more aggressive to metals than alkaline ones, although some corrosion may take place even in neutral or alkaline media. For this reason, it is essential to control the pH of heating and cooling systems. pH will also influence scaling and biological fouling.

Chlorine

Many different chemical agents are employed for microorganism control in re-circulating water systems. The primary purpose of the chemical agent is to kill or inhibit the growth and accretion of organisms.

Unless the chemical agent is present in sufficient quantity or is highly toxic, it is not uncommon for the chemical agent, in extremely dilute concentrations, to actually stimulate the growth of microorganisms.

Chlorine is probably the agent most widely employed for control of microorganisms. In the absence of substances that cause a high chlorine demand, chlorine is usually the most economical method of treatment.

It is not satisfactory to feed chlorine without first chemically testing the water to determine the residual of free chlorine that is present. Not only is chlorine one of the most effective slime control agents, but it is also one of the most damaging materials to cooling tower lumber and other vulnerable areas. Consequently, the use of chlorine must be carefully controlled.

A system of control testing ensures that chemical balances are maintained in recommended ranges so that deposits, delignification, and electrochemical corrosion are controlled.

Establishing a reliable water test program requires qualified personnel and proper facilities for testing. Independently testing samples of water from heating and cooling systems is the only way to determine the treatment required and to monitor the results.

Figure 7.17 A water treatment test laboratory. Building owners need to have available to them an independent means of testing the water in heating and cooling systems.

BUILDING LOCATION AND PROBLEM IDENTIFICATION

Building Name	Sample No.
Building Address	
Sample Drawn by	Date
Tests Completed by	Date
Recommendations	
Type of Treatment	

HEATING WATER TEST

Temperature of Sample	°C/F
pH (Measure of Hydrogen Ions)	pH
Fe ++ Ferrous Iron Oxide	ppm
Conductivity	mm
Corrosion Inhibitor	ppm

COOLING WATER TEST

Temperature of Sample	°C/F
pH (Measure of Hydrogen Ions)	pH
Chlorides	ppm
Conductivity	mm
Corrosion Inhibitor	ppm

Water treatment is necessary if managers expect to control corrosion, biological fouling, bacteria, and other pollutants. An independent test must be made to determine the condition of the water before a decision can be made about the treatment that is needed and to monitor the treatment program. Many sellers of chemicals are more interested in selling their products than in helping overcome the problems.

Figure 7.18   A water test report form   (From Mel A. Shear, *Handbook of Building Maintenance Management*, © 1983, p. 50 [A Reston Publication]. Adapted by permission of Prentice-Hall, Inc., Englewood Cliffs, New Jersey).

Testing control.   A system of control testing ensures that chemical balances are maintained in recommended ranges so that deposits, delignification (destructive action on wood), and electrochemical corrosion are controlled.

Establishing a reliable water-test program requires qualified personnel and proper facilities for testing (Figure 7.17). The personnel must be attentive to results that indicate deficiencies. They should bring them to the immediate attention of those responsible for corrective action.

A control chart listing recommended ranges should be available for ready reference. The testing area must be secluded to prevent contamination from dust, smoke, and fumes.

Results should be recorded immediately on record sheets (see Figure 7.18) and circulated to those responsible. Problems should be followed up, corrected, and properly filed for future reference.

Energy Management

8.1 THE ENERGY CRUNCH

Before 1973 most construction and building management companies paid little attention to the cost of maintenance and operations expenses and their relationship to the success or failure of a project. This attitude resulted in poor workmanship and misapplication of the electrical-mechanical equipment installed in buildings built after World War II. It continued until the year of the energy crunch, when people started to take a second look at the problems that were built into buildings and what it was costing building owners in additional maintenance and operations expenses to operate the buildings and overcome the problems.

In 1973 the cost of oil soared and triggered increases in everything associated with the cost of construction and the cost of maintaining and operating buildings. Since that time, entrepreneurs have been quick to exploit the market by selling building owners a wide variety of energy-saving controls, equipment, tools, materials, and chemicals. In some cases they are trying to control a building's operation by installing a computer programmed to control the electrical-mechanical operations. These buildings are marketed as "smart buildings." The benefits of these savings are often diluted because building owners share the savings with the persons offering the programs, equipment, or advice as they either pay a consulting fee or are charged on a per-building-per-month basis. Other building owners are paying or have paid for energy-saving programs without knowing if they are saving any money or not.

In 1970, when Cadillac Development initiated its planned maintenance and energy management program, it didn't know that the price of oil would rise as it did and that the price of natural gas would also rise from 65 cents per MCF in 1970 to $4.50 in 1982. In 1973, the year of the crunch, the company was already showing substantial savings from its program and was thus in a position to take full advantage of the price rise. The higher the price rose, the more it automatically saved.

The water treatment program that triggered the savings program was also showing results. It pacified the electrolysis problem; leaks in the heating systems were uncovered and corrected; the iron oxide in the heating water was put back in solution; and once the in-suite blend valves and the controls on the heating systems operated properly and the problems brought under control, the fuel and maintenance costs began decreasing.

At the same time, the on-site operating staff and the support-service specialist in the residential division's maintenance and operations department participated in a training and upgrading program. Some of the outside support-service contractors also improved their effectiveness as they were introduced to Cadillac's systems and needs. The planning and budgeting system allowed everyone to participate in the program, and the new recordkeeping system kept accurate records of achievements.

8.2 WHAT IS ENERGY?

A dictionary defines energy as the power or capacity to be active; strength of body or mind to think or to work; natural power vigorously exerted; or the capacity for performing work. It is important that people on a management team understand what is meant by energy and how important it is that many of the technical terms associated with energy management are explained and clarified. In short, team members should have a better understanding of the engineering theories that affect the use of energy explained to them in as simple a form as possible.

Energy originates with the sun and can be converted from one form to another. The efficiency with which energy is converted results in operational savings. Electrical energy can be converted to illumination and to mechanical energy such as that used to power motors. Chemical energy (fuel) can be converted to heat.

Successful maintenance programs (which include energy) and the effective management of the consumption and cost of energy need the commitment, support, participation, involvement, and dedication of every one on construction and building management teams; from the building owner or the chief executive officer of a large company to the on-site operator of an individual building. Operations control of the electrical-mechanical equipment by knowledgeable on-site staff and the availability of knowledgeable consulting services specialists to support management are two keys to success. In this program, each building becomes the management system and individual profit center. Using this management concept and organizing information requirements to fit the plan are additional keys to success.

Many buildings prior to the energy crunch—and too many since then—were built without considering the cost of maintenance or energy. Because of this it is important that the information systems used are such that management can develop records that will show a building's present cost and energy consumption base. Management must know the present status of each building to measure realistically the future success of the program.

All built-in problems can easily be documented using the information system suggested in this book. Information about the present condition of each building is also essential and is gathered using the inspection procedures described and the knowledge of structural and electrical-mechanical specialists that must be made available to support management. It may be necessary to develop in-house specialists, or they may be sought from outside sources.

Because each building is its own business unit, all the information gathered should be reported for individual buildings. The things that need to be done can be priced and ranked, properly budgeted, then carried out. What is important is to be able to do whatever will give the building the highest return on investment while, at the same time, having a minimal impact on the profit for the building. The program we explain in this book will allow managers to do that.

Regardless of how efficiently a building is constructed, it cannot operate effectively without the full cooperation and understanding of the on-site operating staff. If anyone, the manager, the on-site operator, or the support-service technician, does not understand or accept the mode of operation, he or she, can literally cause the program to fail.

8.3 A PLANNED MAINTENANCE AND ENERGY MANAGEMENT PROGRAM

Objective

A successful planned maintenance and energy management program should reduce the cost of maintenance and operations to its lowest possible level without making the occupants of the buildings feel uncomfortable and without downgrading the structure or the electrical-mechanical equipment. Maintenance and operations expenses include building additions or replacements;

equipment additions or replacements; repair and maintenance expenses; the salaries of the on-site staff; and the cost of fuel, electricity, and water. The account classifications and budget-builder working papers illustrated in Chapter 5 give the breakdown of all of the maintenance and operations expense classifications.

Purpose of the Plan of Action

1. To define the maintenance and energy management accountabilities of people on the management team.
2. To set objectives and a means of monitoring and measuring the results of the program.

Goal of the Program

1. To reduce the cost of maintenance and the consumption of energy to its lowest possible level without making the building occupants feel uncomfortable.
2. To continue the program until there are no further opportunities to save money.

OBJECTIVE OF THE PROGRAM

1. To double the life of components that wear out and need replacement.
2. To reduce the cost of corrective maintenance.
3. To identify everything that would hinder management's achievement of the purpose of the program by regularly inspecting the buildings and arranging for support-service specialists to investigate, report, and supervise the correction of more serious problems.
4. To correct any deficiencies as soon as they are discovered unless the cost to correct them exceeds an amount predetermined by the building owner.
5. To keep written records of all deficiencies or retrofit measures on the renovation proposal forms (see Figures 5.38 and 5.39) and to value analyze and establish priorities for those that would cost more than the amount predetermined by the owner.
6. To upgrade the knowledge of everyone on the management team so that he or she will be more qualified to make the right decisions about the correction of deficiencies and the feasibility of retrofit measures and to otherwise contribute to assure the success of the program.
7. To develop building profiles and energy audits on the forms developed for this purpose for each building in the management portfolio or for any buildings being purchased or newly developed and built.

8. To develop and use a system of recordkeeping on the forms developed for this purpose (see Figures 5.1 to 5.35).

Scope of the Plan of Action

To assure the success of the program, it is necessary to identify all the maintenance requirements for each building in the management portfolio. The maintenance requirements include prevention, correction, repair, redesign, retrofitting, or renovation. Everything is then ranked and built into the budgets for the year during which the work is expected to be completed.

All possible energy-related measures, renovations, and retrofits are listed separately and form an addendum to this plan. To assure the success of this program, managers, on-site operating staff, support-service specialists, and outside contractors should be qualified to carry out effectively the maintenance services functional accountabilities identified on each of their charters of accountability and explained in Chapter 6.

8.4 SUPPORT-SERVICE SPECIALISTS

In general, the design, construction, and building management industry does not have the support-service specialists that it needs to help it make the right decisions. Studies have shown that many decisions made by developers, designers, builders, owners, managers, operators, and people who provide consulting and support services are made by gut feel, conventional wisdom, or ignorance. Specialized consulting and support services fall into several clearly defined areas of expertise that are discussed in Chapter 1. Until people are trained to provide this service to managers, the decision-making process will not be what it should be, problems will continually be built into new buildings, and management will continue to have problems dealing with them.

Specialists are needed to develop master action plans such as outlined in Chapter 4. Maintenance activities that are recurring, even if they occur every other year, must be included in each building's plan and budgets each year, or in the year that they are to be carried out, and treated differently than renovations or retrofits. Specialists identify things that require redesigning, renovating, or retrofitting; they recommend the solutions to these major problem-solving expenditures, develop specifications, tender the work, and monitor the job as it is being done. Traditionally building managers take on this responsibility without having the knowledge or the skills needed to assure the best value for the money being spent. In many cases, they abdicate their responsibility by relying on the contractor to be the specialist.

This book clearly explains what these responsibilities should be and the kinds of specialists that are required. People with this knowledge and expertise saved Cadillac Fairview over $5 million in 1981 (see the details in Chapter 12).

The Purpose of the Support-Service Specialist

- To provide specialized housekeeping, groundskeeping, structural, or electrical-mechanical support services to owners or managers of buildings.
- To help owners, managers, and operators develop maintenance and energy management programs for buildings.
- To help owners, managers, and operators prepare their annual budget projections. This includes the planning of a suitable maintenance and energy management program for each building being managed, that would include prevention; correction; redesign; retrofitting; renovation; repair and maintenance; on-site staff salaries; the consumption and cost of fuel, electricity, and water.
- To help owners and managers make decisions by providing consulting services when they are considering the purchase or development of a new project or need problems assessed and recommendations for solving them.
- To assist the owner or manager in taking over a new building.
- To help owners or managers develop building profiles and energy audits for the buildings being managed.
- To provide as requested, but at least on an annual basis, hands-on, written inspections of buildings for owners or managers.
- To help owners or managers upgrade the knowledge of their on-site staffs.
- To provide emergency services to their clients.
- To help owners or managers provide safety, security, comfort, ambience, and a sense of well-being for the occupants of the buildings being managed.

8.5 MEASURES TO BE CONSIDERED

There are numerous opportunities in buildings for reducing the cost of repairs and maintenance, fuel, electricity, and water. In many cases, these reductions can be achieved through simple practical actions carried out by the on-site staff, consultants, or support-service specialists. To take advantage of these opportunities to save, the people involved need the right information, and they need to know what they are doing.

All the maintenance and energy-saving measures that are listed in the following pages and also detailed with the budget-builder working papers will, if implemented, substantially cut a building's operational costs and add to a building's profits. Before you implement these measures, there are a few things that must be kept in mind:

1. All the measures will not apply to all buildings. Tailor the measures to the identified needs of each building. Remember that each building should be considered as its own business unit, and as such, it competes only against itself.

2. Each building must be fine-tuned to assure that it is operating in its as-built condition before making any changes. That means that all no-cost measures must be initiated and that the operating costs are such that there are no more opportunities to save available before spending money for retrofit measures.

3. Average the previous three years' maintenance and operations expenses by using the account classifications illustrated in Figures 5.1 to 5.5 and Figures 5.32 to 5.35 as a way of organizing the information.

4. All measures that require an outlay of cash must be costed and ranked so that the one having the greatest saving potential with the least cost would be commenced first. The others would then be implemented in a logical sequence.

5. All opportunities to save that are missed become immediate losses and could make the difference between a profit and loss for a building. These measures then become a matter of utmost urgency.

The measures that follow are organized in such a way that you can easily review them. They are all classified by the various building services and electrical-mechanical systems. The measures should be assessed and classified into either recurring or nonrecurring categories. It will be necessary to determine how often the recurring activities are done, who will do them, and how much they cost. This information is then entered on the budget-builder working paper (see Figures 5.6 to 5.31) for each building. If the work is being done by the on-site staff, it will have to be included in their schedule of duties. If the work is being done by a contractor, specifications will need to be developed, and contracts, detailing what is expected, signed with them.

If the measure is classified as a renovation, retrofit, or nonrecurring activity, then the renovation proposal procedure outlined in Chapter 5 will need to be followed.

Plumbing and Drainage Systems

- Clean sanitary drains and catch basins.
- Service domestic hot-water storage tanks.
- Service valves as required.
- Service pumps as required.
- Open, close, and service swimming pools, fountains, and cooling towers.
- Lower water pressure.

- Water grounds after sunset.
- Install pool covers on swimming pools.
- Insulate exposed pipework.
- Install high-efficiency boilers.

Heating Systems

- Service and calibrate outdoor resets and blend-valve controllers.
- Replace old controllers with solid-state or microprocessor-based central system controls.
- Use a central control system.
- Service the burners and monitor their efficiency on a regular basis.
- Inspect and service heating boilers on both the fire side and the water side.
- Clean heat exchangers on atmospheric heaters.
- Inspect and service hot-air furnaces.
- Add and monitor water treatment to the heating systems, the cooling tower, whirlpools, swimming pools, and decorative fountains.
- Inspect and top up, if necessary, the glycol in fresh-air heaters and ramp heating.
- Inspect and service all liquid-to-liquid heat exchangers to assure that they are not plugged and are operating efficiently.
- Inspect and service direct domestic hot-water heaters.
- Inspect and service pumps and valves.
- Install timers on all incinerator burners.
- Install an hour counter on electrically heated snow-melting areas. Assure that the light signal and the switch are located where they can be monitored and shut off when not needed.
- Reduce temperatures for heating garages and fresh-air supply to the buildings. Turn them off completely when the weather warrants.
- Clear obstructions from make-up supply air openings.
- Install a thermostat to shut down the garage heat during mild weather.
- Lower the temperature of the domestic hot water to 120°F, and set back the temperature even lower during low-use periods.
- Blank off unnecessary heaters.
- Tune up apartment corridor air-supply heaters and add electric ignition for the gas burner instead of a pilot light.
- Install snow-sensing control system on heated ramps.
- If feasible, cover heated ramps and turn off the heat.

- Add in-suite thermostatic control valves, especially on the sunny side of a building without blend valves and outdoor reset or on/off sensors.
- Install sequence controllers on multiple boilers and heaters. Isolate off-line boilers.
- Change heating system zoning.

Cooling Systems

- Fully maintain and service chillers. Once a week, rotate oil filter handle, operate purge as required, and check purge drum for water. Quarterly, check oil in purge compressor, oil purge compressor motor, check purge belt tension, and clean all water strainers.
- Regularly inspect and service cooling towers, and add and monitor water treatment.
- Individual or fan-coil units must be regularly serviced by either in-house or outside service technicians.
- Service all pumps, valves, and motors on a regular basis.
- Add zone-demand reset to multizone and dual-duct systems.
- Convert multizone and dual-duct systems to variable-volume systems.
- Isolate off-line chillers.
- Use central control system.
- Shut down completely during unoccupied periods.
- Reduce the maximum cooling load as much as possible.
- Keep the condenser water and evaporator water tubes clean by adequate water treatment, periodic observation, and periodic cleaning.
- Reset the chilled water temperature as the total heat content (enthalpy) of the outdoor air rises.

Electrical Services

- Where feasible, convert indoor fixtures from incandescents to fluorescents and outdoor fixtures to high-pressure sodium-vapor.
- Use a single bulb of higher wattage rather than several low-watt bulbs: Two 60-watt bulbs produce less light than one 100-watt bulb, although they consume about 20 percent more energy.
- Use lampshades that are wide at both ends.
- When buying appliances, compare wattage consumption. Buy the appliance that consumes less power.
- The waste of energy because an appliance cannot function efficiently is obvious. Dust and dirt in controls, valves, pumps, motor bearings, and

fans, aside from the waste of energy, could lead to failures that are costly to repair. Keep electrical-mechanical equipment and equipment rooms clean.

- Add photocells to outdoor lighting and in any indoor area that is windowed.
- Where indoor lighting is on the same circuit as the outdoor lighting, separate them.
- Adjust timer clocks as required and turn off unnecessary lights.
- Adjust lighting to a reasonable level. Do not use bulbs with wattage higher than necessary. Regularly clean walls, ceilings, bulbs, and fixtures to ensure maximum reflection.
- Use white paint for the ceilings and walls of underground garages and equipment rooms.
- Arrange lighting so that it can be group relamped.
- Clean fixtures and lamps on a regular basis.
- If feasible, install programmable lighting.
- Put reminders on switches that should be turned off manually. If necessary, use switches with pilot lights for out-of-the-way lights or equipment that may be forgotten.
- Fully maintain elevators and escalators.
- Investigate peak shedding, load cycling, and power-factor improvement as possible methods of reducing the cost of electricity. Your local utility company bill will reveal any penalties that you are paying for low-power factor situations.
- Use a "total energy balance" approach for maximum energy utilization and savings rather than concentrating on a single area.
- Assure that the staff and the tenants understand conservation.

Fire-Control Systems

- Test and service alarms, voice communication, and standby batteries.
- Test and service standby power generator.

Structure

- Inspect and repair roofs (inverted roofs are the most energy efficient).
- Inspect and repair brickwork.
- Inspect and repair or replace caulking.
- Inspect and repair structural concrete.
- Inspect and repair sidewalks and asphalt paving.

- Standardize locks, keys, and building hardware and assure that they are maintained.
- Provide painting and decorating services when required.
- Service windows and doors when required.
- Retrofit or replace windows.
- Insulate exposed floors.
- Seal against infiltration.

8.6 QUICK-FIX MEASURES

There are several easily accomplished ways in which owners and managers can reduce the consumption of energy in their buildings by

- Reducing lighting levels
- Stopping equipment
- Reducing make-up air
- Minimizing exhausting of air
- Insulating where feasible
- Sealing cracks
- Adjusting controls
- Reducing the temperature of domestic hot water
- Reducing the use of water
- Reviewing maintenance activities and initiating a more effective program
- Adjusting the outdoor reset control so that it supplies the right blend of heating water to the building

8.7 BUILDING OPERATOR'S RESPONSIBILITIES

All maintenance and energy-related activities are initiated by the owner or manager and performed by either the on-site operating staff, an in-house support service, or an outside contractor. In addition to the energy-related responsibilities listed separately, the building operator is responsible for documenting all tenant maintenance requests, for following them up, and for correcting problems, if possible, or reporting the problem to the owner or manager, who would call in the contractor.

The operator must also respond to all emergencies—fire, flood, lack of heat, power failure, and other such problems that could be considered emergencies—and must be aware of all valves and controls and their purposes so that they can be activated in the event of an emergency.

The building operator should be qualified to carry out the following maintenance and energy-related functions:

- Carry out daily "look, listen, and touch" inspections.
- Record data on operating logs at the same time every day.
- Report all abnormal conditions as soon as they are noticed.
- Keep electrical-mechanical equipment clean of dirt, dust, rust, and other contaminants. Paint and color-code them.
- Carry out the lubrication programs recommended by manufacturers.
- Assure that all time clocks are properly set to conform with the rising and setting sun.
- Keep temperature control settings as directed. Controllers should not be changed without the approval of the owner or manager.
- Keep belts, sheaves, and drives operating properly. Use the right size belts and assure that they are properly aligned and replaced at the first sign of slippage or cracking.
- Regularly check the condition of bearings, and at the first sign of any unusual noise notify the owner or manager so that they can be serviced.
- Change filters as required.
- Monitor boiler and burner efficiency by checking the readings recorded on the operating logs each day, immediately report anything that is not normal; chart the operations by plotting them on a heating performance graph on a daily basis.
- Monitor cooling system efficiency by checking the readings recorded on operating logs every day. Immediately report anything that is not normal.
- Report all leaks in heating, cooling, or plumbing systems immediately.
- Keep lighting intensities at proper levels. Clean fixtures when relamping.
- Check the exterior of the building for worn or broken weatherstripping. Arrange for replacement as soon as wear is noticed.
- Check all doors and door closers to assure that they are operating correctly. Immediately report any problems to the owner or manager.
- To assure that the electrical-mechanical systems are operating as designed, the operators should understand them. In this regard operators should seek training and upgrading from the owner or manager.
- Assure that all air vents are operating properly and that there is no problem with air locks in the heating system.

The building operator should carry out the following maintenance and energy-related tasks in each apartment unit at least once a year.

- Make sure that the heating baseboard convectors are not blocked or covered with dust.
- Check all shut-off valves, especially hot-water valves, to assure that they are not leaking.
- Replace all tap washers and O rings in all the faucets in the suite.
- Check all washer seats and replace them if they are damaged.
- Replace swing-spout O rings, as leaks in them are the major cause of countertop deterioration, and loss of the hot water wastes energy.
- Water closet tanks should be inspected for float adjustment, water level. and defective ball and flapper valves.
- Clean shower heads and aerators.
- Check bathroom wall tiles for hairline cracks, soggy grout, or faulty caulking. A straightened paper clip is ideal for probing for signs of softening resulting from water penetration.

All energy retrofit measures must be assessed on their potential return on investment and ranked. All recurring measures must be planned, organized, assigned, directed, and monitored before you spend any money on retrofits. Records must be kept of the results of the program. Only when there are no further opportunities to reduce the costs with the existing conditions should you consider investing in a retrofit or renovation. All potential retrofits must also be ranked, and the one showing the highest return on investment should be commenced first. Do not be swayed by a salesperson promising miracle results. Stick to your plan!

How Energy Is Used in Buildings

9.1 HEAT AND HEAT TRANSMISSION

The Flow of Heat

Heat can be transferred to other substances, such as air or water, but cannot be destroyed. To designate a rate of flow, the *British thermal unit* (Btu) is used. This term indicates the amount of heat that flows from one substance to another in one hour.

Btu Factors

Although the illustrations used here are mostly for natural gas, management should also be aware of the Btu factors for electricity and coal. Management may want to know the number of Btu's per hour (Btu/hr) a building would need to offset its heat loss at any particular time. It is for this reason that this information is included. By using records of operation and heating performance graphs illustrated in Chapter 10 to keep constant control of each building's pulse, heartbeat, and blood pressure, it should not be necessary to use these figures to make comparisons with other buildings. Buildings should not be competing with other buildings, nor should the results of their energy savings be compared—not even buildings such as those referred to in Chapter 12, which appear to be identical.

The following list shows the Btu output of various fuels:

1 gal residential #2 fuel oil = 168,000 Btu
1 gal light industrial #4 fuel oil = 173,000 Btu
1 gal medium industrial #5 fuel oil = 180,000 Btu
1 gal medium industrial #6 fuel oil (less than 1% sulfur) = 180,000 Btu
1 gal medium industrial #6 fuel oil (maximum 2% sulfur) = 182,000 Btu
100 cu ft natural gas (1 therm) = 100,000 Btu
1,000 cu ft natural gas (1 MCF) = 1,030,000 Btu
1 kWh electricity = 3,412 Btu
1 ton coal = 25,200,000 Btu
1 ton refrigeration = 12,000 Btu/hr
Chilled water—1 Btu/lb/°F

Degree-Days

To offset weather variables from one year to another when estimating fuel and power consumption, the United States government, in 1936, began using a *degree-day* calculation. A degree-day is the number of degrees the mean daily outdoor temperature is below 65°F, or 18°C. On a day when the mean temperature is 40°, the degree-day for that day is 25. This formula was determined by using a residential single-family house, not a building; however, if everyone uses the same degree-day base, we are, in effect, comparing "apples with apples."

Record-keeping forms used to monitor operational effectiveness, and utility consumption and cost-tracking forms give management month-to-month degree-day information as well as the annual total. These records usually show that the weather seems to have a fairly regular up and down cycle from year to year. Degree-day figures are available from your local weather bureau either by phone or by reports that are issued on a regular basis and to which management can subscribe.

9.2 THERMAL CHARACTERISTICS OF A BUILDING

Many people believe that it is necessary to prepare an energy audit before you can develop an energy management program. Cadillac Development was able to develop a very successful program without using information gathered in an energy audit. Because of the general belief that this is necessary and because it is never a bad idea to have information about a building, some basic ideas about energy audits are included here. Energy goals for each building can be developed from these records. To establish a meaningful energy consumption base, it is a good idea to average the consumption per degree-day for the previous three years. Your energy goal should be to reduce these figures to the lowest possible level from those averages.

Energy audits allow building owners and managers to calculate the potential for saving energy in their buildings. They also indicate the areas in which management is most likely to save energy. The examples included here are for multiple-unit apartment buildings with interior corridors. This means that other buildings should use different statistics and calculations for their energy audits.

9.3 PREVIOUS YEARS' RECORDS

The most important thing for management to do is to gather the fuel, electricity, and water bills for the past 36 months for each building in the portfolio. Using the monthly cost and consumption forms discussed in Chapter 5, record the information. Although you have 36 months of billing, the first bill is used only to determine accurately the number of days that were included on the first bill. The forms will have only 12 months of information, and those 12 months do not necessarily have to be from January to December. You may wish to match your records to the company year end or to the heating and cooling season. The important thing is that you average the consumption and cost of fuel, electricity, and water from a previous 36-month period, if possible, so that you have an accurate record of the building's performance before you start the program.

Current Maintenance and Operating Costs

As with energy bills, it is important that the records you use for repair and maintenance expenses are also averaged for the previous years and that they are available for each building in your management portfolio. The account classifications discussed in Chapter 5 are recommended as a format for organizing the information. If you find it difficult to break down your previous information into the account classifications recommended, you will have to develop a budget by using these forms and forget about the past. Once all the maintenance and energy programs are built into the budgets and carried out for a few years, you will find that there will be a continuity of maintenance that will repeat itself each year. Knowing how to "do the right things right," establishing a plan of action such as explained in Chapter 2, building the cost of the program into your budgets, and then carrying out the program on a regular year-to-year basis is the secret to success.

9.4 SETTING MAINTENANCE AND ENERGY TARGETS

Maintenance and energy targets are best established by starting with targets based on past experiences. Develop the program by keeping in mind that the objective is to reduce the cost of maintenance, on-site staff salaries, and the cost and consumption of fuel, electricity, and water to its lowest possible level without downgrading the structure, the equipment, the ambience, or the comfort and well-being of the occupants of the buildings.

Initially Cadillac Fairview's program concentrated on reducing the cost of fuel. This meant that the first priority was to clear up the corrosion problem in the heating systems and to assure that the domestic water heating, storage, and delivery system was operating as efficiently as possible.

The first task was to fine-tune the outdoor reset controller and assure that the valves throughout each building were operating properly. Heating performance graphs (an example of which is shown in Chapter 10) indicated on a day-by-day basis that the fuel was being used in accordance with the design criteria established by the engineer who designed the system. This fact alone accounted for savings, but Cadillac found that it could operate much below these design criteria figures for much of the heating or cooling seasons and so encouraged operators to reduce the temperatures even further without receiving any complaints from the tenants.

It is important that building owners, managers, and support-service technicians understand heat loss and heat gain and other terms that are generally used when people try to sell you energy-saving plans or equipment. It is difficult to make intelligent value analysis decisions about them without having a basic knowledge of records, calculations, and procedures related to a building's maintenance and operations expenses and energy use.

Energy Use in Buildings

The energy used varies greatly among residential, commercial, industrial, and institutional buildings. A residential building or hospital is in use virtually 24 hours per day, 365 days a year; a school or office building is in use only part of the day. In these buildings, equipment can be turned off when not in use, but in hospitals or apartment buildings, it is more difficult to shut things down.

One factor that affects the rate at which a structure loses heat is its construction. This includes not only the material used but also the air leakage between the inside of the structure and the outdoors. Another important factor affecting heat loss rates is the difference between indoor and outdoor temperature. An additional factor in heat loss is the wind velocity. For most locations, designers consider a 15 mph wind a suitable allowance for wind velocity.

There are several components that affect the energy consumed by a building. Each of them can be classified as being either weather sensitive or occupant sensitive. The weather-sensitive components are affected by the outside temperature, the internal heat gained, and the heat lost from the building. The occupant-sensitive components are those that are related to occupant use and must be replenished.

Many Buildings Are Overdesigned

Location of buildings, either within a city or in different parts of the country, have a great effect on the amount of energy that is required to heat or cool them. Temperatures could vary between 30° and 70°F for 75 percent of the time, and therefore 75 percent of a building's energy use and waste would take place in that period.

It is not unusual for engineers to design for extreme weather for an entire season, when either the heating or cooling system is used, rather than for the more moderate temperatures that prevail 75 percent of the time. To save energy it is important to have control over the inside comfort temperature, irrespective of the outside temperature during that time.

A substantial portion of the energy waste associated with boilers and chillers is due to part-load performance. Heating and air-conditioning systems operate at less than full load for a considerable time during an annual cycle. Since the energy crunch, the trend has been to smaller progressive-use equipment with controls for staging start-up when required, rather than continuously running larger equipment when it is not needed. Units can thus be shut down when they are not required. In this situation the equipment would more likely operate at its rated capacity and show greater savings.

Figure 9.1 illustrates in chart form the various energy-use patterns in buildings. It should be understood that these patterns would vary in commercial, residential, industrial, or institutional buildings. Each building should have its own energy-use pattern, and the energy used would have to be supported by individual meter readings in each building.

Insulation

Well-insulated buildings with low internal heat gain have a higher potential for saving energy. The opposite is true for buildings with a high internal heat gain. It is also true that well-insulated buildings lack heat gain from the outside. Engineers sometimes explain this by saying, "what is good for the heat is good for the cold."

Because of internal heat gain, the insulation that is installed to keep the heat out when it is 90° or 100°F outside also keeps the internally generated

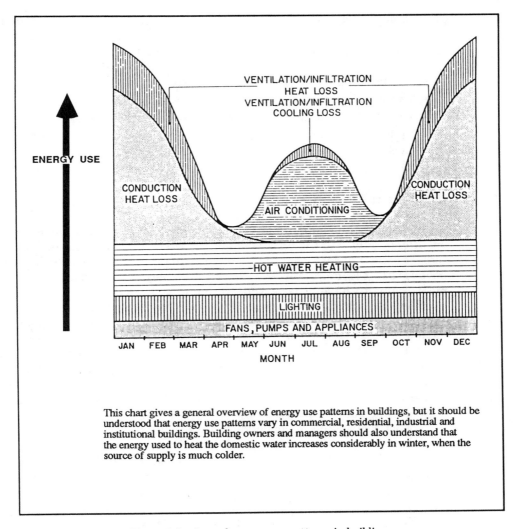

This chart gives a general overview of energy use patterns in buildings, but it should be understood that energy use patterns vary in commercial, residential, industrial and institutional buildings. Building owners and managers should also understand that the energy used to heat the domestic water increases considerably in winter, when the source of supply is much colder.

Figure 9.1   Annual energy-use patterns in buildings.

heat from leaking out when it is 50° or 60°F outside. If that internally generated heat cannot leak out of the building, it will have to be removed using mechanical energy, with either fan energy or air conditioning energy.

To properly monitor and control energy use in buildings it is necessary to separate the weather-sensitive and the non–weather-sensitive energy consumption if management wants to control their use. Controlling the relationship between the outside and inside temperature is essential to controlling the weather-sensitive energy use. Cutting down the use of lighting, fans, pumps, appliances, and domestic hot water is essential to the control of the occupant, or non–weather-sensitive, energy use. The major structural and electrical-mechanical components can be classified as follows:

- The building envelope (weather sensitive)
- The ventilation system (weather and occupant sensitive)
- The electrical-mechanical equipment (weather sensitive)
- Lighting, appliances, and other user-related components (occupant sensitive)
- Heating the domestic water (occupant and weather sensitive)

Heat Loss and Heat Gain

The consulting and support-service specialists, not the owner, manager, or the on-site operator, are the ones who are expected to understand technical matters. It is not our intention to try to make you into an expert; we do, however, believe that it is important for everyone on construction and building management teams to have a basic understanding of heat loss and heat gain, heat transfer, British thermal units (Btu's), degree-days, comfort, flow of heat, structure, and electrical-mechanical systems; and to recognize components and have a basic knowledge of how the electrical-mechanical systems work.

During the heating season, extreme temperatures are of short duration, occur late at night, and have minimal impact on occupant comfort. On the other hand, during the cooling season, extreme outdoor temperatures span longer periods of time. Because they occur during the working day, they have a greater impact on occupant comfort.

Most surfaces used in a building are a composite of several materials. The rate at which heat flows through this combination of materials is called the *U value*, or overall coefficient of heat transfer. The resistance to heat loss, through roofs, walls, windows, and doors is referred to as an *R value* (see Figure 9.2). The more energy we lose, the more we need to replace the loss. This energy is measured in Btu's.

The conduction heat loss in Btu's for walls, windows, ceilings, doors, and floors exposed to outdoor temperatures is the product of the design temperature difference times the U factor times the area of each building component. Heat loss is shown mathematically as follows:

$$H = U \times A \times (t_i - t_o)$$

where

H = heat loss
A = area of surface
t_i = inside temperature
t_o = outside temperature

"R" VALUES OF ROOFS & WALLS	°F	°C
Air Space 1/2"	0.91	0.51
Air Space 1"	1.00	0.56
Air Space 2"	1.02	0.57
Ceiling Space	0.93	0.52
Common Brick	0.80	0.44
Concrete Block 4"	0.71	0.39
Concrete Block 8"	1.11	0.62
Exterior Air Film	0.17	0.29
Extruded Polystyrene 1"	5.00	2.78
Extruded Polystyrene 2"	10.00	5.56
Face Brick	0.44	0.24
Fibreboard 1"	3.00	1.67
Fibreboard 2"	6.00	3.33
Furring 1"	0.94	0.52
Gypsum Board 3/8"	0.32	0.17
Gypsum Board 1/2"	0.45	0.25
Interior Air Film	0.68	0.38
Mortar 1"	0.20	0.11

"R" VALUES OF ROOFS & WALLS	°F	°C
Plaster 3/4"	0.15	0.08
Plaster 1/2"	0.13	0.07
Poured Concrete 4"	0.32	0.17
Poured Concrete 8"	0.64	0.36
Reflective Air Space	1.83	1.02
Roof Built-up	0.33	0.18
Roof Inverted	0.33	0.18
Vapor Barrier	0.06	0.03
"U" VALUE OF WINDOWS		
SINGLE GLAZED		
Steel Sash	1.13	2.03
Aluminium Sash	1.24	2.23
Balcony Doors - Aluminium	1.24	2.23
DOUBLE GLAZED		
Steel Sash	0.73	1.31
Aluminium Sash	0.79	1.42
Wood	0.64	1.15
Storm Doors	0.39	0.70

The resistance to heat loss ("R" value) of building materials measures heat flow resistance in terms of how effective it is for the thickness being used and is measured in degrees. The more effective the material, the higher the "R" value. Heat flow from the interior of the building (referred to as the "U" value) to the cooler exterior is determined by multiplying the heat flow characteristics of a given assembly of materials by the area of the material involved ("A") by the difference between the inside temperature desired and the average low temperature on the outside of the structure.

• To calculate the "U" values divide 1 by the "R" value.
• Heat loss and heat gain is measured in Btu's per hour (Btuh).
• Heat loss is shown mathematically as U x A x (Temperature inside - temperature outside) = Btuh.
• Heat gain during the summer is shown as U x A x (Temperature outside - temperature inside) = Btuh.

Figure 9.2 The resistance to heat loss ("R" value) of various building components (From Mel A. Shear, *Handbook of Building Maintenance Management*, © 1983, p. 573–75 [A Reston Publication]. Adapted by permission of Prentice-Hall, Inc., Englewood Cliffs, New Jersey).

Heat gain is shown mathematically as follows:

$$H = U \times A \times (t_o - t_i)$$

Figures 9.3, 9.4, and 9.5 can be used as a guide to help you calculate heat loss and heat gain in existing buildings by measuring lengths, widths, and heights if the as-built plans are not available.

So far, we have considered the ways in which a building loses heat by conduction or transmission of the heat through the outside shell of the structure. A building can also lose heat by having cold outside air enter and displace warm air. When this leakage occurs through cracks and is not under control, it is called *infiltration*. When air is brought in or exhausted through openings designed for this purpose—usually by controlled methods—it is called *ventilation*.

Infiltration occurs mainly around windows, doors, frames, and between foundation walls and sill plates. In a double-hung home window, air might leak in at 20 cubic feet per hour per foot of crack if the wind is blowing at 15 miles per hour.

Many energy-management programs use building energy audits to determine the thermal characteristics of a building so that they can accurately measure the heat loss and heat gain and the amount of energy required to offset them (Figures 9.6 and 9.7). It is very difficult for the average owner or manager of a building to gather, interpret, and use this information. In many cases the information, if misunderstood or not gathered correctly, could lead to the wrong assumptions.

As an example, most people think that an all-glass high-rise office building is energy inefficient. In fact, the opposite may be true because the internally generated heat from equipment and people is allowed to leak out through the glass, thus lowering the air-conditioning load.

In Cadillac's energy-management program, we used the information gathered on the operational logs to record the actual operation of the building at the time the program was started. This information was recorded on heating performance graphs along with the daily temperature at the building. We used the average heating-water-supply design temperatures used by our design engineers as a base from which to monitor the program.

At first we operated the equipment according to the norm established by the design engineers: When the temperature of the supply water was plotted on the graph, it matched the line established by the outside temperature. Then the outdoor reset control was adjusted down until occupants of the building complained (several tenants had been asked to report on the comfort levels in their apartments). Cadillac found that it could operate the building at 10° to 15° below the average criteria used by the design engineers when they designed the building and not receive complaints from the tenants.

Heating complaints were recorded on a specially designed heating maintenance request form (Figure 4.4) and followed up by the on-site operator; if

Most surfaces used in buildings are composites of several materials. The rate at which heat flows through this combination of materials is called the "U" value, or overall coefficient of heat transfer. The resistance to heat loss through roofs, walls, windows, doors, etc., is referred to as the "R" value.

The more energy we lose from a building the more we need to replace the loss. Energy is measured in British Thermal Units (Btus).

To determine the energy requirements for heating or cooling the space in a building, it is necessary to do an analysis of the building's skin that includes: • walls • roofs • exposed floors • glazing • exterior doors (the glazing includes the window frames and also the exterior doors). This illustration shows how to measure a building for this purpose.

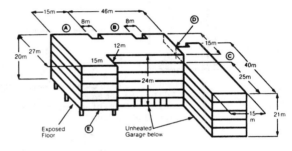

EXPOSED FLOORS	
TO OUTSIDE	sq.m.
27m x 15m	405
TO HEATED GARAGE	
46m x 15m - (2x1x8)	674
40m x 15m - 1 x 1 x 8)	592
TOTAL EXPOSED FLOORS	**1266**

WALLS		GLASS		ROOF	
AREA SIZE	sq.m.	%	sq.m.	AREA SIZE	sq.m.
a (12m + 15m + 27m + 15m + 1) x 20m	1400	15	210	27m x 15m	405
b (46m + [3 x 1m] + 46 x 24m	2280	20	465	46m x 15m - (2 x 1m x 8m)	674
c (15m + [2 x 1m] + 40 + 15 + 25) x 21	2058	20	412	40m x 15m - (1 x 1m x 8m)	592
d (15m x 3m)	45	0			
e (15m x 4m)	60	0			
TOTAL WALL AREA	**5843**	**TOTAL**	**1087**	**TOTAL ROOF AREA**	**1671**
LESS THE GLASS AREA	1078				
NET WALL AREA	**4765**				

Figure 9.3   How to measure a building's wall and roof areas.

To calculate the heat loss for a building, it is necessary to measure the total enclosed floor area of the building. This would include all heated space except the elevator penthouse, storage and locker rooms, garage area, boiler, fan and other electrical and mechanical rooms.

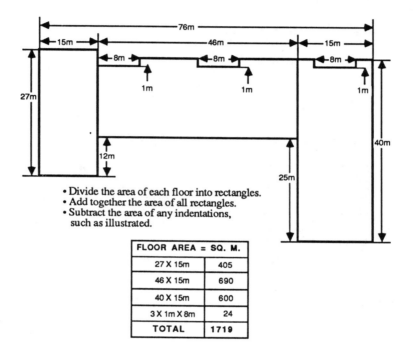

• Divide the area of each floor into rectangles.
• Add together the area of all rectangles.
• Subtract the area of any indentations, such as illustrated.

FLOOR AREA = SQ. M.	
27 X 15m	405
46 X 15m	690
40 X 15m	600
3 X 1m X 8m	24
TOTAL	**1719**

Calculations can be made in either feet and square feet or meters and square meters. If available, use the as-built drawings for measurements. If not, then you will have to actually measure each area. Multiply the calculations for each floor by the number of similar floors. Repeat the calculations for dissimilar floors.

• 1 meter = 3.28 feet • 1 square meter = 10,764 square feet

Figure 9.4   How to measure a building's floor area.

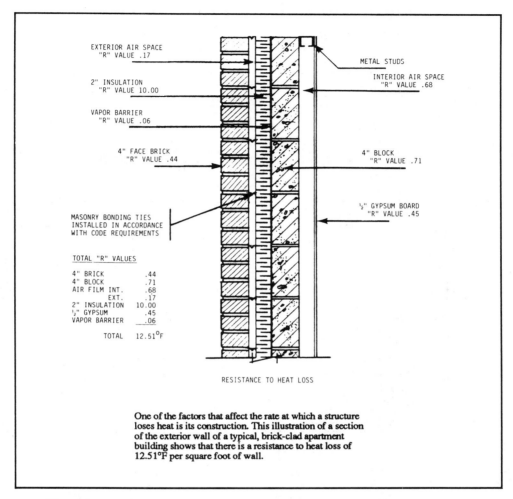

One of the factors that affect the rate at which a structure loses heat is its construction. This illustration of a section of the exterior wall of a typical, brick-clad apartment building shows that there is a resistance to heat loss of 12.51°F per square foot of wall.

Figure 9.5   A typical exterior brick-and-block wall cross section (From Mel A. Shear, *Handbook of Building Maintenance Management,* © 1983, p. 572 [A Reston Publication]. Adapted by permission of Prentice-Hall, Inc., Englewood Cliffs, New Jersey).

not resolved by the operator, the problem was turned over to an electrical-mechanical support-service specialist who usually corrected the problem. It is important to determine whether the problem is confined to an individual unit or whether it is common to the entire building. The form was also designed as a teaching tool. The operator followed a logical sequence of elimination in answering each of the questions in the form. The first "no" answer usually uncovered the problem. It is interesting to know that most of the complaints received were because people were uncomfortably hot, not cold.

Building Number	Building Name				
Building Address					
Date Built	Number of Suites Square Footage			Occupant Mix	

	1 * x	2 =	3	4 **	5 ***
Structural Areas	Sq.Ft. or Sq. Mtrs.	"R" Values	Total "R" Values	"U" Values	Btus/Day Heat Loss
Bearing Walls					
Outside Walls					
Outside Doors					
Glazing - Single or Double - Inc. Frames					
Exposed Floors					
Exposed Concrete					
Roof					
Ventilation	Supply & Exhaust (Heated & Unheated) Garage-Corridor-Suite- 1.95 Btuh/cfm				
			Total Btuh/Day Heat Loss		
Total Btuh/Day Heat Loss —————————— = 1,030,000 Btuh	The Total MCF/Day Fuel Required to Offset the Heat Loss				

    *   To convert square feet to square meters, multiply by 0.093.
  **   To convert the "R" values to "U" values, divide 1 by the "R" values.
***   To calculate the Btus per day, multiply the "U" values by 24.

"R" value is the term used to explain the resistance to heat loss through
roofs, walls, and doors. Most surfaces used in buildings are a composite
of several materials. The rate at which heat flows through this combination
of materials is called the "U" value, or overall coefficient of heat transfer.
"R" and "U" values for various materials are shown in Figure 9.2.

Figure 9.6 A form that can be used to calculate a building's daily fuel requirement
(From Mel A. Shear, *Handbook of Building Maintenance Management*, © 1983, p. 576
[A Reston Publication]. Adapted by permission of Prentice-Hall, Inc., Englewood Cliffs,
New Jersey).

A Do-It-Yourself Energy Audit

Building No.		Building Name						
Building Address			Township					
No. of Suites			Glazing					

Column 1 X 2 = 3 − 4 = 5 X 6 = 7 Plus or 8 = 9
Degree-Days   Minus

Year / Month	Inside Comfort Temp. °F	No. of Bill Reading Days	Inside Monthly Comfort Temp. °F	Average Monthly Outside Temp. °F	Temp. Inside Minus Outside *	Monthly Heat Loss **	Monthly Energy Goal	Actual Fuel Used Each Month	Over or Under Monthly Goal
Jan.	74			1382					
Feb.	74			1202					
Mar.	74			1022					
Apr.	74			752					
May	74			392					
June	74		Heating Domestic Water						
July	74		Heating Domestic Water						
Aug.	74		Heating Domestic Water						
Sept.	74			236					
Oct.	74			542					
Nov.	74			752					
Dec.	74			1120					

* The Celcius comfort temperature is 23°C. The average monthly Celcius comfort temperatures in the Toronto area are as follows: Jan. 750 • Feb. 650 • Mar. 550 • April 400 May 200 • Sept. 130 • Oct. 300 • Nov. 400 • Dec. 620 - totaling 4000.

** To calculate the monthly heat loss for a building (column 6), take the daily fuel requirement from Figure 9.6, and multiply by the number of reading days shown on that building's fuel utility bill.

Figure 9.7 A form that can be used to calculate a building's monthly energy goal (From Mel A. Shear, *Handbook of Building Maintenance Management,* © 1983, p. 603 [A Reston Publication]. Adapted by permission of Prentice-Hall, Inc., Englewood Cliffs, New Jersey).

Chemical Energy

10.1 COMFORT

Over a period of several centuries, buildings have evolved from simple shelters providing minimum requirements of safety and isolation from sometimes hostile external environment into complex systems intended to satisfy many physiological and psychological needs. This evolution has assured building occupants greater comfort and a more productive working environment; however, these improvements have not come without significant costs.

One cannot envision a successful building project without proper heating, cooling, and ventilation systems. More than one third of our energy is consumed in residential and commercial buildings; unfortunately, much of this consumption is unnecessary. The results of Cadillac Fairview's residential division's maintenance- and energy-management program demonstrate that there is a great potential for saving even in buildings that were overdesigned and not that well built. Studies have shown that with proper design, operation, and maintenance of commercial, residential, industrial, and institutional buildings, safe, healthful, and comfortable environments can be provided at much less cost than building owners have traditionally expected.

When designing new buildings or seeking energy and maintenance savings in existing buildings, management must know the building, heating and cooling loads and be able to determine the energy required to efficiently and effectively operate the heating, ventilating, and air-conditioning systems to meet these loads during occupied periods. The final challenge is to bring the actual consumption of energy in line with what is required to keep the building's occupants comfortable.

Air Temperature and Body Heat

The room temperature affects the rate of convective and evaporative body heat losses. Because the room temperature will be below the body temperature of 98.6°F, there will be convective heat loss from the body. Many factors affect the comfort of a body (Figure 10.1). Generally, the body feels more comfortable in a temperature range of between 72°F in the winter and 72°–76°F in the summer.

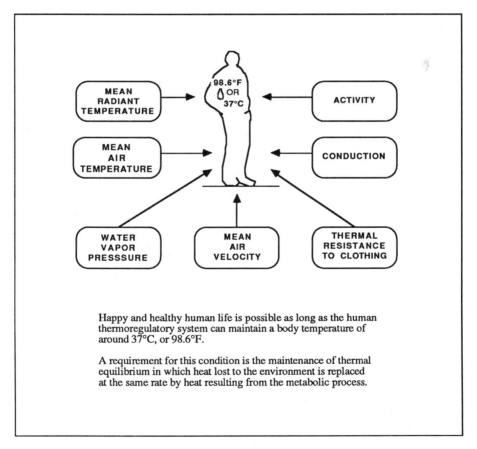

Figure 10.1   Human comfort requirements (From Mel A. Shear, *Handbook of Building Maintenance Management,* © 1983, p. 565 [A Reston Publication]. Adapted by permission of Prentice-Hall, Inc., Englewood Cliffs, New Jersey).

In the summer, comfort is also greatly affected by the relationship between indoor and outdoor temperatures. This is especially true in spaces that people occupy for short periods. A person in a residence or office for a long time becomes accustomed to a 75°F temperature and is comfortable; a person in a space for a short time, generally up to one hour, is comfortable if there is only 10°–15°F difference between the outside and the inside temperatures. This is especially true when it is extremely hot outside. People should not expect the temperature inside to be 75°F when the temperature outside is 95°F.

Space Conditions Affecting Comfort

The conditions within a space (room) that affect the comfort of an occupant (because of the way they affect the rate of heat loss from the body) are:

- Room air temperature (also called dry-bulb temperature)
- Humidity, or moisture content, of the room
- Surface temperatures of surrounding surfaces in the room (also called the mean radiant temperature, or MRT)
- The rate of air motion

An occupant will feel comfortable when each of these factors is within a certain range.

No matter how much heat is introduced into a space, it is very difficult for an occupant to feel comfortable if he or she is sitting next to a very cold surface such as a window. The combination of the body heat loss on the side of the body nearer the window and the cold air coming through any cracks around the window makes this a difficult situation. As an example: The temperature in a person's office was turned up to 76°F and he still felt uncomfortable. By rearranging the office so that there was an interior wall at his back instead of a window, he felt comfortable at 72°F. Encourage people to move away from cold surfaces in the winter.

Comfortable Environment

People feel comfortable within certain ranges of air temperature, humidity, temperatures of surrounding surfaces, and air motion. In areas where people will be basically inactive, such as in classrooms and hospital rooms, higher temperatures will be required than in those spaces where people will be active. Generally, there is a link between humidity and air temperature when both air movement and surface temperatures remain constant. This air-temperature-to-humidity relationship shows that to produce comfort, humidity should decrease as temperature increases. This means that in the winter it would be most economical to provide comfort with lower air temperatures and higher humidity.

Some people normally prefer higher temperatures. Some older people, because of poor circulation, prefer high temperatures. Whether a person will be comfortable or not also depends on clothing and activity. A person wearing a sweater while cleaning a house will need a lower temperature than someone watching television and wearing a short-sleeved shirt.

10.2 AIR CONDITIONING

Heating System

Some hot-water heating systems vary water temperature to radiators to match or offset the building's heat losses. Some older systems vary the boiler water temperature via outdoor reset sensors, and the outdoor condition dictates when the boiler is on or off. More modern systems operate the boilers at a constant temperature and vary the system-supply water temperature through outdoor reset sensors and blending valves to suit outdoor conditions (see Figure 10.2).

Because only 3 percent of the heating season requires full boiler capacity, multiboiler systems have been installed in some buildings. This allows peak operating efficiency of the fuel-burning equipment with additional boilers cutting in or out automatically as outdoor conditions demand. A further refinement is a sequence controller that allows any boiler to be the lead boiler and thus equalizes the running hours of the equipment. The system may also be zoned so that the temperature of the water to the zone in the sunlight, or upper, zone is cooler than the zone in the shade, or the lower area in the building. It should be understood that this system is ineffective at night and when the sun is not shining. This system can be controlled electrically, electronically, or pneumatically (air operated).

Three-Way Blending Valve Operation

This is the most common application of an indoor-outdoor sensing system, known as outdoor reset, for varying the water temperature and it is used in many buildings (Figures 10.3 and 10.4). The master control transmits a signal to the valve operator or electronic controller of the three-way blending valve, which has two inlets and one outlet. The valve operator or controller then positions or repositions the valve stem, which changes the proportion of hot and cool water entering each of the two inlets. The result is a change in the water temperature leaving the outlet and going to the heating system.

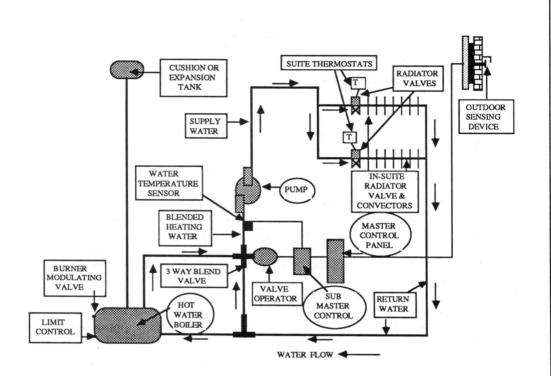

This schematic drawing illustrates the most common application of an indoor/outdoor sensing system, known as the "outdoor reset," for automatically varying the temperature of a heating system's supply water. The master control transmits a signal to the operator or controller of the 3-way blending valve, which has two inlets and one outlet. The valve operator or controller then positions or repositions the valve stem, which changes the proportion of the hotter and cooler water entering each of the two inlets. The result is an automatic blending of the building's heating system's supply water.

To ensure that the inside temperature of the building is comfortable, irrespective of the outside temperature, the controller must be correctly adusted (see Figures 10.20 and 10.21).

Today there are many companies making excellent solid-state controllers that are far superior to the old ones that were installed in many buildings. Owners would be wise to install these new solid-state controllers.

Figure 10.2   How an outdoor reset sensor works.

Some hot-water heating systems vary water temperature to radiators to match or offset a building's heat losses. Some older systems vary the boiler water temperature via outdoor reset sensors, and the outdoor condition dictates when the boiler is either on or off.

More modern systems operate the boilers at a constant temperature and vary the heating system supply temperature through outdoor reset sensors and blending valves to suit outdoor conditions (see Figure 10.2).

Building operators should be trained to monitor the operation of these systems on an operational log (Figure 10.12).

As they do this, they are in effect plotting a building's operational cardiograph.

Figure 10.3   Heating system blending valve control.

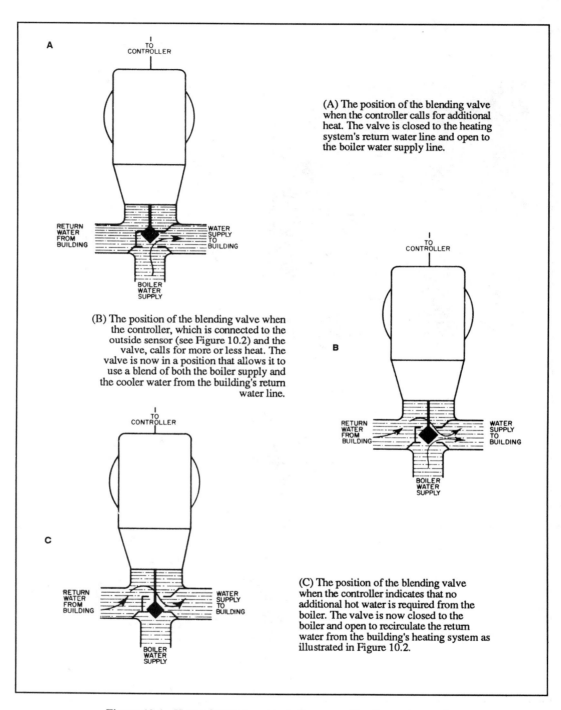

A

TO
CONTROLLER

(A) The position of the blending valve when the controller calls for additional heat. The valve is closed to the heating system's return water line and open to the boiler water supply line.

RETURN WATER FROM BUILDING

WATER SUPPLY TO BUILDING

BOILER WATER SUPPLY

(B) The position of the blending valve when the controller, which is connected to the outside sensor (see Figure 10.2) and the valve, calls for more or less heat. The valve is now in a position that allows it to use a blend of both the boiler supply and the cooler water from the building's return water line.

B

TO
CONTROLLER

RETURN WATER FROM BUILDING

WATER SUPPLY TO BUILDING

BOILER WATER SUPPLY

C

TO
CONTROLLER

RETURN WATER FROM BUILDING

WATER SUPPLY TO BUILDING

BOILER WATER SUPPLY

(C) The position of the blending valve when the controller indicates that no additional hot water is required from the boiler. The valve is now closed to the boiler and open to recirculate the return water from the building's heating system as illustrated in Figure 10.2.

Figure 10.4   How a heating system's three-way blending valve works.

In this system the boiler operates at a fixed boiler water temperature (average 185–200°F), and the blending valves control the water temperature to the system by proportionately blending 200°F water from the boiler with return water from the system. The supply water to the heating system is called the *blend water temperature.*

Corridor air is controlled by a thermostat in the duct, which operates a three-way blending valve set to maintain a corridor temperature suited to the needs of the building. Cadillac's policy was to maintain an air supply temperature of 68°F.

A Simple Energy Goal

After a study of the heating maintenance request reports, it was discovered that buildings could operate at much lower blended-heating-water temperatures than those illustrated in the design engineer's blended-water temperature chart (Figure 10.20) without complaints from the tenants. Many of the buildings in Cadillac's portfolio were actually operating at as much as 15 or 20 percent below design, without any problems with the tenants. This is because most buildings are overdesigned by as much as 25 percent or designed for extreme conditions, when those conditions exist for only a very short period during the heating season.

Cadillac established an energy consumption "bottom-line" level for each of its buildings. It was not necessary to develop a formal energy audit; it was sufficient that each building competed against its previous fuel-use levels. Temperatures were reduced until tenants complained about lack of heat. Although more than $2 million was saved in 1981, the company actually, never reached a "bottom-line" fuel consumption level in any building in its portfolio.

Heat Exchanger

The heat exchanger transfers heat from one liquid to another without mixing the liquids. Different forms of heat exchanges are used for the following purposes in buildings.

- Heating glycol for coils in fresh-air supply fan ducts and for heating piping (either steel or plastic) in exposed entrance ramps for underground parking areas (see Figure 10.5)
- Heating the domestic water

Heat exchangers use two circulating pumps. One circulates the boiler water through the tubes in the heat exchanger; the other pump circulates the heated domestic water to the building, or the heated glycol to areas where the heating coils might be subject to freezing. The temperature of the water being supplied to the building and to heat glycol-filled heat exchangers is controlled

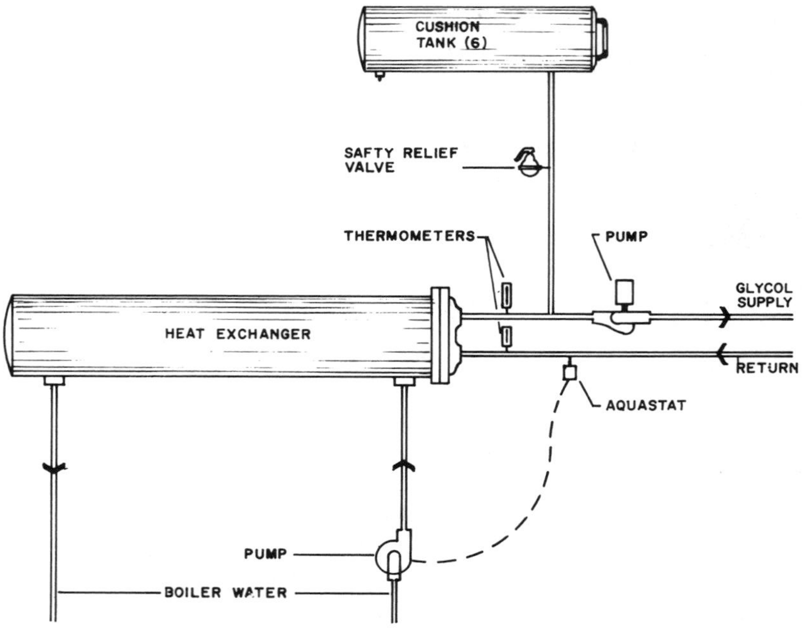

In this system the hot boiler water surrounds a coil of tubes containing glycol. The heated glycol is then pumped into a heating coil over which cold fresh air is passed and heated before it enters the building. This system is also used to heat up any other components, such as sidewalks or entrances to underground garages, that may be subjected to freezing temperatures.

Figure 10.5 Method of heating glycol.

by an aquastat. Domestic water should not be heated over 140°F, and glycol should not be heated over 120°F.

Cooling Systems

All air-cooling and food-storage systems are dependent on adequate refrigeration systems. Refrigeration is necessary for complete year-round air-conditioned comfort and is dependent on the vapor-compression refrigeration cycle.

This cycle is relatively efficient, easy to control, and has a moderate installation cost. Very few cooling techniques provide lower-cost cooling.

The Refrigeration Cycle

Refrigeration is the removal of heat. The operation of the cycle is dependent on a refrigerant that has a low boiling point. (The boiling point of a refrigerant must be low enough to absorb heat—the latent heat of vaporization—at a temperature lower than the temperature to be maintained.) Different substances used as refrigerants have different boiling points to allow their use in various situations. The boiling point of a refrigerant can be changed by varying the pressure on the refrigerant.

A crude system connects a source of liquid refrigerant (commonly Freon 22, which boils at $-41.4°F$, and is contained in the receiver below a condenser) to a coil (evaporator). A valve, installed in the connecting pipe, regulates the flow rate of this refrigerant into the evaporator coil. If warm air (95°F) is blown across the coil, the boiling liquid refrigerant will absorb the heat from this air, reducing the air temperature and accomplishing refrigeration. This condensing process can be achieved with either hot air (by using a fan) or hot water (by using tap water or water from a cooling tower).

In the crude system, the regulating valve makes it possible to adjust the flow so that all the refrigerant is evaporated by the time it reaches the open end of the coil. (In more sophisticated systems, a recovery system is added to the cycle to save the refrigerant for reuse.) The refrigerant is then compressed to increase its pressure and temperature until it becomes a high pressure, hot refrigerant gas. This refrigerant gas is then cooled and condensed to a liquid.

The condensing agent, usually water (from the cooling tower) that can be reused or air (from a fan), is at a temperature lower than that at which the refrigerant condenses at this pressure. The refrigerant then flows from the condenser, as a high-pressure liquid, to the expansion valve, and the refrigeration cycle is repeated (Figure 10.6).

10.3 DOMESTIC WATER

Heating Domestic Water

The plumbing system includes piping to and from heating devices, or a heating storage device that contains enough hot water to satisfy the building occupant's needs. After the fuel needed to heat a building, the next biggest potential for saving energy is to properly control the fuel used to heat the domestic water.

In hospitals and residential buildings the energy used to satisfy the needs

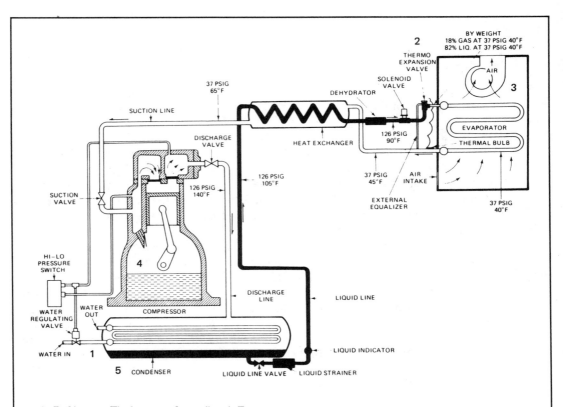

1. Refrigerant. The heat transfer medium is Freon

2. Expansion Valve. The high-pressure refrigerant leaves the condenser that has rejected the heat of the compressor, and the heat absorbed in the space being cooled. The valve controls the amount of high-pressure liquid Freon that is introduced into the evaporator when it passes through the expansion valve. The Freon leaves the expansion valve as a low-pressure refrigerant liquid.

3. Evaporator.The evaporator allows the building air (fan) and/or water (cooling tower) to be cooled as it passes through and/or surrounds the evaporator coil. The Freon changes from a cool low-pressure liquid to a cool low-pressure vapor gas as it passes through the evaporator on its way to the compressor.

4. Compressor. The compressor compresses the low-pressure gas into a high-pressure gas at a much higher temperature. This hot refrigerent gas is then forced through the condenser.

5. Condenser. As the hot refrigerant gas is forced through the condenser where it is cooled until it becomes a liquid again. This cooled high-pressure liquid is then directed back to the expansion valve, as the refrigeration cycle is repeated.

   Cooling Tower. The cooling tower is an extension of the refrigeration cycle and is not illustrated because it is usually remote from the chilling equipment. It is important for people to know that air and water are used to cool the refrigerant.

Figure 10.6   The components of a refrigeration cycle (From Air-Conditioning & Refrigeration Inst., *Refrigeration and Air-Conditioning,* 2nd ed., © 1987, p. 92. Reprinted by permission of Prentice-Hall, Inc., Englewood Cliffs, New Jersey.)

of the occupants can run from 10 to 30 percent of the total energy consumption for a building. In retail stores and office buildings, it is often less than 5 percent. In apartment buildings, 25 percent of the fuel is used to heat the building, 20 percent is used to heat the domestic water, and 15 percent is used to heat the corridor air supply. In apartment buildings, of this 20 percent, occupants use hot water for bathing (30 percent), cooking (14 percent), and laundry (11 percent). In office, industrial, or institutional buildings, the hot water needs may be for other purposes. These heating devices may be a direct or indirect heat exchanger that may use oil, gas, electricity, or solar energy to function (see Figure 10.7).

Direct or Indirect Heating Systems

The geographic location of a building should be considered when deciding about the most economical way to heat and store domestic hot water and whether to use a direct or indirect heater.

In cooler climates, an indirect heater is usually installed because the building heating boilers are used for most months of the year. A well-designed system usually has a series of smaller boilers that can be sequenced to match a building's heating requirements over the entire winter season. In this way, during the fall and spring, when demand is lower, only the boilers dictated by the building's demand are used. During the coldest part of the winter, all the boilers are needed.

In this situation separate boilers should be installed to heat the domestic water. Because domestic water use is dictated by the occupants and not by the weather, these boilers should ideally have separate meters so that the fuel used to heat the domestic water can be kept separate from the fuel used to heat the building. In some projects each individual apartment unit may have its own hot water heater. Each unit has its own utility meter, and the occupants pay for the energy used to heat their domestic water. In warmer climates, it might make sense to use a direct heater or perhaps, solar panels to heat domestic water.

Because domestic hot water use is dictated by the occupants of a building, attention should be directed to the heating of the water relative to any energy management program. Heating the domestic water consumes 20 percent of the energy used by an apartment building and therefore warrants very serious consideration in those types of buildings.

When management is monitoring an energy management program, the fuel used to heat the domestic water should be deducted from the fuel used to heat the building. The fuel used to heat the domestic water is dictated by the amount of water used by the building occupants. The fuel used to heat the building is dictated by the weather.

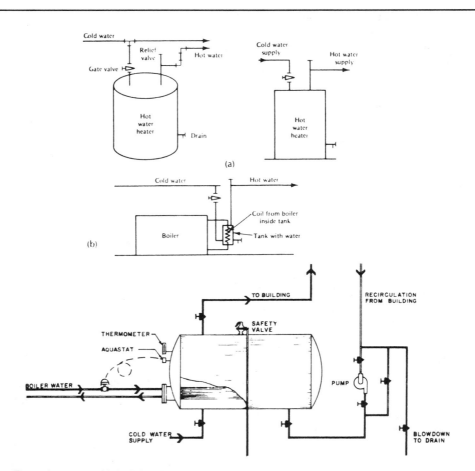

Domestic water used in buildings is heated in two ways: either with a direct heater such as illustrated in (a); or indirectly with a heat exchanger, as illustrated in (b). The heat exchanger is located either inside or outside the tank used to store the water after it is heated.

To maintain a constant temperature of water and to assure the user of instant hot water in all areas of the building, the water is recirulated back to the storage tank and reheated, if required.

The temperature of the water in the storage tank is thermostatically controlled and should not exceed 140°F. If the condition of the tank and the heat exchanger or heater are well maintained, this temperature can be reduced to 120°F, and even lower during low-use periods. Speedy recovery of water temperatures after use is dependent on clean, efficient heating equipment. The savings in fuel costs because of this reduction in temperature and the ability to reheat the water quickly because the heat exchangers are clean are significant when one considers that water is used for 12 months of the year.

Figure 10.7   Methods of heating domestic water.

Energy Used to Heat Domestic Water

It might be thought that occupant, or non-weather-sensitive, systems are constant and that the weather-sensitive systems vary with the changing seasonal climates; therefore, the energy used to heat domestic water would be constant for the entire year. In fact, the water supplied to most buildings is much colder in the areas where winter is cold enough to freeze water than it is in the summer or in warmer southern areas. It could be as much as 17 percent colder in winter, and over a 12-month period the energy required to heat the water could be as much as 5 percent higher than most people believe. Conversely, it could mean that hospitals, hotels, and apartment buildings, which use most of the domestic water, would consume less energy to heat their buildings than is generally believed and more to heat the domestic water.

Figure 9.1 is an overview of energy-use patterns in buildings for a 12-month period. We must, however, realize that management needs accurate information and meaningful records if it expects to make the right decisions about saving maintenance or energy expenses in buildings.

Temperature Control

Controlling the temperature of domestic water is one of the best ways to save energy. This cannot be done unless the heating, storage, and distribution system is the right one; the thermostats are properly located on the storage tanks; and the heating and recovery system is efficient and well maintained. In many systems the temperature of the water in the storage tanks is kept much too high. There are two reasons for this. First, the heat recovery system may be inefficient, and the operator may think that a shortage of hot water can be overcome by raising the temperature. Second, management may be unaware of the need to service and maintain the system.

Reductions in hot-water temperature provide proportional reductions in hot-water energy consumption. While it has been thought that lower hot-water temperature would result in higher hot-water consumption, experience has shown that this is not the case. The hot-water consumption does not change as the temperature changes, because most people use hot water at whatever temperature it may be set at. In most domestic water systems people expect to add cold water because the temperature is usually too hot. It is best to supply water at the correct temperature so that it is not necessary to add cold water.

Servicing the Domestic Hot-Water Storage Tank

Heating domestic water can be costly, and one of the prime goals of the Cadillac energy conservation program was to reduce the temperature of the domestic water. This was difficult to do if the heat exchanger in the storage tank was plugged with iron oxide and the tank itself was full of deposits that covered the heat exchanger coils, reducing its efficiency (see Figure 10.8).

After encountering problems maintaining hot water in an apartment building, especially during high-use periods, Cadillac opened up one of the storage tanks as a part of the investigation. To say that what we found inside the tank was a shock would be an understatement. The inside of the storage tank was completely cleaned out and then covered with a cement wash to protect it from corrosion. The outside of the heat exchanger coils was also cleaned because it was completely surrounded with a jelly-like material and the debris illustrated in Figure 10.8a and 10.8b.

Although the cleaning was of some help, the system was still not working efficiently, and it was decided to open the tank again to remove the heat exchanger coil. This allowed a complete cleaning of both the inside and the outside of the coil.

The coil was taken to the maintenance department and immersed in a fiberglass-lined bath equipped with a heater and recirculation pump. The water was treated with the same chemical (Nutek) that was used to overcome the corrosion problem in the heating system. This proved to be an excellent and effective way to clean the heat exchangers and make them like new (Figures 10.8c and 10.8d). Some people use muriatic acid, which is highly toxic and corrosive, to clean the heat exchangers. The system described above is perfectly safe and effective.

It was found that this cleaning was needed every other year. It is strongly recommended that plumbing and heating contractors develop and provide this service for their customers.

The success of this program was evident in the fact that the temperature in the storage tanks was reduced to 120°F from 140°F; the temperture was further reduced during low-use periods. The source of heating the domestic water and the storage tank must be kept in a clean, efficient condition if the lowest possible temperature is to be maintained while still meeting the needs of the building occupants.

There have been many energy-saving measures sold to building owners. Some are quite good; many are not so good. But servicing the domestic water heating and storage system paid big dividends.

Three major benefits of this program were:

1. Complaints about a shortage of hot water practically disappeared.
2. Cement-lining the storage tank protected it from corrosion and thus greatly prolonged its life.
3. The temperature of the water stored in the tank was reduced by 20°F and further set back during low-use periods.

(a)　(b)

(c)　(d)

(e)

(a) The condition of the heat exchanger that has just been removed from a domestic hot water storage tank. As the water is recirculated back to the tank, everything in the piping system eventually gathers around the heat exchanger, reducing the efficiency of the heat transfer to the water.

(b) This bag of garbage was just removed from this same tank.

(c) The heat exchanger emersed in a bath of heated water treated with a chemical. This bath cleans the outside of the tube bundle as well as the iron oxide (evidence of corrosion in the heating system) that accumulates within each tube.

(d) When the black substance flowing from the interior of the tubes was analyzed, it was found that iron oxide was present in the system. To pacify the electrolysis that creates this problem requires the right water treatment program (see Figure 2.1). Notice the difference in the tubes after they are removed from the bath.

(e) The inside of the tank after it was cleaned and protectively cement washed. By cleaning up the tanks and the heat exchanger tubes we were able to reduce the storage temperature of the water in the tank from 140°F to 120°F as well as further reduce the temperature during low-use periods. This maintenance program contributed substanially to the success of Cadillac Fairview's residential divisions' maintenance and energy saving program.

Figure 10.8 Servicing the domestic water storage tank and the heat exchanger.

Heat Losses From Uninsulated Piping

Heat losses from uninsulated piping can cause as much as a 30°F temperature drop from the storage tank to the most remote user in the building. It may not make sense to insulate these pipes in existing buildings, but design engineers should take a close look at value analyzing the cost against the savings potential of insulating these pipes over the life span of a building.

When you are considering the waste of energy in a building, one factor that should not be overlooked is the heat loss from bare piping. This heat loss can be substantially overcome by adding insulation. The amount of heat loss and potential savings can easily be determined by referring to Figure 10.9. Using a 1.5-inch pipe as an example, we find that

- We lose 4,370 Btu/(hr)(100 ft) of bare pipe, at 3 cents per kWh, which would cost $336.59 per year.
- If we add 1-inch of fiberglass, it costs only $63.23 at 3 cents per kWh, saving $273.36 per year per 100 linear foot of pipe.

As with all other energy-saving measures, this option would have to be considered on its merit and allotted its place in the priority sequence of energy-saving measures.

Leaking Faucets Are Expensive

To assure that you are taking full advantage of the potential for saving energy by effectively controlling the way you heat, store, and deliver domestic water, you must make sure that the hot water is not dripping or running down the drain at the faucets. It would be a shame to have a good maintenance program in the equipment room without assuring that all leaks were uncovered and corrected. Leaks can occur in faucets, valve pack glands, pump seals, and in pipes. The loss-of-water chart shows how serious a problem this can be (see Figures 10.10 and 10.11).

The saving of fuel because of Cadillac's maintenance program was far better than was expected. In some buildings where there were two storage tanks, one tank was eliminated, and there were no problems with hot-water shortages. In other buildings, with two storage tanks of the same pressure, it was possible to repipe the tanks in series so that one tank stored the water while the other was used for both heating and storing.

There is a great potential for saving money by properly servicing the domestic water heating systems. Arrange to start the program as soon as possible. It is interesting to note that this maintenance program would be needed even if there were no energy crunch. This is an excellent example of doing the right things right.

COPPER TUBING HEAT LOSSES AND THE
POTENTIAL FOR SAVINGS BY INSULATING THEM

Nominal tube size (in.)	Outside diameter of tube (in.)*	Insulation thickness (in.)	Heat loss Btuh/ 100 ft.	Approx. ($) cost/ year †
0.50	0.62	0	1,852	142.64
		0.50	635	48.91
		1.00	471	36.27
		1.25	400	30.80
0.75	0.88	0	2,530	194.87
		0.50	789	60.77
		1.00	567	43.67
		1.50	472	36.35
1.00	1.12	0	2,836	218.43
		0.50	859	82.80
		1.00	610	46.98
		1.50	504	38.82
1.25	1.38	0	3,784	291.45
		0.50	1075	82.80
		1.00	741	57.07
		1.50	601	46.29
1.50	1.62	0	4,370	336.59
		0.50	1,209	93.12
		1.00	821	63.23
		1.50	660	50.83
2.00	2.12	0	5,567	428.78
		0.50	1,485	114.45
		1.00	985	75.87
		1.50	779	60.00

The above heat losses are based on 70°F ambient temperature;
130°F domestic water temperature; still air; and Fiberglas Canada's
preformed pipe insulation statistics.

*Outside dimensions of tubing were obtained from ASTM C-585

Heat loss calculations courtesy of Fiberglas Canada Inc., Technical
Services Dept.

† The costs are based on the following factors: 1 kWh = 3,412 Btus;
   the cost of 1 kWh was 3¢ in Toronto in 1987; the cost calculations
   were made by the author.

Figure 10.9   The potential savings by insulating copper tubing used in domestic water systems. (Courtesy of Fiberglas Canada Inc., Technical Services Dept.)

LOSS OF WATER STATISTICS

ONE DROP PER SECOND	1 day loss 1 week loss 1 month loss	= 1 gal. & 1 pt. = 8 gallons = 34 gallons	(4.26 liters) (30.28 liters) (128.69 liters
TWO DROPS PER SECOND	1 day loss 1 week loss 1 month loss	= 2 2/3 gallons = 26 gallons = 100 gallons	(13.88 liters) (98.41 liters) (378.5 liters)
DROPS TO A STREAM	1 day loss 1 week loss 1 month loss	= 24 gallons = 175 gallons = 700 gallons	(90.84 liters) (662.38 liters) (2,649.5 liters)
1 1/16" STREAM	1 day loss 1 week loss 1 month loss	= 64 gallons = 575 gallons = 2,500 gallons	(317.94 liters) (2,176,38 liters) (9,462.5 liters)
1/8" STEAM	1 day loss 1 week loss 1 month loss	= 260 gallons = 1,800 gallons = 7,800 gallons	(984.1 liters) (6,813 liters) (29,523 liters)
3/16" STREAM	1 day loss 1 week loss 1 month loss	= 425 gallons = 3,000 gallons = 12,750 gallons	(1,608.62 liters) (11,355.6 liters) (48,258.75 liters)
1/4" STREAM	1 day loss 1 week loss 1 month loss	= 925 gallons = 6,500 gallons = 27,750 gallons	(3,501.13 liters) (24,602.5 liters) (105,033,75 liters

Surveys done in apartment buildings found that there are many leaking hot water faucets that require servicing. The statistics illustrated on this chart help quantify the amount of heated domestic water that is wasted. By using the form illustrated in Figure 5.32 you can calculate the cost per gallon of heating that water in each building. It is one of the reasons why each apartment unit should be inspected once a year to assure that this type of problem, and others, do not get out of hand. Tenants should be encouraged to report problems, and the management staff should be trained to correct them as soon as possible.

Figure 10.10 The amount of hot water that is wasted by a leaking faucet (From Mel A. Shear, *Handbook of Building Maintenance Management,* © 1983, p. 593 [A Reston Publication]. Adapted by permission of Prentice-Hall, Inc., Englewood Cliffs, New Jersey).

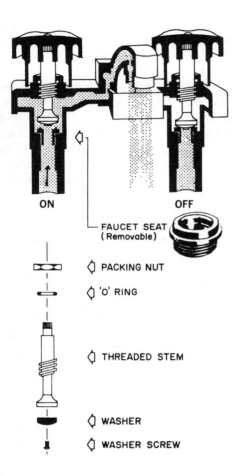

ON   OFF

FAUCET SEAT
(Removable)

◊ PACKING NUT

◊ 'O' RING

◊ THREADED STEM

◊ WASHER

◊ WASHER SCREW

The cause of a leaking faucet can be quickly traced to any of three common defects, all of which can be easily repaired by the building operator.

The first common cause of leaking is a worn washer. A worn washer cannot maintain a water-tight seal and should be replaced as soon as possible.

The second cause of leaking is a problem with the faucet seat. When the flat surface of the seat, against which the washer compresses, becomes rough, it will be impossible to prevent recurring leaks by merely installing new washers. Such roughness is caused by the corrosion or abrasion of sand and rust particles embedded in the washer.

If new piping is not flushed out after it is installed, the sand and dirt in the pipe could cause this type of problem, even if the building is a new one. If the seat is removable, it is easily changed.

The third problem is with the "O" ring. Leaks sometimes develop between the stem and the faucet handle. This is caused by a defective or missing "O" ring. The leak is easily corrected by simply changing the "O" ring.

It should be noted that when the valve stem is removed, the person servicing the valve should check that the washer screw is still in place. It has been found that it is possible for the valve screw to work itself loose and become lodged in the small water line within the faucet body. If this condition exists it will restrict or cut off the flow of water.

Figure 10.11   A leaking faucet.

10.4 MONITORING THE SYSTEMS' OPERATIONS

To help monitor the operation of the heating, cooling, and ventilation systems, Cadillac developed two operational logs in which records were kept by the building operator. Revised samples of the heating and ventilation logs are illustrated in Figures 10.12 and 10.13.

It is also a good practice to attach equipment numbers and a plastic holder with an equipment record card to each piece of electrical-mechanical equipment. All maintenance and data pertinent to each piece of equipment must be recorded on the equipment card: such things as lubrication and filter-changing. Cushion-tank gauge levels, emergency battery conditions, outside temperature, and blended-water temperatures are recorded on the operational log. A graph illustrating the operation of a typical heating system for one month is shown in Figure 10.21).

It is the building operator's responsibility to carry out a "look, listen, and touch" inspection every day. One of the chores the operator is expected to carry out during these inspections is the recording of data requested on the operating logs. By monitoring this information, management can be assured that the equipment is operating according to design and that operational data is available for other purposes; for example,

- It reminds the operator to lubricate and change filters according to the routine that has been established for that building (Figure 10.14).
- It also provides management with some historical data about the operation of a building's heating, ventilation, and cooling systems that could be helpful for troubleshooting problems as well as for monitoring the effectiveness of the maintenance- and energy-management program.

It is important that the manager and the building operator know when temperature and pressure readings are normal for the equipment installed in the building. Operators should be trained to recognize an abnormal condition so that it can be immediately corrected. Anything that is beyond the ability of the operator to correct must be reported to management so that a support-service specialist can correct it.

When building operators visit the equipment rooms and record operational data on logs, they are, in effect, checking the building's "vital signs." To monitor a building's "pulse" and "heartbeat" and efficient use of chemical energy, operators should be trained to fill in the logs as well as to plot on the heating performance graph the outside temperature, the blended-heating-water supply temperature, and the normal operating design temperature (Figure 10.15).

This recordkeeping system is shown in several examples: a hydronic heating-system log (Figure 10.16); a corridor-air-supply log (Figure 10.17); two heating maintenance requests (one shows how a problem with a heating con-

BUILDING NUMBER		PREPARED BY							
BUILDING ADDRESS					CUSHION TANK LEVELS (SHADE IN)				
WEEK ENDING									
ENTER LAST DATE: FILTERS CHANGED				PUMPS & MOTORS LUBRICATED					
WATER ADDED TO STAND-BY BATTERIES				LIST HYDROMETER READINGS					

DAYS OF THE WEEK	TEMPERATURE		BLDG. LOOP TEMP.		BLDG. LOOP TEMP.		BOILER NO. 1		BOILER NO. 2	
	OUTSIDE	TIME	SUPPLY	RETURN	SUPPLY	RETURN	PRESS.	TEMP.	PRESS	TEMP.
SUN.										
MON.										
TUES.										
WED.										
THURS.										
FRI.										
SAT.										

DAYS OF THE WEEK	BOILER NO. 3		BOILER NO. 4		BOILER NO. 5		BLDG. PUMPS		BLDG. PUMPS	
	PRESS.	TEMP.	PRESS.	TEMP.	PRESS.	TEMP.	A PRESS. B		A PRES. B	
SUN.										
MON.										
TUES.										
WED.										
THURS.										
FRI.										
SAT.										

DAYS OF THE WEEK	SUN.	MON.	TUES.	WED.	THURS.	FRI.	SAT.
FIRE PUMP PRESSURE							
SUMP PUMPS CHECKED							
RAMP HEAT ON/OFF							
TRACER WIRE ON/OFF							
WATER TREATMENT TANKS O.K.							
PUMP ROOM TEMPERATURE							

DAYS OF THE WEEK	DHW TANK TEMP	HEAD PRESS.	DOM. WTR. PUMP 1		DOM. WTR. PUMP 2		LWR. ZN. PRESS.		UPR. ZN. PRESS.	
			SUCTION	DISCHARGE	SUCTION	DISCHARGE	HOT	COLD	HOT	COLD
SUN.										
MON.										
TUES.										
WED.										
THURS.										
FRI.										
SAT.										

Figure 10.12   A daily operating log for a building's mechanical systems.

BUILDING NO.		CHILLER MAKE							
BUILDING NAME		EQUIPMENT NO.							
BUILDING ADDRESS		TIME STARTED:		A.M.		P.M.			
OPERATOR		MON	TUES	WED	THURS	FRI	SAT	SUN
WEEK ENDING	TIME							
VOLTAGE	1							
	2							
	3							
AMPERAGE	1							
	2							
	3							
DEMAND LIMIT SETTING %								
CONDENSER WATER - IN °C / °F								
CONDENSER WATER - OUT °C / °F								
CONDENSER WATER PRESS. DIFF. IN PSIG								
CHILLED WATER - IN °C / °F								
CHILLED WATER - OUT °C / °F								
CHILLED WATER PRESS. DIFF. IN PSIG								
OIL GUAGE PRESS. IN PSIG								
OIL SUMP PRESS. IN PSIG								
OIL LEVEL								
OIL TEMPERATURE SUMP °C / °F								
OIL TEMPERATURE COOLER °C / °F								
OIL TEMPERATURE BEARINGS °C / °F								
EVAPORATOR GUAGE PRESSURE								
CONDENSER GUAGE PRESSURE								
FREON SUCTION TEMPERATURE °C / °F								
FREON CONDENSING TEMP. °C / °F								
FREON EVAPORATOR TEMP. °C / °F								
CHEMICAL READINGS CHECKED YES/NO?								
COOLING TOWER CHECK	1. WATER LEVEL							
	2. BELTS							
	3. OIL LEVEL							
	4. BLEED							
	5. NOZZLES							
WATER LEVEL IN EXPANSION TANK - SHADE IN LEVELS								
PURGE DRUM PRESSURE IF USED IN PSIG								
OUTSIDE TEMPERATURE °C / °F								
CHECK PURGE FOR WATER - YES/NO?								
FREQUENCY OF PURGE CYCLE IN MIN.								
THE SPREAD BETWEEN CONDENSER WATER OUT TEMP. AND CONDENSING LIQUID REFRIGERANT TEMP.								
CONVERT CONDENSER PRESSURE TO TEMPERATURE & COMPRESS TO LIQUID CONDITION. TEMPERATURE SHOULD BE WITHIN 2°F								
ROTATE OIL FILTER HANDLE WEEKLY - YES NO ☐ ☐								

DAYS OF THE WEEK	DATE AND TIME LOG TAKEN	CORRIDOR AIR SUPPLY UNITS					
		GLYCOL COIL			HEAT EXCHANGER		
		SUPPLY	RETURN	AIR TEMP.	SUPPLY	RETURN	BLEND TEMP
MON.							
WED.							
FRI.							

Figure 10.13   A chiller and ventilation system daily operating log.

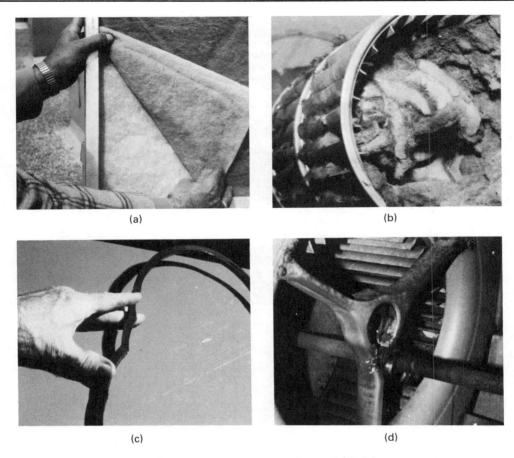

(a)   (b)

(c)   (d)

(a) A throwaway filter that has been allowed to plug up with dirt. Building operators
   should be taught to regularly schedule the replacement of filters long before they
   reach this condition.

(b) A fan that has been allowed to completely plug up with lint. This situation is common
   in buildings where building operators are not taught to carry out daily "look, listen,
   and touch" inspections.

(c) Building operators should also be taught how to inspect belts for signs of slippage
   and indications of cracking. Inspections of the belts would have revealed signs of
   cracking and slippage long before they reached the conditions illustrated. Belts should
   be replaced at the first sign of these problems.

(d) What happens when air handling equipment is neglected. In this case an unlubricated
   bearing has worn right through the support bracket. In many cases when the shaft is
   severely damaged and left unobserved, the broken pieces have completely destroyed
   the fan housing. At the first sign of noise the fans must be shut down and serviced

Figure 10.14   Poorly maintained fans.

This heating performance graph is used to plot a building's operational "cardiograph." Each morning the on-site staff plot the daily outside temperature, the design temperature recommendations, and the actual performance of the building's heating system. If the heating system varies from the design temperature recommendations for the building, a qualified person "fine-tunes" the blend-valve operator for maximum efficiency. This activity provides substantial savings in fuel costs if the on-site staff are properly trained to monitor and adjust the controls.

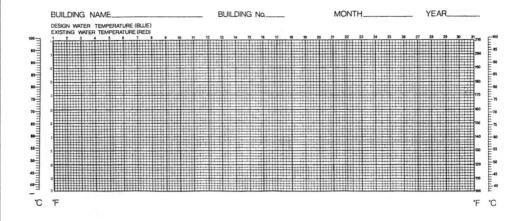

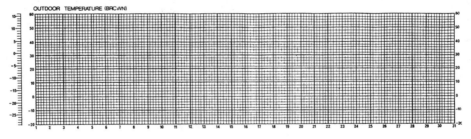

NOTE: FOR CONSISTENCY OF RECORD KEEPING, LOG READING MUST BE TAKEN AT THE SAME TIME EVERY DAY.

Every building operator should be supplied with a year's supply of heating performance graph charts and should be taught how to plot the daily outside temperature, the accepted normal design supply temperature for the building, and the actual temperature of the heating water supply. That is the way management can monitor the operation of the outdoor reset controller. If the temperature is running above the comfort level set for the building, the operator should know either how to adjust the controller or whom to call to have the problem overcome. If plotted on a daily basis, these charts will alert the operator to any condition that is not normal, allowing management the opportunity to immediately correct the problem.

Figure 10.15   A heating performance graph.

BUILDING NO. 176	DATE WHEN PUMPS AND MOTORS WAS LAST LUBRICATED Nov. 7, 1980
BUILDING ADDRESS 40 High Park Ave. Toronto	CUSHION TANK LEVEL
WEEK ENDING November 15th, 1980	EMERGENCY BATTERIES FULL FAST CHARGE Nov. 11th 1950 WATER ADDED ✓
PREPARED BY J.P. Bain	HYDROMETER READINGS 1250

* OPERATIONAL LOGS SHOULD BE COMPLETED EVERY MORNING   * ATTACH COPIES OF ALL HEATING MAINTENANCE REQUESTS   * REPORT ALL LEAKS AND UNUSUAL READINGS IMMEDIATELY

NOV. DAY DATE	TEMPERATURE OUTSIDE TEMP.	TIME TAKEN	BOILER NUMBER 1 PRESS PSIG	SUPPLY TEMP.	RETURN TEMP.	STACK TEMP.	BOILER NUMBER 2 PRESS PSIG	DESIGN SUPPLY TEMP.	RETURN TEMP.	STACK TEMP.	DOMESTIC HOT WATER HTR. ON/OFF	SUPP. TEMP.	RET. TEMP.
SUN. 4	39°F	7:30A.M	110	186°F	172°F	550°F		139°F					
MON. 10	28	8.00 A.M	110	198	188	200		154	BOILER		ONLY USED		
TUES. 11	23	8.00 A.M	110	180	170	550		161	OFF		WHEN DOMESTIC		
WED. 12	23	8.00 A.M	110	192	180	250		161	NOT		WATER IS HEATED		
THURS. 13	34	8.00 A.M	110	184	172	550		146	NEEDED		WITH A		
FRI. 14	36	8.00 A.M	110	190	180	200		144			SEPARATE		
SAT. 15	32	8.00 A.M	110	186	174	200		149			HEATER		

DAY	ZONE PUMP NO. 1 UPPER BLEND TEMP.	RETURN TEMP.	PRESS. DIFF.	ZONE PUMP NO. 2 LOWER BLEND TEMP.	RETURN TEMP.	PRESS DIFF.	COLD WATER BOOSTER PUMP PRESS.	HEAT EXCHANGER PUMP ON/OFF	SUPPLY	RETURN	DOMESTIC HOT WATER STORAGE SUPPLY	RETURN
SUN.	138°F	132°F	.	136°F	132°F		140	OFF	148°	110°F	128°F	
MON.	144	136	NO	144	138	NO	130	ON	196	170	110	NO
TUES.	154	146	GUAGE	156	150	GUAGE	135	ON	180	160	118	GUAGE
WED.	150	142		152	148		130	ON	190	170	118	
THUR.	142	136		140	136		135	OFF	140	90	126	
FRI.	138	132		138	134		130	ON	190	170	110	
SAT.	140	134		144	136		140	OFF	140	110	128	

When building operators visit the boiler room and record the operational data on this log, they are, in effect, checking the building's "vital signs." To monitor the "pulse" and "heartbeat," management must be aware of what is normal operation.

To monitor the efficient use of energy, operators should be trained to plot on a heating performance graph (see Figure 10.21) the outside temperature, the blended heating supply water temperature, and what is considered the normal operating design temperature (see Figure 10.20).

Figure 10.16   A daily operations log for a hydronic heating system.

BUILDING NO. 176		LAST DATE FILTERS CHANGED *Oct. 15TH 1980*	
BUILDING ADDRESS *40 HIGH PARK AVE. Toronto*		LAST DATE BELTS CHANGED *August 10TH 1980*	
WEEK ENDING *NOV. 15TH, 1980*		LAST DATE EQUIPMENT LUBRICATED *SEPT. 8TH 1980*	
PREPARED BY *J. P. BAIN*		CUSHION TANK LEVEL	

CORRIDOR AIR SUPPLY UNIT - 1

NOV. DAY / DATE	OUT SIDE TEMP	TIME LOG TAKEN	DISCH AIR TEMP.	HEAT EXCHANGER *SOUTH*			GLYCOL COIL *SOUTH*		
				SUPPLY TEMP.	RETURN TEMP.	BLEND TEMP.	SUPPLY TEMP.	RETURN TEMP.	DISCH. AIR TEMP.
SUN. 9	39°F	9:30 A.M	64°F	186° F	106°F	114°F			
MON. 10	28	9:30	64	198	114	124	NOT		
TUES. 11	23	9:30	64	180	122	132	REQUIRED.		
WED. 12	23	9:30	64	192	118	128			
THUR. 13	34	9:30	64	184	108	116			
FRI. 14	36	9:30	64	190	106	112			
SAT. 15	32	9:30	64	186	110	118			

GARAGE RAMP HEATING   GARAGE HEATING

NOV DAY/ DATE	FIRE PUMP PRESS.	SUMP PUMPS CHECK'D.	HEAT EXCHANGERS			RAMP GLYCOL		PRIMARY PUMP NO.		
			PUMP ON/OFF	SUPPLY TEMP.	RETURN TEMP.	SUPPLY TEMP.	RETURN TEMP.	PRESS. DIFF.	SUPPLY TEMP.	RETURN TEMP.
SUN. 9	155	✓	—	OFF	—	OFF				
MON. 10	150	✓	—	OFF	—	OFF		HEAT		
TUES. 11	150	✓	ON	180°F	165°F	152°F	150°F	NOT		
WED. 12	150	✓	ON	185	175	156	144	ON		
THUR. 13	150	✓	ON	180	170	156	144			
FRI. 14	150	✓	ON	180	175	156	142			
SAT. 15	150	✓	ON	180	170	158	144			

To avoid corrosion problems with steel ramp heating pipes, the heat of the liquid in those pipes should not be allowed to exceed 110°F. If plastic pipes are are used, it is even more critical because they become very pliable if they are overheated. Once they cool off, they become very brittle and crack.

Figure 10.17   A daily corridor air supply operations log.

MAINTENANCE REQUEST

—HEATING—   18818

BUILDING 40 HIGH PARK AVE.	SUITE # 1815	DATE 12/NOV
RESIDENT'S NAME MORRIS POCOCK	PHONE # RES: 767-6021	BUS:

REQUEST:

APT. TOO COLD

JP Berin REQUEST RECEIVED BY	RESIDENT'S CONSENT I WISH TO HAVE THE REQUEST ATTENDED TO AND I HEREBY AUTHORIZE CADILLAC FAIRVIEW RESIDENTAL MANAGEMENT TO ENTER MY APARTMENT SHOULD IT BE NECESSARY TO USE A SERVICE AGENCY OTHER THAN CADILLAC FAIRVIEW RESIDENTIAL MANAGEMENT OR SHOULD MORE THAN ONE VISIT BE REQUIRED FOR CORRECTION. I ALSO SIGNIFY MY CONSENT.	_See note attached_ RESIDENT'S SIGNATURE	12/NOV DATE

INSTRUCTIONS:
1. NUMEROUS CALLS MAY INDICATE THAT THE PROBLEM IS IN THE BOILER ROOM. COMPLETE SECTION B AND LIST SUITE NUMBERS IN THE COMMENTS SECTION.
2. IF PROBLEM IS IN THE SUITE VALVE COMPLETE SECTION A PART 1 AND IF PROBLEM IS STILL UNCORRECTED COMPLETE PART 2.

A. CONDITIONS IN SUITE

PART 1

	YES	NO
1. ARE THE CONVECTOR ISOLATING VALVES OPEN FULLY?	✓	
2. IS THE SUITE VALVE FREE TO TURN?		✓
3. DOES THE SUITE VALVE OPERATE ON DEMAND FROM THE THERMOSTAT?		✓
4. THE RESIDENT'S THERMOMETER READING IS	69 °F	
5. THE SETTING ON THE THERMOSTAT IS WARMER	°F	
6. THE THERMOMETER READING ON THE THERMOSTAT IS	68 °F	
7. THE DRY BULB READING IN THE SLING PSYCHROMETER IS:		

LIVINGROOM	BEDROOM	BEDROOM
68 °F	68 °F	/ °F / °F

PART 2

	YES	NO
8. IS ANY PART OF THE CONVECTOR BLOCKED OFF BY FOIL, PAINT, ETC.?		
9. IS THERE AN AIR CONDITIONER OR SLEEVE INSTALLED IN THE SUITE?		
10. HAS WEATHER STRIPPING BEEN INSTALLED AROUND THE SUITE ENTRANCE DOOR?		
11. ARE THE EXHAUST VENTS IN THE KITCHEN AND BATHROOMS OPERATING PROPERLY?		
12. IS THERE A HUMIDIFIER IN USE IN THE SUITE?		
13. IS THERE ANY HEAT GENERATING DEVICE NEAR THE THERMOSTAT (LAMP, T.V., ETC.)?		
14. ARE THERE ANY NOTICEABLE COLD AIR DRAFTS FROM BALCONY DOORS OR WINDOWS?		
15. ARE THE OPENINGS IN THE CONVECTOR COVERS CLEAR OF ALL WINDOW DRAPES?		
16. ARE THE CONVECTOR FINS FREE OF DUST AND CARPET LINT?		

B. CONDITIONS IN HEATING SYSTEM

1. BOILER PRESSURE	110	PSI
2. BOILER SUPPLY TEMPERATURE	192	°F
3. BOILER RETURN TEMPERATURE	180	°F
4. BLEND WATER TEMPERATURE	150	°F
5. BUILDING RETURN TEMPERATURE	142	°F
6. OUTDOOR TEMPERATURE	23	°F

DESIGN 161

COMMENTS:
FOUND FLAIR VALVE STUCK IN CLOSED POSITION
FREED FLAIR VALVE AND REPLACED MOTOR
OPERATION OK NOW
TEMP. IS ABOUT 71°F ALREADY

JP Berin
INSPECTOR'S SIGNATURE

C. MANAGEMENT OFFICE

P.M. — INDICATE BY CHECK DOCUMENTS REQUIRED.

✓	SUPPLIER	DATE ISSUED
WORK ORDER #		
PURCHASE ORDER #		

WORK TO BE DONE

RECEIVED BY
P.F. MTCE. DEPT.

NOV 17 1980

Figure 10.18 A heating maintenance request in which the operator freed a seized valve and replaced a burned-out motor.

MAINTENANCE REQUEST

—HEATING—   18815

BUILDING	40 HIGH PARK AVE.	SUITE # 1708	DATE 11.10.80

RESIDENT'S NAME		PHONE # RES:	BUS:

REQUEST: CHECK APT. COLD

RESIDENT'S CONSENT

I WISH TO HAVE THE REQUEST ATTENDED TO AND I HEREBY AUTHORIZE CADILLAC FAIRVIEW RESIDENTAL MANAGEMENT TO ENTER MY APARTMENT SHOULD IT BE NECESSARY TO USE A SERVICE AGENCY OTHER THAN CADILLAC FAIRVIEW RESIDENTIAL MANAGEMENT OR SHOULD MORE THAN ONE VISIT BE REQUIRED FOR CORRECTION. I ALSO SIGNIFY MY CONSENT

REQUEST RECEIVED BY   RESIDENT'S SIGNATURE   DATE

INSTRUCTIONS:
1. NUMEROUS CALLS MAY INDICATE THAT THE PROBLEM IS IN THE BOILER ROOM. COMPLETE SECTION B AND LIST SUITE NUMBERS IN THE COMMENTS SECTION.
2. IF PROBLEM IS IN THE SUITE VALVE COMPLETE SECTION A PART 1 AND IF PROBLEM IS STILL UNCORRECTED COMPLETE PART 2.

A. CONDITIONS IN SUITE

PART 1

	YES	NO
1. ARE THE CONVECTOR ISOLATING VALVES OPEN FULLY?	✓	
2. IS THE SUITE VALVE FREE TO TURN?	✓	
3. DOES THE SUITE VALVE OPERATE ON DEMAND FROM THE THERMOSTAT?	✓	
4. THE RESIDENT'S THERMOMETER READING IS	74 °F	
5. THE SETTING ON THE THERMOSTAT IS	x °F	
6. THE THERMOMETER READING ON THE THERMOSTAT IS	74 °F	
7. THE DRY BULB READING IN THE SLING PSYCHROMETER IS:	74	

LIVINGROOM	BEDROOM	BEDROOM	
74 °F	74 °F	°F	°F

PART 2

	YES	NO
8. IS ANY PART OF THE CONVECTOR BLOCKED OFF BY FOIL, PAINT, ETC.?		✓
9. IS THERE AN AIR CONDITIONER OR SLEEVE INSTALLED IN THE SUITE?		✓
10. HAS WEATHER STRIPPING BEEN INSTALLED AROUND THE SUITE ENTRANCE DOOR?		✓
11. ARE THE EXHAUST VENTS IN THE KITCHEN AND BATHROOMS OPERATING PROPERLY?	✓	
12. IS THERE A HUMIDIFIER IN USE IN THE SUITE?		✓
13. IS THERE ANY HEAT GENERATING DEVICE NEAR THE THERMOSTAT (LAMP, T.V., ETC.)?		✓
14. ARE THERE ANY NOTICEABLE COLD AIR DRAFTS FROM BALCONY DOORS OR WINDOWS?		✓
15. ARE THE OPENINGS IN THE CONVECTOR COVERS CLEAR OF ALL WINDOW DRAPES?		✓
16. ARE THE CONVECTOR FINS FREE OF DUST AND CARPET LINT?	✓	

B. CONDITIONS IN HEATING SYSTEM

1. BOILER PRESSURE	108	PSI
2. BOILER SUPPLY TEMPERATURE	197	°F
3. BOILER RETURN TEMPERATURE	180	°F
4. BLEND WATER TEMPERATURE	126	°F
5. BUILDING RETURN TEMPERATURE	120	°F
6. OUTDOOR TEMPERATURE	40	°F

COMMENTS:
DRAPES IN L.R. TO FLOOR
    "   " B.R. " "
TEMPERATURE AT CONVECTOR IN L.R. 105°
    "   "   "   " B.R. 105°
FLAIR VALVE CONTROLLED

INSPECTOR'S SIGNATURE

C. MANAGEMENT OFFICE

P.M. – INDICATE BY CHECK DOCUMENTS REQUIRED.

	SUPPLIER	DATE ISSUED
WORK ORDER #		
PURCHASE ORDER #		

WORK TO BE DONE

Figure 10.19 A heating maintenance request indicating a problem with draperies that covered the heating convector.

Traditionally design engineers have designed hydronic heating systems for buildings so that the supply temperature of the water in the system is 193°F when the outside temperature is 0°F. The supply temperature line shown on this chart reflects that thinking.

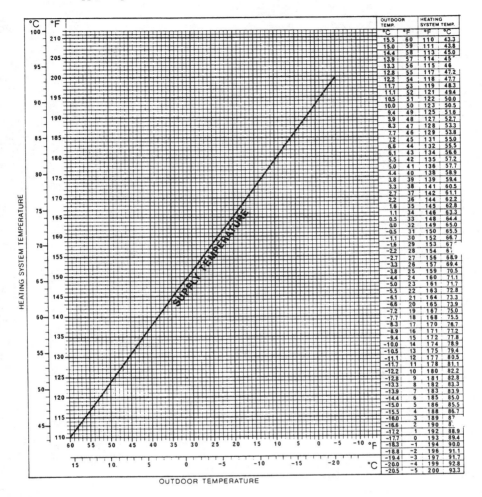

OUTDOOR TEMP.		HEATING SYSTEM TEMP.	
°C	°F	°F	°C
15.5	60	110	43.3
15.0	59	111	43.8
14.4	58	113	45.0
13.9	57	114	45
13.3	56	115	46
12.8	55	117	47.2
12.2	54	118	47.7
11.7	53	119	48.3
11.1	52	121	49.4
10.5	51	122	50.0
10.0	50	123	50.5
9.4	49	125	51.6
8.9	48	127	52.7
8.3	47	128	53.3
7.7	46	129	53.8
7.2	45	131	55.0
6.6	44	132	55.5
6.1	43	134	56.6
5.5	42	135	57.2
5.0	41	136	57.7
4.4	40	138	58.9
3.8	39	139	59.4
3.3	38	141	60.5
2.7	37	142	61.1
2.2	36	144	62.2
1.6	35	145	62.8
1.1	34	146	63.3
0.5	33	148	64.4
0.0	32	149	65.0
−0.5	31	150	65.5
−1.1	30	152	66.7
−1.6	29	153	67
−2.2	28	154	6 .
−2.7	27	156	68.9
−3.3	26	157	69.4
−3.8	25	159	70.5
−4.4	24	160	71.1
−5.0	23	161	71.7
−5.5	22	163	72.8
−6.1	21	164	73.3
−6.6	20	165	73.9
−7.2	19	167	75.0
−7.7	18	168	75.5
−8.3	17	170	76.7
−8.9	16	171	77.2
−9.4	15	172	77.8
−10.0	14	174	78.9
−10.5	13	175	79.4
−11.1	12	177	80.5
−11.7	11	178	81.1
−12.2	10	180	82.2
−12.8	9	181	82.8
−13.3	8	182	83.3
−13.9	7	183	83.9
−14.4	6	185	85.0
−15.0	5	186	85.5
−15.5	4	188	86.7
−16.0	3	189	87
−16.6	2	190	8 .
−17.2	1	192	88.9
−17.7	0	193	89.4
−18.3	−1	194	90.0
−18.8	−2	196	91.1
−19.4	−3	197	91.7
−20.0	−4	199	92.8
−20.5	−5	200	93.3

If we consider each building as its own business unit, it would compete only against itself in relation to the repair and maintenance expenses, the cost of on-site salaries, and the consumption and cost of electricity, water, and fuel. An analysis of three years of energy bills would provide the base from which management could begin a building's energy management program. A suggested indoor comfort temperature for a building in the Toronto, Canada, area could be 74°F. Management would adjust the blended water temperature not only to achieve this desired inside temperature but even to reduce that temperature below this figure. The actual comfort temperature would be reached when the tenants first complain. This would mean that each building would actually have its own comfort supply temperature and that a design temperature line should be plotted on each building's design temperature chart and its results only compared with this "tailored" base.

Figure 10.20 A hydronic heating system design temperature chart.

255

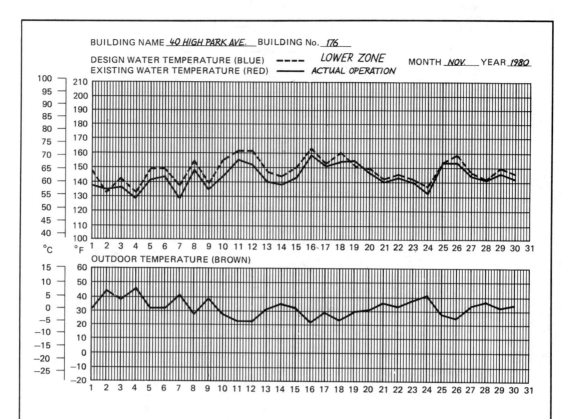

BUILDING NAME *40 HIGH PARK AVE.* BUILDING No. *176*

DESIGN WATER TEMPERATURE (BLUE) ———— *LOWER ZONE*   MONTH *NOV.*   YEAR *1980*
EXISTING WATER TEMPERATURE (RED) ———— *ACTUAL OPERATION*

OUTDOOR TEMPERATURE (BROWN)

In this example the operating temperature of the heating supply water is slightly below the design for the building. It is not uncommon to find that a building can actually operate 15 to 20% below the design guide temperature (see Figure 10.20) without receiving any complaints from the tenants. The reason for this over-design is that engineers traditionally design heating systems for the most extreme winter weather, when, in fact, extreme weather is experienced for only 25% of the season. Matching the heating water supply to meet the actual comfort needs for a building during the spring and fall is how building owners can really save money. The right information in the hands of knowledgeable workers is the secret to saving these maintenance and energy expenses.

Figure 10.21   A heating performance chart that has been plotted by the on-site building operator.

vector on/off valve was resolved [Figure 10.18], the other shows that the problem was caused by the tenant's draperies that blocked the convection of air over the step-over radiator [Figure 10.19]); the design engineer's blended-water temperature chart (Figure 10.20); and a completed heating performance graph (Figure 10.21).

Electrical Energy

11.1 LIGHTING AND ELECTRIC POWER

The lighting energy in a building is either function related, as in a commercial or institutional building, or nonfunction related for residential buildings. Non-function-related lighting can be defined as the lighting used in parking lots, lobbies, corridors, stairwells, and mechanical rooms. Function-related lighting includes such things as office space, merchandising areas, work areas, or classrooms.

11.2 MANAGING ELECTRICAL ENERGY

The specific goal of electrical energy management is to reduce the waste of electrical energy consumption to its lowest possible level while maintaining reasonable occupant comfort.

A building's electrical system basically consists of lighting and motor loads. Lighting should provide the illumination required by the occupants for their daily activities and should shut down when not required. Motor loads are

This chapter is from Mel A. Shear, *Handbook of Building Maintenance Management,* © 1983, pp. 578–85 (A Reston Publication). Adapted by permission of Prentice-Hall, Inc., Englewood Cliffs, New Jersey.

required to power the components of the plumbing, heating, ventilation, and air-conditioning systems.

A successful energy-management program should reduce electrical energy by controlling manually or automatically the following:

1. Lighting
2. Power factor of motors
3. Reuse of heat generated by people, lights, equipment, appliances
4. Controls that
   - Turn energy-using equipment on or off when not required
   - Regulate temperatures to match a building's heat loss or heat gain
   - Alert operators to problems

To be successful, the entire management team must acquire an understanding of electrical-mechanical efficiencies and heat-recovery techniques. To monitor progress, the right system of recordkeeping must be developed and maintained.

11.3 LIGHTING

The electrical energy consumed by lighting in a building can range from 20 percent to as high as 50 percent, depending on the building. Because many apartment buildings are bulk metered, the incentive for tenants to turn off lights or to reduce wattage is removed because the landlord pays the bills in those buildings.

In commercial buildings, the selection of lighting is often made for aesthetic rather than practical purposes. To overcome this problem, energy audits must be developed that would study ways to reduce the wattage. Further substantial savings can be achieved by shutting down lighting and equipment when not required.

It has been shown that the electrical energy cost for lighting constitutes the greatest share of the overall total electrical energy costs. These costs break down as follows:

- 70 percent for the utility company
- 20 percent for maintenance (replacing bulbs, cleaning)
- 10 percent for the cost of bulbs

How to Reduce Operating Costs

The first step in reducing operating costs is to reduce lighting levels where they exceed the requirements for the area by initiating any or all of the following actions:

1. Use task lighting where practical (see Figure 11.1).
2. Remove fixtures that are not required.
3. Remove the lamps or disconnect the ballast.
4. Use lower-wattage lamps.
5. Install dummy fluorescent lamps.
6. In buildings with large glass areas, use photoelectric switches to control the lights near the perimeter where the sun is bright and is supplying an overabundance of light.
7. Replace incandescent bulbs with fluorescents where practical.

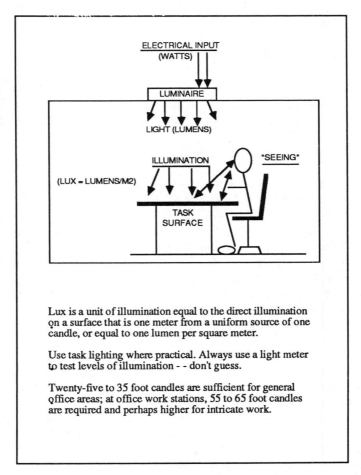

Lux is a unit of illumination equal to the direct illumination on a surface that is one meter from a uniform source of one candle, or equal to one lumen per square meter.

Use task lighting where practical. Always use a light meter to test levels of illumination - - don't guess.

Twenty-five to 35 foot candles are sufficient for general office areas; at office work stations, 55 to 65 foot candles are required and perhaps higher for intricate work.

Figure 11.1 How to use task lighting (From Mel A. Shear, *Handbook of Building Maintenance Management,* © 1983, p. 579 [A Reston Publication]. Adapted by permission of Prentice-Hall, Inc., Englewood Cliffs, New Jersey).

A Guide for Reasonable Light Levels

Always use a light meter to test levels of illumination—don't guess.

- Office work stations: 55–65 foot candles, higher for intricate work
- General office: 25–35 foot candles
- Halls and corridors: 20 foot candles or less

Quality of Illumination

To upgrade the quality of illumination to meet a building's requirements, a knowledge of the most efficient sources that are available is required.

1. High-pressure sodium-vapor: 100 lumens/watt
2. Metal halide: 74 lumens/watt
3. Fluorescent: 67 lumens/watt
4. Mercury vapor: 46 lumens/watt
5. Incandescent: 17 lumens/watt

Importance of Painting, Cleaning, and Control

Unless fixtures and lamps are properly maintained, 50 percent of the illumination produced and 50 percent of the electricity going through the meter is wasted.

Proper maintenance of lighting fixtures includes cleaning and washing fixtures and lamps as well as surrounding walls and ceilings. Lighting fixtures become less efficient as fine dirt collects on them, and losses of 10 percent to 25 percent are not uncommon. Fluorescent tubes must be dusted as often as necessary. Proper maintenance also includes repair or replacement of defective components of the lighting system.

If surrounding walls and ceilings are unpainted concrete, the reflectance of light is very low. To overcome this and also to make cleaning easier, the walls and ceilings of underground garages, public areas, and equipment rooms should be painted white. Painting will increase the reflectivity by 80 percent. In offices, nonreflecting colors should be used, as this will increase the amount of reflected light from a fixture's reflector.

Natural light should be used whenever possible. Photocells, timers, and better switching systems should be used to turn off lights in unused areas and after hours. Electronic systems of programmable lighting are now being marketed that efficiently control the turning on or off of all the lights in a building.

Cleaning and security-staff operations should be arranged so that all lighting, except security lighting, is switched off whenever an area is unoccupied. Cleaning time for each area should be as short as possible, and the amount of lighting switched on during cleaning should be held to a minimum.

Lamp Life

As a rule, operating an incandescent bulb rated 130V will double the life of a bulb.

A 6-hour burning cycle for a fluorescent tube will extend its life 25 percent. A 12-hour burning cycle will extend its life 60 percent.

Group Relamping

Group relamping is recommended because it organizes the bulb-replacing effort and saves labor costs. It also eliminates the need to have a large number of spares on hand, which is very costly.

To gain as much use out of the old bulbs as possible:

- Replace lamps in the usual way until 20 percent have been replaced. *Then change them all.* Long-life incandescent bulbs that are rated for 130V service should be used.
- Four-foot, 40-watt fluorescents will need changing every three years; they should last 30,000 hours if they burn continuously.
- When you do the first group relamp of an older installation, you will lose half the life of all the lamps. To help defray the cost, the bulbs removed could be used to replace burned out bulbs in vacant units.
- Other than at the time of group relamping, you should date the base of each bulb when it is changed. In this way you will know exactly how long the bulb lasted.
- Keep the newest bulbs for use in the building; throw away bulbs that have been used for 80 percent or 85 percent of their life expectancy.

Return Air Through Light Fixtures

Some systems allow the return air to pass through the light fixtures in the room (Figure 11.2). This reduces the amount of air flow required to cool the room and thus reduces overall fan horsepower, because a large amount of the heat never enters the conditioned space. The building energy consumption can be reduced even more if the heat extracted from the lights is recovered and reused to satisfy a heating need in the building.

In a contemporary office building both sensible and latent heat are generated within an occupied space by people, lights, and equipment. People generate about 75 watts/person as sensible heat and 60 watts/person as latent heat. In an air-conditioned building, the equipment heat should be collected and

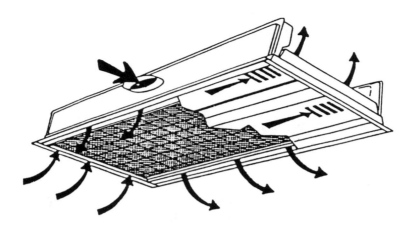

Some systems allow return air to pass through light fixtures in a room. This reduces the amount of air flow required to cool the room and, thus, reduces overall fan horsepower because a large percentage of the heat never enters the conditioned space.

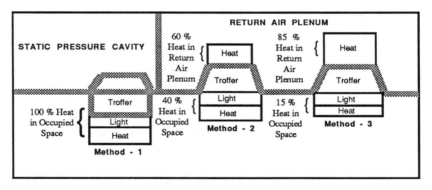

Method 1 - With surface-mounted or suspended light fixtures, all heat is left in the occupied space. The fixture troffer is recessed into the static pressure cavity.

Method 2 - With fixture toffer installed in the return air plenum, 40 percent of the heat is in the occupied space.

Method 3 - The heat transfer and air supply fixture is installed similar to method 2. When this type of fixture is used only 15 percent of the heat is in the occupied space.

Figure 11.2 A system that allows air to pass through light fixtures. (From Lee Kendrick, *Energy Conservation and Management for Buildings,* © 1977 by Lee Kendrick. Adapted by permission of the author and publisher, The Office of Lee Kendrick, Consulting Engineer, Energy Management Division.)

mixed with the return air during the heating season. Ideally, during the cooling season it should be rejected directly to the outside.

Lights are especially wasteful of energy because both the lights themselves and the air-conditioning equipment needed to remove the heat from the lights consume electrical energy.

Fluorescent Lamps

Fluorescent lamps are a widely used source of artificial illumination because they are efficient, economical to operate, and readily available.

The main factors affecting the luminous efficiency of a fluorescent lamp are:

- Design
- Materials used in its construction
- Reflector used in the lamp
- Method of installation
- Ambient temperature
- Voltage and frequency of the electrical input
- Cleaning and maintenance

11.4 CONSUMPTION BY APPLIANCES

There are several reasons why it is useful to know the power consumed by various electrical appliances.

1. To conserve energy—as energy is measured by a watt-hour meter, and because many appliances are rated in amps, it will be necessary to convert amperes to watts to calculate the energy used. *This is done by multiplying the amps drawn by the voltage.*
2. To properly wire a circuit.
3. To resolve electrical problems (blown fuses).

The name plates on electrical devices will usually give you sufficient information so that you can calculate power consumption or the current carried.

Unnecessary consumption adds up quickly in any building. Making people aware of consumption should alert them to saving energy by turning off lights and by not using appliances or running motors unnecessarily.

Using a cost rate of 6.5 cents per kWh, the listing shown in Figure 11.3 can be used as an approximate guide to estimated annual kWh appliance consumption.

Appliance	kWh	Cost
Air Conditioner (6,000 Btu)	500	32.50
Car Block Heater	456	29.64
Clock	18	1.17
Clothes Dryer	900	58.50
Coffee Maker	100	6.50
Dehumidifier	400	26.00
Dishwasher (not including hot water)	300	19.50
Electric Blanket	125	8.25
Electric Kettle	150	9.75
Electric Shaver	1	
Electric Stove	1200	78.00
Electric Water Heater	4000	260.00
Food Waste Disposer	25	1.62
Frying Pan	180	11.70
Fan (furnace)	800	52.00
Hair Dryer	15	.97
Humidifier	200	13.00
Iron	120	7.80
Kitchen and/or Bathroom Fan	50	3.25
Refrigerator (12 cubic feet)	850	55.25
Frost Free	1200	78.00
Freezer (14 cubic feet)	1200	78.00
Frost Free	1600	104.00
Television (color solid state)	450	29.25
Toaster	40	2.60
Vacuum Cleaner	40	2.60
Washing Machine (not hot water)	50	3.25

This table was prepared to help you understand the energy consumption and cost of appliances that are used every day by many of us. The costs are calculated at the rates charges in Toronto, Ontario, Canada, when they averaged 6.5¢ per kWh.

If we use a 1,000-watt appliance for one hour, it will consume exactly one kilowatt hour (kWh). This is recorded by the electric meter and will eventually figure in the electric bill.

Figure 11.3 Appliance energy costs (From Mel A. Shear, *Handbook of Building Maintenance Management,* © 1983, p. 582 [A Reston Publication). Adapted by permission of Prentice-Hall, Inc., Englewood Cliffs, New Jersey).

11.5 THE ELECTRIC BILL

Understanding Your Electric Bill

If you do not understand your electric bill, you cannot possibly establish a successful electrical energy management program. One of the most costly and misunderstood billing concepts is the "demand charge." We will try and explain this part of your electric bill first.

Power demand.   Many electric utility companies have specific demand provisions in their rates. Controlling peak demand can mean a substantial savings.

If we ignore the effect of power factor, the energy consumption characteristics of any electrical device may be expressed in terms of the device's steady-state kW rating. By assuming steady-state conditions, we temporarily ignore the power surge experienced during the start-up of many motor-driven devices. Some building engineers are concerned about the starting surge of a large piece of equipment. They believe that it somehow "peaks out" on the demand meter and causes a high demand charge on the next bill. That is not the case.

Kilowatt demand.   Any electrical device has a kW rating simply because of its power consumption characteristics. The situation changes whenever we connect the kW rated device to a source of electrical power. The device will only exert a kW demand equal to its kW rating as soon as it has operated at its rated load for 20 minutes. The demand meter does not register until that time.

The demand meter.   Except for loads supplied on a "flat-rate" basis, the use of demand-indicating kilowatt-hour meters for commercial and industrial buildings is practically universal (see Figure 11.4). These are really two meters in one—a kilowatt-hour (kWh) meter that "counts up" the energy used and a (thermal) demand meter that indicates both the present and peak loads that have occurred during a billing period. The demand meter is reset each time the kWh meter is read.

Demand meters usually have a 90 percent rise time of about 20 minutes; that is, from a cold start the meter will rise to 90 percent of the true load value in 20 minutes, 99 percent of the true load in 40 minutes, and 99.9 percent in one hour. They are, therefore, not affected by surging motor starting currents, which usually last for 1 minute.

Demand Charges

Demand charges cannot be eliminated. They are the real cost for a utility, but they can be minimized. Minimizing demand is to the utility's and the custom-

By means of a small motor that runs faster or slower depending on how much current is entering, the meter registers the amount of electricity that is consumed. As the motor runs, it turns numbered indicators to register the cumulative total energy used. The indicator numbers show kilowatt hours, usually abbreviated kWh, and these are the figures that appear on the billing.

The red indicator (on the left) on a demand meter reads the highest actual demand consumption. When the black indicator maintains a position for 20 minutes and then drops back to a more constant position, it pushes the red indicator into the peak demand position.

One killowatt hour is equivalent to 1,000 watts consumed in one hour.

Figure 11.4 The electrical demand meter. (Courtesy of Ontario Hydro.)

er's benefit alike, and a building owner will obtain more electrical energy per dollar if the peak demand is leveled off (Figure 11.5).

Demand-charge revenue is used by a utility company to recover its fixed-asset investment in generators, transmission, and distribution lines. As these demand charges make up a substantial part of some customer's bills, it is obvi-

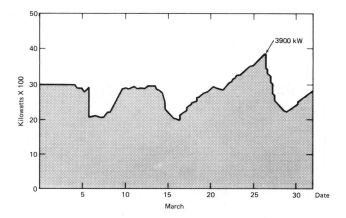

Figure 11.5   An electrical demand recording chart illustrating the point at which a building reached its peak demand. (Courtesy of Ontario Hydro.)

ously very important that all developers, designers, building owners, managers, and operators have an understanding about how these charges are calculated.

From a common 100-watt light bulb to a huge, 1,000-ton centrifugal chiller, every electrical device that consumes power has a kW rating. The kW rating of power-consuming electrical equipment is equal to its steady-state power consumption expressed in watts and divided by 1,000 watts/kW. For the light bulb, the kW rating would be 100 watts divided by 1,000 watts/kW or .1kW. For the chiller (at about .8 kW/ton with auxiliaries), the kW rating would be 1,000 tons times .8 kW/ton or 800 kW. Notice that we still do not have kW demand, only kW rating, ignoring the power factor and under steady-state operating conditions. Any electrical device will exhibit a kW demand equal to its kW rating as soon as it is operated at its rated load for 20 minutes.

In a typical building there is a wide spread between the amount of power used in optimum operation and the maximum demands that will be made for short periods on the supplying utility's facilities. The impact that demand has on the electric bill may not be fully realized from a cursory inspection of the billing rate structure (see Figure 11.6).

11.6 MECHANICAL ENERGY

Motor Loads

A motor does not use 100 horsepower just because its nameplate says it is a 100 Hp motor. Its actual use of power is based on the motor's driven load. A

Keep this stub for your record				Please return this portion of bill with payment and include account number on all checks				
Months	Code	Gross Amount		Months	Reading	kW hrs Consumed	Code	Gross Amount
10	07	19,031.68		10	17280	707200	07	1,931.68
10	15	1.61		10		Tax 11	15	1.61
10	11	4.20		10			11	4.20

Reading Date Feb. 11, 1977	Gross Amount				Gross Amount
	19,037.49			19,037.49	
Meter Reading	10% Discount	CUSTOMER'S NAME		1,903.58	10% Prompt Payment Discount
4624	1,903.58	BUILDING NAME			
kW hours Cons.	Net Amount	ADDRESS		17,133.91	Net Amount if Paid Before Discount Date
707200	17,133.91	CITY			
Billing Demand 17280					

Discount Date March 9, 1977	Account Number	Account Number	Reading Date Feb. 11, 1977	Discount Date March 9, 1977

NOT SHOWN ON THIS BILL ARE THE FOLLOWING RATES:

Demand Charge	$2.20 per kilowatt
First 100 x Demand kW hours	4.57¢ per kilowatt
Second 100 x Demand kW hours	1.9¢ per kilowatt
Remainder of kW hours	1.12¢ per kilowatt

CONVERTING THESE RATES TO THE ACTUAL BILL ILLUSTRATED ABOVE:

Billing Demand - 1,728 kW, and the actual kWh consumed - 707,200

Demand Charge	1,728 x $2.20 =	$ 3,801.60
First Energy Charge	100 x 1,728 x 4.57¢ =	7,896.96
Second Energy Charge	100 x 1,728 x 1.9¢ =	3,283.20
Balance of Energy Charge 707,200 - 2(100 x 1,728) = 361,600 x 1.12¢ =		4,049.92

GROSS AMOUNT OF BILL = $19,031.68

Managers who do not understand the electric bill cannot possibly establish and monitor successful electrical energy management programs. One of the most costly and misunderstood concepts is the "demand charge." Leveling off the demand charge in a billing period can significantly add to the savings in electrical energy costs.

Demand charges cannot be eliminated. As these demand charges make up a substantial part of some building owners' bills, it is obviously very important that all developers, designers, builders, owners, managers, operators, and support service technicians have an understanding of how these charges are calculated.

Figure 11.6 A typical electric utility bill (From Mel A. Shear, *Handbook of Building Maintenance Management,* © 1983, p. 588 [A Reston Publication]. Adapted by permission of Prentice-Hall, Inc., Englewood Cliffs, New Jersey).

100 Hp motor may use a fraction of its nameplate rating. Most motors have more capability than the load to which they are connected. As loads are reduced during a building's unoccupied periods, this overcapacity becomes even greater.

The Power Factor

A motor also has another characteristic that affects power consumption. A motor uses up to 30 percent of its nameplate rating without any load just to provide the required magnetization of the windings to operate the motor. Thus, when using a 100 Hp motor, 30 Hp is used to give off unwanted heat to the motor's windings. As 1 Hp uses 746 kW, 30 Hp consumes 22.38 [(746 × 30) ÷ 1000] kW per day needlessly. This unnecessary consumption multiplied by all the motors in a building could be a factor in high power-demand charges on your electric bill. If the motor could be reduced to 75 Hp from 100 Hp and still carry the load, only 22.5 Hp would be used instead of 30 Hp. *Match the motor to the driven load to save energy.*

Load Factor

Load factor is defined as the number of hours of use. How long lights burn or motors run determines the load factor. In most businesses, records are kept on a monthly cycle over a 12-month period, including records concerning energy consumption. This allows all of the seasonal variations that take place over the course of a year to be considered.

Load factor is important because we must know, for example, how long a motor is used and how much it is used. A 1 Hp motor that is used with a 100 percent load factor is going to consume more energy than a 10 Hp motor used with a 5 percent load factor. Therefore, in an analysis of a building's use of electrical energy, the circulating pump motor is more critical than the motor on the garage door operator.

Efficiency of Motors

Motors under 20 Hp and installed in buildings in the past 25 years are not very efficient. Today, most motor manufacturers make high-efficiency motors. It usually pays to replace motors under 20 Hp and with *high load factors* with new high-efficiency motors.

Another concern with motors is that their part-load efficiency is poor, expecially at less than 25 percent capacity. Many motors used in buildings are larger than needed, resulting in operation at light loads. It may even be worth considering moving the motors to equipment closer to their rated capacity.

Useful conversion factors

I = ampere, a unit of current

E = volt, a unit of pressure

W = watt, a measure of power

R = ohm, a unit of resistance

kW = 1,000 watts, a measure of power

Hp = horsepower; 1 Hp = 0.746 kW.

When measuring the operating efficiency of a motor, record the nameplate data; the manufacturer; the horsepower (Hp); the voltage (E); the amperage (I); and what the motor powers.

Energy efficiency formula (eff)

$$\frac{\text{Energy output}}{\text{Energy input}} \times 100 = \% \text{ efficiency}$$

1 kW = 1.35 Hp = 3,413 Btu
1 Hp = .746 kW = 2,544 Btu

For example, if motor output is 2.5 Hp, motor input is 2.25 kW.

$$\text{Efficiency} = \frac{2.5 \text{ Hp}}{2.25 \text{ kW} \times 1.35 \text{ Hp}}$$

$$= \frac{2.5 \text{ Hp}}{3.00 \text{ Hp}} \times 100 = 82.5\%$$

Motor data records give you the energy output in each of the electrical-mechanical systems. The energy input would require the use of an ammeter to check the actual power (voltage and amperage).

The *power factor* (pf) is the ratio of the actual power to the apparent power. Where the efficiency (eff) is unknown, use 85 percent.

To find the power factor:

$$\text{Single-phase circuits: pf} = \frac{W}{E \times I}$$

$$\text{Two-phase circuits: pf} = \frac{W}{E \times I \times 2}$$

$$\text{Three-phase circuits: pf} = \frac{W}{E \times I \times 1.73}$$

To find amps where Hp is known:

Single-phase circuits: $I = \dfrac{Hp \times 746}{E \times eff \times pf}$

Three-phase circuits: $I = \dfrac{Hp \times 746}{1.73 \times E \times eff \times pf}$

To find Hp where amps are known:

Single-phase circuits: $Hp = \dfrac{I \times E \times eff \times pf}{746}$

Three-phase circuits: $Hp = \dfrac{I \times E \times eff \times pf \times 1.73}{746}$

Selling a Major Energy-Saving Retrofit Measure

12.1 WHY A $300,000 ENERGY-SAVING RETROFIT MEASURE

When Cadillac Development started its maintenance and energy management program in 1970, the maintenance and operations department of its residential division pledged to assess all potential for savings. This group also pledged to do the no-cost or low-cost things first, before they spent any money on retrofit energy measures. This policy caused it to resist signing contracts for computer controls or other energy-saving measures that were being offered at the time. By 1979 the company had reduced the cost of maintenance and energy substantially; it was at this stage that Cadillac started to look at other ways to save.

Background

To confirm some of the claims being made about the effects on a building project of poor initial design and misapplication of equipment, Cadillac Development decided to experiment with four identical buildings planned for its University City project in the Keele and Finch area of North York, a township located north of Toronto. Each of the buildings was at the same angle to the sun, each contained 370 apartments, and each was heated hydronically and had outside reset controls that automatically blended the heating supply water to the buildings (see Figure 12.1).

One of four 23-story buildings used in Cadillac Development residential division's energy-saving experiment, one of the most unusual and innovative energy management concepts ever attemped. All the buildings are oriented at the same angle to the sun; the Canwell waste (including human waste) recycling system was installed in one of the buildings; and this same building was designed as a super energy-efficient building. The two buildings involved in the retrofits mentioned in detail on Figures 12.2 and 12.3 were designed just like many of the apartment buildings that were being built in Toronto at that time. Comparisons of the fuel consumption records that were kept indicated that the most efficient building used half the fuel of the least efficient building of the four used in the experiment. It follows, then, that many buildings in the Toronto area use 10 to 20 percent more fuel than they should, and better design and construction practices could have reduced energy costs by a further 30 percent. This may be true in many other areas of the world.

Figure 12.1   One of four identical buildings that were used in an energy saving experiment.

First Building

The first building was designed and built with single-glazed windows, was traditionally insulated, heated with three packaged firetube boilers in a subbasement boiler room, and equipped with forced-draft burners capable of using either gas or oil.

The ventilation system was heated by water-to-glycol heat exchangers in the make-up air supply to the corridors. Stale air was exhausted centrally by fans that removed air from rest rooms and kitchens in each unit. The corridors were pressurized so that the air was forced into each unit around the suite entrance doors. Because the exhausted air was heated and then picked up additional heat in the building before being exhausted into the atmosphere, about 9,300 Btu/hr were wasted.

The domestic water was heated by a water-to-water heat exchanger inserted in a storage tank using one of the boilers that heated the building.

Second Building

The second building was built exactly like the first except that the domestic water and the corridor fresh-air supply were heated by 23 boilers that were heated by 23 atmospheric burners with no alternative (oil) fuel source. Research at the time of the retrofits showed that the building did not warrant double-glazing: The payback relative to the then-current cost of natural gas was not economically feasible.

Third Building

The third building was built exactly the same as the second except that it was double-glazed. At that time, few apartment buildings in Toronto were built with double-glazed windows. It is much less expensive, however, to install them initially than to change them after the building is built.

Fourth Building

The fourth building was the state of the art at that time. Cadillac Development cooperated with Canada Mortgage and Housing Corporation, in Ottawa, and the Ontario Research Foundation in Oakville, Ontario, and allowed them to build a Canwell recycle system in the building. This meant that all the waste—including human waste—generated by the building's occupants could be recycled. The building had double-glazed windows, and extra insulation was added. The roof was an inverted roof, commonly called an upside-down roof because the insulation is on top.

The building was heated by three watertube boilers with forced-draft gas/oil burners located in a rooftop boiler room. The heated exhausted air was recycled back into the building after passing over charcoal filters to remove contaminants. The domestic water was heated by one of the three boilers.

These four buildings were the focal points of an experiment to document accurately the cost-benefit ratio of various structural and electrical-mechanical building components explained in this chapter.

Cost and Consumption Statistics

At the time of the retrofit, the first and third buildings consumed about 37,000 MCF of natural gas per year. The second building consumed about 45,500 MCF per year, and the fourth building consumed about 22,750 MCF per year. The cost of natural gas in the winter of 1979–1980 was $2.35 per MCF for interruptible gas and $2.59 per MCF for straight gas. By May 1981 the cost of interruptible gas rose to $3.29 per MCF.

For the first building, $86,950 was spent for fuel in that year; for the second building, $117,845; for the third building, $95,830; and for the fourth, $53,462.

It seemed logical that Cadillac Development should explore the feasibility of retrofitting the heating plants in the second and third buildings and adding heat recovery to their ventilation systems. (See Figures 12.2 to 12.6.)

Why the Inefficient Equipment Was Installed

A technical committee had been established many years before the installation of the atmospherically heated boilers. The specifications suggested by that committee did not recommend these boilers. In spite of this, and in spite of the fact that the specifications called for the installation of Bryan watertube boilers, three buildings were furnished with heating boilers and furnace heaters equipped with atmospheric burners. The first of these three apartment buildings to have this type of equipment installed showed high energy use and had other problems, such as cold corridors and a lack of hot water. In spite of this, it was decided to install them in the two other buildings.

After the electrical-mechanical support-service experts in the maintenance and operation department assured the company that it could further reduce the high costs of heating energy, it was decided to research the potential for savings in the three buildings with heating boilers and furnace heaters equipped with atmospheric burners.

As Cadillac studied the feasibility of retrofitting the first building, three startling facts were uncovered. The first was that the company installed the atmospheric boilers and furnaces to save $20,000 when they built the building. The second was that the company invested only $90,000 in that building when it was built. The third shock was that it was going to cost more than $300,000 to replace the heating plant and to install heat-recovery equipment on the exhaust air system.

Research revealed that the company needed only $9,000 profit to achieve a 10 percent return on its initial investment and that the $20,000 savings that appealed to the development officer when the building was built would now cost the company $500,000 by the time it replaced the equipment. If the equipment was not replaced, cash flow generated by this building would be used up

The building studied is located at 470 Sentinel Road, in the City of Toronto, Ontario, Canada. It is one of four identical buildings that were deliberately built differently to compare the effects of double-glazing; heat recovery from the exhausted air; and the difference in the performance of firetube and watertube boilers equipped with oil/gas forced-draft burners; and boilers equipped with atmospheric burners.

One of the advantages of oil/gas burners is that they were charged at the lower interruptible rate at that time. Originally, this building was heated by 15 boilers equipped with atmospheric burners that also heated the domestic water. Eight furnaces heated the corridor air supply. The buiding consumed 45,500 MCF of natural gas annually before the retrofit.

It was estimated that the building would save 6,825 MCF as a result of improved burner efficiency; 5,801 MCF by recycling the heat exhaused by the corridor air; $3,500 for burner service; and 24¢ per MCF by paying the interruptible rate instead of the straight gas rate. These savings were all available if we removed the heating plant and replaced the heaters with watertube boilers equipped with forced-fuel dual-fuel burners and added some sort of heat-recovery equipment to recover the heat wasted when we exhausted the stale air from the building.

The cost of this retrofit was $300,000.

Date	Cost of an MCF of Gas	Missed Opportunity to Save	Losses	Cost of Burner Service for 23 Burners	Total Loss	Effect on Cash Flow
1979	$2.95	IN MCF				$883,097
1980	3.53	12,626	$44,570	$3,500	$48,070	835,027
1981	4.03	12,626	50,883	3,500	54,383	780,644
1982	4.60	12,626	58,080	3,500	61,580	719,064
1983	5.25	12,626	66,287	3,500	69,787	649,277
1984	6.00	12,626	75,756	3,500	79,256	570,021
	TOTAL OF LOST OPPORTUNITY TO SAVE				**$313,076**	

The cash flow for this building in 1979 was $883,097. We predicted that the cost of natural gas would increase each year by 15 to 20 percent. This chart shows what would happen to the cash flow if the changes in the heating system were not made. We called the losses the "lost opportunity to save." We predicted that if we would have decided not to make the changes, the losses would have reduced the cash flow to $570,021 by 1984.

At that time, we could not predict the increase in interest rates and inflation that followed this investigation. Experiences since then indicate that the loss would be much greater because the cost of repair and maintenance and the cost of on-site staff salaries increased since then by at least 10 percent per year, adding a further benefit to this project.

All savings go directly into cash flow and profits, while all "lost opportunities to save" come right off the profits for the building. When you overcome the loss and also make the savings, you double the benefits.

Figure 12.2   Energy-loss economics. An explanation of the lost opportunity to save for a building that was poorly designed and equipped with the wrong heating plant.

This chart was used to detail the potential benefits available to the building at 470 Sentinel Road if we removed the 23 boilers and heaters equipped with atmospheric burners and replaced them with 3 watertube boilers with dual-fired, forced-draft burners and installed recuperators to recover the wasted heat lost with the exhausted air leaving the building.

This is a single-glazed, 370-suite building. Because the boiler room is on the roof, the cost to remove and replace the equipment was much more than it would have been if the boiler room was in the basement. The cost of this retrofit was $300,000. The figures shown on this chart are the actual savings up until the year 1982 and are estimated after that.

POTENTIAL SAVINGS CALCULATIONS

Improvement in burner combustion efficiency - 15% of 45,500 MCF = 6,825 MCF
Recycling of heat exhausted with the stale air 45,500 - 6,825 @15% = 5,801 MCF
TOTAL POTENTIAL FUEL SAVINGS = 6,825 + 5,801 = 12,626 MCF per year.

A savings of 12,626 MCF @ $5. per MCF = $63,130.
Potential savings for burner service maintenance for 20 burners =   3,500.
Potential savings for preferred, dual fired burner gas rate - 45,500 - 12,626 = 32,874 @15¢ =   7,890.
TOTAL ANNUAL POTENTIAL FOR SAVINGS = $63,130 + $3,500 + $7,890 = $74,520.

Date	Cost of Fuel	Fuel Savings in MCF	Fuel Cost	DOLLAR		SAVINGS	
				Rate Difference	Burner Service	Total Savings	Effect on Cash Flow
1979	2.71	12,626					$ 883,097
1980	3.29	12,626	$41,540	$7,890	$ 3,500	$52,930	936,027
1981	3.79	12,626	47,853	7,890	3,500	59,243	995,270
1982	4.36	12,626	55,049	7,890	3,500	66,439	1,061,709
1983	5.01	12,626	63,256	7,890	3,500	74,646	1,136,355
1984	5.76	12,626	72,726	7,890	3,500	84,116	1,220,471

TOTAL SAVINGS $ 337,374.

The cash flow for this building, spread between the loss if the retrofit were not done, and the savings gained by making the change, is calculated by recovering the "lost opportunity to save," $48,070 detailed on Figure 12.2, and adding the savings of $52,930 detailed here, totalling $101,000 in the first year after the retrofit.

Figure 12.3   Energy-saving retrofit economics. The potential-savings calculations that were used to convince Cadillac Development to remove and replace the heating plant.

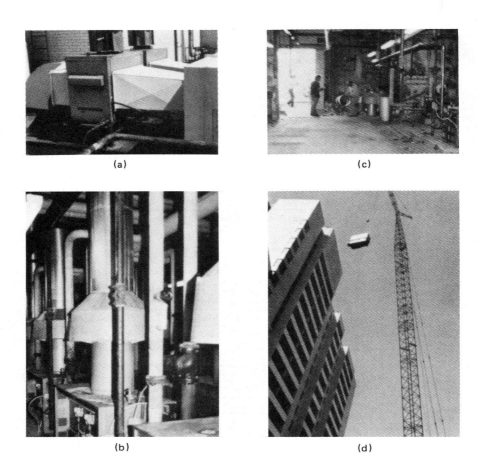

(a)

(c)

(b)

(d)

(a) The furnace heaters installed to heat the fresh air supply to the building.
They were removed and replaced with heat-recovery recuperators (see Figure 12.6).

(b) The original installation of the atmospheric heating boilers that were removed
and replaced with watertube boilers.

(c) The empty rooftop boiler room and the hole in the wall through which the
heating boilers (b) were removed and through which the new boilers were moved
into the building.

(d) The new equipment being hoisted to the roof of the 18-story building, not one of the
four used in our energy management experiment, and how the old equipment was
removed. It wasn't easy.

Figure 12.4   Retrofitting a rooftop heating plant.

Top: The installation of the new heat-recovery recuperators. They pick up the heat from the exhausted air, which is then used to heat the fresh air being brought into the building
Bottom: The new Bryan watertube boilers that were installed in the building. It was discovered after the first year of operation that one of those boilers was not needed, and it was subsequently removed and installed in another building that we retrofitted. Design engineers advised us at the time we installed them that we needed four boilers for this building when we actually needed only three. This is interesting because even though we were replacing equipment that was misapplied and overdesigned, the engineers still tended to overdesign.

Figure 12.5   The heat-recovery apparatus and the new watertube boilers that were in-stalled to replace the original equipment.

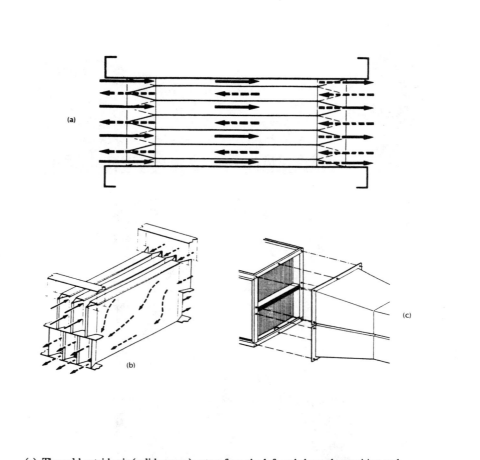

(a) The cold outside air (solid arrows) enters from the left end above the partition and flows toward the right end. The cold air passages are alternated so that heat from the warm exhausted air can be picked up without cross-contamination of the two streams by the smells of the building.

(b) The warm air enters above the center partition. Because the exits above the partition are closed, the air is forced to leave the recuperator below the partition.

(c) How the recuperator is fitted into the duct.

Figure 12.6 How the heat-recovery apparatus works. (Courtesy of Remington/Indusco Inc., 55 Judson Street, Toronto, Ontario, Canada M8Z 1A4.)

quickly if the cost of fuel increased by 15 percent each year and if, because of rent controls, the company could not get substantial increases in rental income to cover the additional expense.

This information, presented in Figures 12.2 and 12.3, was all that was needed to obtain approval for the renovation. During the planning process, design engineers recommended the installation of four 1.5 million Btu/hr Bryan watertube boilers. Their calculations and decision were based on the standard design criteria used at the time. After the first winter, Cadillac found that one of the boilers had not been used for the entire winter, thus confirming its suspicion that design engineers traditionally overdesign—in this case by 25 percent. Further study revealed that in one other building the same thing was true. It was decided to reduce the cost of the retrofit renovations by removing the two unnecessary boilers and installing one in each of the other two buildings. The first year's documented results in the building in which Cadillac replaced the first heating plant confirmed that the company should explore the possibility of doing the same thing in the other two buildings.

These changes, costing approximately $1 million, would not have been necessary if, when the buildings were built, the development, design, and construction team had followed the specifications recommended by its technical committee.

12.2 ENERGY-LOSS ECONOMICS

This experience highlights the importance of communication; the importance of the decision-making process, when management experiences problems created by the wrong decision, and the costly solutions required to overcome them; and the importance of making the right decision when buildings are built.

As explained previously, the traditional development approach was to either "mortgage out" or heavily leverage a project by investing as little as possible. To mortgage out, it is necessary to artificially inflate the pro forma financial projections and to cut the cost of construction to the bone. In large companies, development officers tend to use these or other schemes for selling their projects to the people responsible for financing new projects.

When people cut the cost of construction by taking a "buy now, pay later" approach, the project is placed in jeopardy for as long as it exists, unless inflation and a heavy demand for shelter fill the buildings and push up the rent levels. In Cadillac Development's case, the facts showed that the savings of $20,000 for the heating plant ended up costing $500,000.

To convince the company that it would be wise to retrofit the other two buildings, it was necessary to provide more economic facts to support the proposal than were necessary when the building was first built. It was decided to explore the cost-benefit effect of the initial development and design decision and how the change would affect the cash flow for the building. This was done to support the recommendations we were making to remove and replace the heating plant and to add a heat-recovery system.

The combination of 15 percent increases in fuel costs and other additional expenses would come right out of the cash flow for the building and reduce that figure by $313,076 by 1984 (Figure 12.2).

12.3 ENERGY-SAVINGS ECONOMICS

As Cadillac studied the effect of the savings potential on the cash flow, it found it as startling as the loss if it did not undertake the retrofit (see Figure 12.2). Projections showed that by 1984 the savings would amount to $337,374 (Figure 12.3). In effect, if the retrofit was not done, the company would lose $313,076; if the retrofit was done, the company would save $337,374, making a total savings of $650,450 and paying off the cost in five years.

It was shown that in the first year Cadillac would save the loss of $48,070 and gain the saving of $52,930, making a total savings of $101,000 in the first year. Adding to the factors that encouraged the company to complete these retrofit measures was the rumor that the cost of natural gas was going to double in time. On the strength of all these things, the project was approved.

12.4 THE RESULTS OF THE RETROFIT MEASURE

Figures 12.7 and 12.8 detail the results that were achieved in the first twelve months after the retrofits were completed. Both buildings are included because it helps to compare a building with single-glazed windows (Figure 12.7) with one that has double-glazed windows (Figure 12.8). In this case, the double-glazed building uses about 5,000 MCF natural gas less than the building with single-glazed windows.

Before the renovation results detailed in Figure 12.8, the average gas consumption was 45,500 MCF per year. After the renovation the consumption was reduced to 33,427 MCF—a reduction of 12,073 MCF at $3.496 per MCF, or $42,207 for just the fuel. The original projection was for a gas savings of 12,626 MCF and a cost savings of $47,853 in 1981, somewhat more than was actually saved. The projected cost of fuel was less than the predicted cost of $4.03/MCF, and this accounts for most of the shortfall.

12.5 THE RESULTS OF THE MAINTENANCE AND ENERGY MANAGEMENT PROGRAM

Cadillac Development's planned maintenance and energy management program was begun by the company's residential maintenance and operations de-

(Natural Gas)

BUILDING NUMBER	181	ACCOUNT NUMBER	72	BUILDING NAME	THE PRINCETON

BUILDING ADDRESS	40 FOUNTAINHEAD RD. TOWNSHIP NORTH YORK

NO. OF SUITES	370	METER NO.
		UTILITY ACCOUNT NO. 7 – 01 – 0833 – 999 – 2

RATE CLASSIFICATION INTERRUPTIBLE # 140	RATE INCREASE DATES MARCH – JULY – AUGUST OCTOBER – NOVEMBER

DATE CONTRACT EXPIRES	MINIMUM CONSUMPTION

IF NO SEPARATE METER, USE THE SUMMER FUEL CONSUMP. AS FUEL USED FOR DOM. WTR.	* AVERAGE FUEL USED PER DAY TO HEAT DOMESTIC WATER 24 MCF

NAME OF UTILITY COMPANY CONSUMER'S GAS	PHONE NO. 492 – 5407
	CONTACTS

CALL (416) 676-3083 FOR DEGREE DAY INFORMATION	GLAZING DOUBLE .

YEAR	1981/82	ENERGY USED IN THOUSAND CUBIC FEET (MCF)					TOTAL COST PER MONTH	ELAPSED DEGREE DAYS CELCIUS
DATE METER READ	NO. OF READ DAYS	*VOLUME USED	LESS FUEL FOR DOM. WATER	FUEL USED TO HEAT BLDG.	RATE			
1981 MARCH 24	31	4487.8	744	3743.8	$ 3.141	$14096.	558
APRIL 25	32	2848.0	768	2080.0	3.141	8946.	313
MAY 18	23	1678.0	552	1126.0	3.141	5271.	201
JUNE 26	39	1016.6	936	80.6	3.141	3193.	HEATING
JULY 25	29	624.7	696	-71.3	3.426	2140.	THE
AUG. 27	33	528.9	792	-263.1	3.451	1825.	DOMESTIC
SEPT. 28	32	911.3	768	143.3	3.451	3145.	WATER
OCT. 28	30	1946.7	720	1226.7	3.492	6797.	357.5
NOV. 12	15	1049.0	360	689.0	3.496	3667.	437
DEC. 18	36	4252.5	864	3388.5	3.496	14865.	648
1982 JAN. 14	27	4228.3	648	3580.3	3.496	14781.	870.8
FEB. 12	29	5369.5	696	4673.5	3.496	18770	715.7
ANNUAL TOTALS	356	28941.3	8544	20397.3		$97497	4101

This report shows the actual results of the energy-saving retrofit completed at 40 Fountainhead Road for the first complete year after the change. Before the retrofit, this building consumed 37,000 MCF of natural gas per year; after the retrofit it consumed 28,941 MCF.

A savings of 8,059 MCF, or $36,265, at $4.50 per MCF..

Figure 12.7   The actual fuel consumption results of the energy-saving retrofit measure for a building with double-glazed windows.

(Natural Gas)

BUILDING NUMBER	182	ACCOUNT NUMBER	72	BUILDING NAME	THE CARLTON		

BUILDING ADDRESS	470 SENTINEL ROAD	TOWNSHIP NORTH YORK

NO. OF SUITES	370	METER NO.
		UTILITY ACCOUNT NO. 7-01-08307-999-6
RATE CLASSIFICATION INTERRUPTIBLE #140		RATE INCREASE DATES MARCH - JULY - AUGUST OCTOBER - NOVEMBER

DATE CONTRACT EXPIRES	MINIMUM CONSUMPTION
IF NO SEPARATE METER, USE THE SUMMER FUEL CONSUMP. AS FUEL USED FOR DOM. WTR.	AVERAGE FUEL USED PER DAY TO HEAT DOMESTIC WATER 22.6 MCF
NAME OF UTILITY COMPANY CONSUMER'S GAS	PHONE NO. 492-5407 CONTACTS
CALL (416) 676-3083 FOR DEGREE DAY INFORMATION	GLAZING SINGLE

YEAR	1981/82	ENERGY USED IN THOUSAND CUBIC FEET (MCF)					TOTAL COST PER MONTH	ELAPSED DEGREE DAYS CELCIUS
DATE METER READ	NO. OF READ. DAYS	*VOLUME USED	LESS FUEL FOR DOM. WATER	FUEL USED TO HEAT BLDG.	RATE			
1981 MARCH 21	39	3395.3	881.4	2513.9	3.141	10665.	558
APRIL 4	27	2509.8	610.2	1899.6	3.141	7883.	313
MAY 23	36	2993.7	813.6	2180.1	3.141	9403.	201
JUNE 26	34	819.1	768.4	50.7	3.141	2573.	HEATING
JULY 25	29	661.9	655.4	6.5	3.432	2272.	THE
AUG. 27	33	620.9	745.8	-124.9	3.451	2143.	DOMESTIC
SEPT. 18	22	467.4	497.2	-29.8	3.451	1613.	WATER
OCT. 17	29	2502.5	655.4	1847.1	3.480	8709.	357.5
NOV. 12	26	2565.4	587.6	1977.8	3.496	8968.	437
DEC. 18	36	5342.0	813.6	4528.4	3.496	18674.	648
1982 JAN. 14	27	4884.0	610.2	4273.8	3.496	17074.	870.8
FEB. 12	29	6664.8	655.4	6009.4	3.496	23298.	715.7
ANNUAL TOTALS	367	33427.2	8294.2	25133.0		113,275.	4101

Before the retrofit at 470 Sentinel Road, the average fuel consumption was 45,000 MCF per year. This report shows that this was reduced to 33,427 MCF in 1981-1982.

A reduction of 12,073, or a savings of $42,328 at $3.50 per MCF in the first full year of operation. In our projections of savings (Figure 12.3), we estimated that we would save 12,626 MCF of fuel.

This building actually saved $84,511 in the first year, $42,328 that the building would have lost because of the misapplication of the heating equipment, and $42,328 for the savings. In 1987 the cost of an MCF of natural gas in Toronto is around $5.

Figure 12.8 The actual fuel consumption results of the energy-saving retrofit measure for a building with single-glazed windows.

partment in 1970. From 1971 to 1979, records were kept to document the savings accomplished by this program.

These records were detailed each year for each building on budget-builder working papers, using account classifications (Figures 5.1 to 5.5) that were also used to record actual maintenance and operations expenses for each building. These records were kept on a month-to-month and year-to-year basis in a format that is explained in Chapter 5. Consistent recordkeeping was important because it allowed management to compare with ease the results of the program during a given period of time. This could not have been done if the records were not detailed properly or if their form had changed from year to year.

While the maintenance and energy management program was in effect, inflation ran wild and increased some costs by as much as 20 percent. Cadillac's repair and maintenance costs for each classification, however, increased very little; in many cases, the costs decreased.

Cost and consumption records were kept for fuel, water, and electricity. Fuel consumption records were also kept by degree-days so that accurate year-to-year comparisons could be made. These comparisons were especially important because during the nine years from 1970 to 1979, the cost of natural gas rose from 65 cents per MCF to $4.50. There was no pattern to the increases, and changes occurred at any time during the year.

Figure 12.9 details the maintenance expense savings achieved by the program (the figures are very conservative), and Figures 12.10 and 12.11 show the energy expenses savings.

The savings detailed below are the results of a pledge made by Cadillac Fairview's residential division's maintenance and operation group in 1970. At that time, they initiated a planned maintenance and energy management program in which they projected a savings of 10 percent in maintenance expenses and a 20 percent reduction in energy consumption.

To compound the savings, because any opportunities missed become automatic losses, inflation escalated the cost of everything by at least 10 percent per year. In 1981 alone, the program saved over $3 million in maintenance expenses and $2 million in the cost of natural gas. The inflationary factor could conceivably double the figures shown here.

DETAILS OF THE SAVINGS ACHIEVED IN A 17,000-SUITE PORTFOLIO	SAVINGS
• housekeeping supplies, materials, chemicals, tools, & equipment	$ 84,000
• extended life of 1 million sq. ft. of corridor carpet	109,135
• efficiency of the groundskeeping program	100,000
• extended life of roofing by inspections and maintenance	135,000
• maintaining building hardware & controlling locks & keys	12,000
• extended life of brickwork & structural concrete	120,000
• extended life of asphalt paving by inspections & maintenance	60,000
• extended life of heating boilers because of water treatment	100,000
• efficient sanitary drain cleaning program	100,000
• savings because of a reduction in turnover of on-site staff by training	60,000
• in-house maintenance department savings	
savings in labor costs	400,000
savings in appliance service	330,000
savings by providing materials at cost	25,000
• profits from laundry machine income and doubling of the life of equipment	1,000,000
• savings achieved by negotiating a long-term elevator maintenance contract with a discount for volume	400,000
TOTAL CONTRIBUTION TO THE PROFITS IN 1981	**$3,035,135**

It was found that by doing the right things right, Cadillac Fairview was able to extend the life of a building's components that wear out and need replacement, by 100 percent. Experience showed that to do the right things right, the management team needed the right decision-making information and the right consulting and support services, and the people on the team needed to be assigned the functional responsibilities that best suited them. A professional approach to the way people on a building management team are recruited, interviewed, hired, assigned responsibilities, trained, and upgraded is needed to assure success

Figure 12.9   Details of the savings achieved by a successful maintenance management program in a 17,000-suite apartment building portfolio.

Degree-day consumption records were kept by Cadillac Fairview's residential maintenance and operations division from 1971 to 1979 in the format illustrated below. The fuel used in its 17,000-suite apartment building portfolio was natural gas, and the records were kept in thousands of cubic feet (MCF).

Year	The fuel used to heat the buildings and the domestic water.	Less fuel used to heat the domestic water.	Equals the fuel that is used to only heat the buildings.	Divide by the annual fahrenheit degree-days in Toronto, Canada.	Equals the fuel used per degree-day to heat the buildings.
1971	1,271,806	280,046	991,760	6,734	147.08
1972	1,312,416	280,046	1,032,370	7,000	147.48
1973	1,118,752	280,046	838,706	6,216	134.93
1974	1,193,971	280,046	913,925	6,632	137.80
1975	1,101,401	280,046	821,355	6,226	131.92
1976	1,202,918	280,046	922,872	7,020	131.46
1977	1,110,358	280,046	830,312	6,592	125.96
1978	1,150,787	280,046	870,741	7,250	120.10
1979	1.069,491	280,046	789,445	6,584	119.90

The figures illustrated above are the annual degree-day fuel consumption figures for Cadillac Fairview's 17,000-suite residential portfolio. In 1970 Cadillac Development's maintenance and operations department pledged to reduce the consumption of natural gas by 20 percent. Each year, except 1972, they reduced the fuel consumption from 147.08 MCF in 1971 to 119.9 MCF in 1979. A reduction of 27.18 MCF per apartment suite, or 18.5 percent.

The cost of an MCF of natural gas rose from 65 cents to $4.50 per MCF during this nine-year period.

The savings in 1981 was 27.18 MCF x $4.50 x 17,000, or $2,079,000.

Figure 12.10   The actual consumption per degree-day per suite records for nine years of an energy management program in a 17,000-suite apartment building portfolio.

The objective of an energy management program is to maintain an inside comfort temperature irrespective of the outside weather conditions. A successful program would be one that reduced the consumption of energy to its lowest possible level without making the occupants of the building feel uncomfortable.

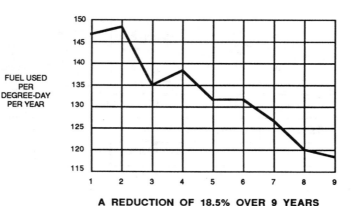

A REDUCTION OF 18.5% OVER 9 YEARS

In 1979, when the cost of natural gas was $4.50 per MCF in Toronto, Cadillac Fairview's residential division saved 27.18 MCF per degree-day per suite in their 17,000-suite apartment portfolio and saved $2,079,000.

Anyone who has an energy management program such as Cadillac Fairview's in place automatically adds the savings to the profits. For those who do not have the right energy management program in place the missed "opportunities to save" are automatically translated into losses.

Figure 12.11   The energy savings detailed in Figure 12.10.

Summing Up

13.1 THE PROBLEMS AND SUGGESTED SOLUTIONS

Most people in the construction and building management industry will recognize the problems articulated in this book and how they affect the way we develop, design, build, manage, operate, and service buildings—problems such as

- Rent controls
- Mortgaging out
- Building flipping
- Poor or fragmented communications
- Inadequate decision-making processes
- Recordkeeping systems that are poor or nonexistent about previous, present, or future costs
- Inadequate planning for the future
- Low productivity
- Poor initial design
- Misapplication of equipment
- Unprofessional management
- Inadequate or nonexistent training programs

Solving these problems now that they have been identified may appear to be an impossible task. It is not easy, and that is why they have not been overcome. Let us review some of the more positive suggestions for doing just that.

All businesses are faced with two basic problems. The first one is the problem of economics, changing markets, and so forth. In the construction and building management industry it is difficult and sometimes impossible to make a building economically viable if it is poorly built, in the wrong location, or overmortgaged. This problem is compounded when a building is first over-mortgaged and then resold (or flipped) several times, adding new mortgages in the process. Unless management can generate sufficient income to pay the additional debt load, this situation is practically impossible to overcome. The other issue is people, not only the people who occupy buildings but also the people who own, manage, operate, and service them.

Both of these issues must be resolved if management expects to be suc-cessful. When owners of residential, commercial, industrial, or institutional buildings are developing a building-business management plan, it must be such that it deals effectively with both of these issues. The program outlined in this book is the best way of doing that.

One major obstacle to the success of the construction and building man-agement industry is the organizational and communication fragmentation that exists between the people who develop, design, and build buildings and those who are responsible for managing them after they are built. It is practically impossible to do the right things unless there is some factual feedback from management that would overcome the misapplication of equipment problems; feedback would also help avoid the structural problems that occur when a building is poorly constructed. To make other than "gut feel" decisions about these very important matters, the decision makers must have accurate infor-mation about the cost to build, the cost to maintain and operate, and the cost to renovate or retrofit.

A Common Team with a Common Purpose

To overcome this roadblock to success (the organizational climate within the industry and within large companies), everyone involved must be considered part of a construction and building management team. Everyone must be guided by the same purpose and have the same objectives. Unless a favorable organizational climate is established for the people in this industry, most of the problems will not be overcome. In fact, the organizational climate within most companies in this industry is so bad that even if everyone on construction and building management teams knew exactly what to do to be successful, the organizational climate would not allow the right things to happen.

The cycle of inflation that our economy has been through since 1973 makes it a matter of utmost urgency that decisions are made about the nature of this business; and about the organization of the management team, what we call the people on that team, and their responsibilities, authority, and functions. Without agreement about a united construction and building management industry, it will be impossible to decide about the kinds of people needed, their training needs, their career paths, and whether or not they are successful. It is also important that decisions are made about the kinds of information these people need, how it is kept, how it is stored, and how it is used.

The Canadian government publishes the *Canadian Classifications Directory of Occupations*. This directory is used to define the skills requirements for the people listed. Training programs are developed and funded through community colleges from these lists. Similar lists are kept by other countries. Most of the people included on the suggested construction and building management business unit chart and other organizational charts in this book are not included in the CCDO listings, and if they are, their responsibilities are vague or completely incorrect.

The construction and building management industry must reach agreement on the industry unification and the organization of the people involved as soon as possible. *Nothing else will fit into place until this is resolved.* People's roles must be clearly defined, there should be no overlapping of responsibilities, and everyone on a management team must have a specific purpose.

13.2 THE IMPORTANCE OF THE INDUSTRY

To show how important this industry is to the economy let us review some figures. Studies by my colleagues in 1983 showed that more than one million people manage and operate buildings in Canada and the United States. If we add the people who develop, design, build, and service buildings, we could conservatively say that the design, construction, and building management industry provides employment for at least two million people. If we add the people who are involved in the manufacture and distribution of the products, materials, equipment, tools, supplies, and chemicals used by these people, we could add many more to these numbers.

In 1987, in the United States, the Institute of Real Estate Management's Certified Property Managers (CPMs) managed more than $872.5 billion in real estate assets. They supervised more than 8.05 billion square feet of commercial space encompassing office buildings, shopping malls, retail strip centers, and industrial properties, and 11.2 million residential units encompassing apartments, condominiums, cooperatives, and federally assisted housing.*

The need for the information systems, people, and educational programs outlined in this book is obvious; as is the amount of money that can be saved

*IREM Fact Sheet, July 1987.

by assuring that the people who develop, design, build, manage, operate, and service buildings have the proper information, consulting and support services, and qualifications to handle their responsibilities.

The Savings Potential

It is estimated that $2.5 billion was spent in 1983 to maintain and operate buildings in Toronto, Ontario. This amount of money was spent to maintain and operate 800 schools, 50 hospitals, 6,000 apartment buildings, 640 office buildings, and many industrial facilities. The study also revealed that there were 540 million square feet of office space and 517,761 apartment units in these buildings. These expenses were for renovations, retrofits, on-site staff salaries, repair and maintenance, fuel, electricity, and water. There is a potential savings of at least 10 percent of the renovations, retrofits, repairs and maintenance expenses and 20 percent of the energy bills if the people who manage, operate, and service buildings have the right information and know what to do.

Something to Remember

Every opportunity to save that is missed becomes an automatic loss. Conversely, all savings are automatically added to the profits of privately owned buildings and would automatically reduce the subsidies for publicly owned buildings. In the first year of the establishment of a planned maintenance and energy management program, the savings benefits double because you overcome the loss and also make the saving.

The Importance of the Consulting and Service Specialists

The importance of service contractors and in-house or consultant specialists cannot be overemphasized. In an economy where one out of every five dollars spent for end-use goods or services is a construction dollar, and another dollar or more is spent for repairing and maintaining existing structures, these specialists are very important because they are the people we need to support the property managers and on-site operators. The specialists are best qualified to overcome the problems built into buildings and to help train the people who are technically weak.

Unfortunately, the construction and building management industry has not yet realized this fact, and we do not have enough of these skilled people available. Without their input and without having data bases available about concepts, development criteria, design specifications, construction, maintenance, and operational and replacement costs, it is almost impossible to value analyze the potential for savings or to take advantage of the savings potential. The people responsible for making the critical decisions about developing, designing, building, managing, or operating buildings will never make the right choices without the right data base information or without feedback from consulting support service specialists.

13.3 THE PEOPLE ISSUE

The best way to zero in on the importance of the construction and building management industry is to analyze the issues involved. The first issue is people and their basic need for shelter. Buildings are important because they provide shelter for people.

Aside from other key criteria such as proper location, design, and construction, the success of a building means assuring that you have the right-decision making information and that the information is communicated to the right people. It is not uncommon for people in the industry to be concerned about whether a building is owned publicly or privately or whether it is an office; a hotel or motel; a school or university; a hospital, factory, condominium, cooperative, or industrial plant; or some other type of building and not realize that it is the way people develop, design, build, manage, and occupy a building that is the real issue.

Achievement of the construction and building management objective of maximizing income while reducing the cost management services to its lowest possible level without downgrading the structure, the electrical-mechanical equipment, the ambience, or comfort of the occupants requires the united support of the many disciplines that are active in the industry.

Professionals involved in building science, energy managers, computer technologists, building managers, and those who provide materials, parts, supplies, tools, equipment, chemicals, labor, and vehicles must all share the goal of making each building business unit successful.

13.4 THE INFORMATION ISSUE

All these decision makers must have the right information available to them before they can make the right decisions about location, financing, construction, managing, operating, and servicing a building over its life span. Decisions made by the developer, designer, builder, manager, operator, and people who provide support services for them must all be based on achievement of a common long-term profitability goal because they all play a role in making a project viable.

In the United States, people who own rental buildings have an estimated income of $500 billion per year. Of this amount the major portion is spent on paying for building debt loads, taxes, repairs and maintenance, renovations, retrofits, on-site staff salaries, fuel, electricity, and water. Yet most property managers spend most of their time leasing and collecting rents and very little time learning more about managing the physical plant.

Managers can assure that they collect market rental fees only if they are not restricted by rent controls. The location, quality of design, and construction can also have a tremendous bearing on the rental fees that can be collected by management. To achieve maximum income, managers must be knowledgeable about marketing techniques and possess entrepreneurial skills that help find innovative ways of achieving this goal.

The ultimate success of a building project depends heavily on management's ability to control the repair and maintenance expenses, the on-site staff salaries, nonrecurring major renovations or retrofits, and the cost of fuel, electricity, and water. In fact these are the only expenses that management can control. That is the reason why it is important that the people who develop, design, and build buildings are cognizant of the long-term effect of the dollars they invest in development, design, and construction.

They must know how much it costs to operate and replace components that will wear out. Major design decisions and decisions about materials and methods show the greatest savings potential when they are considered during the design stage of a building's life. Making changes after a building has been operational is very costly. It can cost anywhere from three to ten times the original cost to correct mistakes made in the development, design, and construction stage of a building's life span (see Chapter 12).

The secret to making the right decisions is to have available the right information about the cost of components, the cost to operate them, and the cost to repair or replace them.

Information Does Not Necessarily Mean Automation

It is not uncommon for people to be overly concerned about computers rather than the information that they provide. They get hung up on automation rather than on the problems that need to be solved and spend an uncontrollable amount of money to develop software that does not get the right things done, when this money would be better spent to help people develop the skills they need to make the right things happen in the industry, and especially in each building.

This book outlines as clearly as possible the information systems required by the people who develop, design, build, manage, operate, and service buildings. More specific information about buildings is available in many other fine books that should be included in a special catalog for our industry.

A computer and appropriate software can provide construction and building managers with a suitable building-business management information system. With a computer, you can access existing business data or file systems through a computer network.

Once managers have the right decision-making information available, whether it is kept manually or stored in a computer data base, they can more easily make the right decisions about the most complex problems related to their buildings. It is not mandatory that this information be kept in a computer data base. The computer is an aid with which to make these decisions, provided that the right decision-making information is stored in the data base file or file system that is developed for this purpose.

Match the Information System to the Building

For the industry to be successful it is essential that a system be expressly developed to meet the needs of the design, construction, and building management industry and that tailor-made systems be developed to suit each building business unit in a management portfolio. Each building is unique and must therefore have its own system.

Maximizing Income

To maximize rental income, managers must know how to professionally market their buildings and how to develop the entrepreneurial skills that would allow them to find innovative ways of achieving their goals. If buildings are located in areas that have rent controls, it is very difficult to get market rents for their space. Thus it is essential that managers have the skills they need to effectively, economically, and smoothly control renovations, retrofits, maintenance, and operations expenses, on-site staff salaries, and the cost of fuel, electricity, and water.

The ideal situation for maximizing profit is to achieve market rent levels while, at the same time, adding the savings from an effective maintenance and energy management program to the profits for a building.

The Benefits of the Right Information System

The right data base of information allows management to choose from many possible alternatives as they develop the right program. The right program provides the following benefits:

- It helps management formulate long- and short-term plans and objectives, especially related to continuity of care maintenance, energy management, or any other specific project.
- It helps balance future plans with current problems by providing specifications and cost to build, cost to operate, and cost to replace data, assuring that management sets realistic goals and then uses the information about actual expenditures to monitor the results of the plan.
- It could help developers, designers, builders, managers, operators, consultants, and service specialists keep abreast of new ideas and technology

through feedback from within and without each building business unit through common construction and building management data bases.

13.5 THE KNOWLEDGE ISSUE

If, as predicted, information, people, and excellence will be inexorably linked, human capital will replace dollar capital, and information will surpass material goods as a basic resource, then creating the right organizational climate, skills development, and information systems must be a matter of major concern. It is not enough for engineers and architects to just design; for developers to be able only to develop new projects; or for planners and builders merely to plan and build. All of them, including property managers and the support service trades, must learn how to be more professional business managers.

Training Institutions Are Not Satisfying the Needs

It is generally felt within our industry that universities and community colleges have not been able to satisfy the educational needs of the construction and building management industry. Certainly they are able to graduate fine architects, engineers, interior designers, landscapers, plumbers, electricians, mechanics, carpenters, appliance service experts, and other specialized people. Rarely do they teach them to conduct businesses.

How Important Is Our Industry?

The construction and building management industry is important because it provides shelter, a basic necessity of life. It is important because the industry and its spin-offs, suppliers of tradespeople, materials, parts, tools, equipment, chemicals, and vehicles could account for as much as 30 percent of a country's gross national product (GNP).

In the United States, building owners may spend as much as $250 billion on maintenance and operations in existing buildings and $300 billion annually to build new buildings. Of their estimated $500 billion in rental income, they spend $25 billion on management fees, $113 billion or more on principal, interest, and first mortgage payments. If they are saddled with second and third mortgages, many more billions of dollars could conceivably be added to these figures.

The only way building owners can get the funds to pay the amount of money demanded by these extra mortgages is to raise the rents or possibly defer maintenance, retrofits, or renovations for a few years. If they do defer maintenance, there comes a time when someone will have to catch up by spending the inflated dollars to correct them, or tear down the building. The problems only get worse; they do not disappear. This approach eventually causes further problems, as the structural defects, deterioration of the electrical-mechanical equipment, and a general downgrading of the housekeeping and groundskeeping make it impossible to get the rents needed or to keep good tenants.

The $250 billion in operating expenses more or less breaks down as follows: $97 billion for taxes; $63 billion for renovations, retrofits, and repair and maintenance; $30 billion for on-site staff salaries; $30 billion for fuel; $20 billion for electricity; $5 billion for water; $5 billion for insurance; and $5 billion for sundry expenses.

Depending on the professionalism of developers, designers, builders, managers, and operators of buildings, the operational expenses could rise to $275 billion from $250 billion or drop below $250 billion if the people in management are professionals. We should be aware that the profit for each building varies, depending upon the income, debt load, and operating expenses for each.

It could be said that much of this enormous amount of money is wasted because decision makers do not have the right information available to them, and the people involved are usually not properly trained to handle their responsibilities.

The government of Ontario has already found that there is a need for this upgrading and has pledged to provide leadership in this regard. It has also supported research in identifying industry problems and training needs. Skills development has already been identified as one of the major problems, and the government has also given a high priority to job retention and job-creation incentives. This type of leadership in helping the construction and building management industry identify and overcome its problems should be encouraged in all countries.

13.6 THE CHALLENGE

Managers of buildings face greater challenges than ever before. Inflation has escalated the cost of land, financing costs, and operations costs to the point where building projects quickly lose their viability. Added to this is the large number of buildings that are overmortgaged, poorly built, and undermaintained. First-class managers are needed to make all building business units successful.

Many people in leadership positions within the industry are more interested in maintaining their positions than in improving the management process. They tend to resist any suggestions for the changes that are so urgently needed to cope with the problems we are facing. The management concepts recommended in this book suggest a fundamentally different approach to managing information and people.

The system proposed in this book was developed to help decision makers in the construction and building management industry to solve problems. The management system applies the concept of identifying problems, collecting pertinent data to help solve them, and then guiding management in the follow-up process to assure that the problems have been solved without creating new ones. It is designed primarily to unite all those in the industry under a common industry-recognized purpose and to encourage them to strive to reach their full potential while they are helping improve the performance of the industry.

A commitment is needed, not only from the head of each business unit or profit center but also from everyone on each building's management team. They all must strive to achieve not only their personal goals but also the goals of their enterprises and the goals of the industry.

People Do the Job Because They Want To

The suggested organizational hierarchy is conducive to helping people satisfy their emotional needs and the need of their enterprise. *The best people can fail if the organization of the management team is inappropriate or if someone on that team purposely wants it to fail or prefers to maintain the status quo.*

By clearly defining responsibilities and authority we empower people to get their jobs done because they want to and at the same time encourage their abilities and personalities to develop naturally. They seem to assume leadership roles within the functional accountabilities assigned to them. In many cases intuition and reason seem to be in balance both in problem solving and in their ability to make decisions. Intuition guides analysis, and because resource support people specialize in specific functions, such as housekeeping, groundskeeping, structural services, or electrical-mechanical systems, they become better and better as a matter of course.

The construction and building management industry must strive to achieve excellence in the way it develops, designs, builds, manages, and operates buildings. It should make it difficult for the "fast buck," or "hit-and-run," entrepreneur to distort the viability of building projects. Achievement of excellence can be accomplished only by assuring that all people involved are professionals and that they are trained to handle the responsibilities assigned to them. Aside from the professional training, they also need the right decision-making information and the right support to handle problems that are beyond their ability.

A Review of Some Important Issues

Let us briefly review some important issues that are covered in this book.

1. The purpose of a planned maintenance services program is to reduce the costs of maintenance services; on-site staff salaries; and fuel, electricity,

and water to their lowest possible levels without downgrading the structure, the electrical-mechanical equipment, the ambience, or the comfort of the occupants of the building being managed.

2. Management must take the following actions if it wants to establish a meaningful maintenance services program, monitor the results, identify flaws, and upgrade it:
   - Identify the key functional accountabilities and properly organize the management team.
   - Prepare charters of accountabilities for all the people on that team.
   - Assign responsibilities and give people the authority to do their jobs.
   - Prepare building profile surveys.
   - Decide about the maintenance needs.
   - Decide who is to do the work.
   - Agree on a chart of expense accounts.
   - Build the costs for the program into a budget.
   - Write specifications and/or standards for the maintenance program.
   - Know how to professionally tender the work being done by outside support service contractors.
   - Use the chart of expense accounts to monitor results.
   - Adjust management's actions to overcome any flaws.

3. The following benefits emerge from a suitably planned and executed program:
   - The cost of maintenance services will decrease by at least 10 percent.
   - The cost of energy will decrease by at least 20 percent.
   - Each building business unit's master action plan will be communicated to everyone on the management team and the costs will be included in a budget.
   - All capitalized expenses or major renovations and retrofits are isolated and receive special attention.
   - The budget provides a basis for comparison to the master action plan for each building business unit.
   - Management is helped to plan for future needs.
   - The budget provides a basis for communication concerning activities in the budget.
   - The budget provides an opportunity for communication about possible revisions to plans, programs, etc.
   - The budgeting process necessitates participation by everyone on the management team as far down the line as necessary.
   - The planning process provides a means of analyzing all planned activities and their costs on a systematic basis.
   - Factual feedback is made available to people who design, build, manage, operate, or service buildings.
   - Provision is made for an effective allocation of on-site, in-house, and outside support services personnel and resources.

- Satisfaction of the emotional needs of the people involved is assured by this management plan.
- This program provides a means of assuring a continuity of action and care for buildings.
- The people involved become better and better as they concentrate on their functional responsibilities.

Conclusion

If we consider that the design, construction, and building management industry is a giant organization of subgroups throughout the world, that one subgroup cannot perform effectively without the others, and that the actions of each subgroup affect the others, we have a clear idea of what we are trying to coordinate and make effective.

Of the billions of dollars spent to maintain and operate buildings, the industry can save 10 percent of the cost of maintenance and 20 percent of the energy expense by effectively managing maintenance and operations. Surely the possibility of such savings will encourage governments and the industry to invest in the information systems and educational training needed to make these savings possible.

Index